Drawn to Injustice

THE WRONGFUL CONVICTION OF TIMOTHY MASTERS

Timothy Masters

with Steve Lehto

BERKLEY BOOKS, NEW YORK

THE BERKLEY PUBLISHING GROUP
Published by the Penguin Group
Penguin Group (USA) Inc.
375 Hudson Street, New York, New York 10014, USA

Penguin Group (Canada), 90 Eglinton Avenue East, Suite 700, Toronto, Ontario M4P 2Y3, Canada
(a division of Pearson Penguin Canada Inc.) • Penguin Books Ltd., 80 Strand, London WC2R 0RL,
England • Penguin Group Ireland, 25 St. Stephen's Green, Dublin 2, Ireland (a division of Penguin
Books Ltd.) • Penguin Group (Australia), 250 Camberwell Road, Camberwell, Victoria 3124, Australia
(a division of Pearson Australia Group Pty. Ltd.) • Penguin Books India Pvt. Ltd., 11 Community
Centre, Panchsheel Park, New Delhi—110 017, India • Penguin Group (NZ), 67 Apollo Drive,
Rosedale, Auckland 0632, New Zealand (a division of Pearson New Zealand Ltd.) • Penguin Books
(South Africa) (Pty.) Ltd., 24 Sturdee Avenue, Rosebank, Johannesburg 2196, South Africa

Penguin Books Ltd., Registered Offices: 80 Strand, London WC2R 0RL, England

The publisher does not have any control over and does not assume any responsibility for author
or third-party websites or their content.

DRAWN TO INJUSTICE

A Berkley Book / published by arrangement with Timothy Masters

PUBLISHING HISTORY
Berkley premium edition / June 2012

Copyright © 2012 by Timothy Masters.
Cover photos courtesy of the author.
Cover design by Diana Kolsky.
Interior text design by Tiffany Estreicher.

ISBN: 978-0-425-24792-1

BERKLEY®
Berkley Books are published by The Berkley Publishing Group,
a division of Penguin Group (USA) Inc.,
375 Hudson Street, New York, New York 10014.
BERKLEY® is a registered trademark of Penguin Group (USA) Inc.
The "B" design is a trademark of Penguin Group (USA) Inc.

PRINTED IN THE UNITED STATES OF AMERICA

10 9 8 7 6 5 4 3 2 1

Most Berkley Books are available at special quantity discounts for bulk purchases
for sales, promotions, premiums, fund-raising, or educational use. Special books,
or book excerpts, can also be created to fit specific needs.

For details, write: Special Markets, The Berkley Publishing Group,
375 Hudson Street, New York, New York 10014.

ALWAYS LEARNING   PEARSON

This book is dedicated to my defense team; attorneys David Wymore, Maria Liu, Mike Heher, our investigators Barie Goetz, Josh Hoban, and DNA experts Richard and Selma Eikelenboom.

To Linda Holloway, who did the right thing, consequences be damned. She went against the grain by breaking the "blue code of silence" to right this wrong. For her integrity, many in local law enforcement have ostracized her.

To all the people who wrote to me after my release. Their generosity enabled me to survive the first few years of freedom in this expensive new world.

To David Lane, Darold Kilmer, and Rebecca Wallace and the team at Kilmer, Lane, and Newman LLP who helped ensure I had the means to survive after release.

And most importantly to my family; my sister Serena, brother in law Mario, niece, nephews, aunts, uncles, and all the cousins, who never gave up as they stood by me during the entire ordeal. I do not think I would have survived this without them.

AUTHOR'S NOTE

Many of the events in this book took place ten or twenty years ago. However, I want you to know that most of what was said by the people in this story was recorded: police interrogations were videotaped and later transcribed. Court hearings were recorded by court reporters and later made into official transcripts. Witnesses gave police investigators written statements. Toward the end of my story I obtained copies of documents and transcripts from the investigations and the trial and court hearings.

In writing this story, I have endeavored to tell it as factually accurate as possible. When I put someone's words in quotes—for example, a witness testifying in a courtroom—those words are exactly as they were recorded in the court transcript. Because of that, you will find a few instances where quotes appear to contain "mistakes," where someone has said something incorrectly, with bad grammar or awkward phrasing. I left these errors intact in order to avoid misquoting or misrepresenting anyone and to tell my story as accurately as possible.

INTRODUCTION

Early in the morning of February 11, 1987, someone fatally stabbed Peggy Lee Hettrick of Fort Collins, Colorado, in the back. The killer carefully sliced off one of her nipples and a piece of her clitoris, most likely using a surgical tool. He—almost everyone agrees the killer had to be male—then dumped her body in a field, a hundred feet or so from a street called Landings Drive. Her body was left with her top pulled up, exposing her torso and mutilated breast. Her pants and underwear had been pulled down, exposing her mutilated clitoris. The killer then walked away into the darkness.

I would find out about Peggy's death the next day, when I walked by her body on my way to school, and then later, when I was questioned by local police. I was only fifteen years old, and Peggy Hettrick's death would become the defining moment of my life. While her killer remained at large, the police would hound me for years. They would accuse me of the gruesome killing and tell my neighbors and classmates that I was the prime suspect. After ten years, they would arrest and prosecute me for the murder, even though there was no evidence that I had been involved. Worse, they would ignore evidence pointing to others, letting the real killer evade justice.

To get a conviction without evidence, the police and the prosecutors concocted a theory based upon drawings and stories I had written before the murder and found a psychiatrist willing to testify that these creations proved I had the capacity and motive to kill. They also withheld evidence from my defense team that showed I was innocent. I spent nearly ten years in prison for a murder I did not commit—a decade spent struggling with life in prison and fighting the legal system. My biggest opponents were the City of Fort Collins and the Larimer County District Attorney's Office. Realizing how bad it would make them look if the truth was revealed, they fought my efforts to clear my name.

This is my story, of how I was accused of a brutal and vicious crime I could never have committed and of how I was arrested, convicted, and imprisoned wrongly. This is also the story of how I gained my freedom and have managed to finally begin living the normal life I should have had all along.

1

February 11, 1987

ON FEBRUARY 11, 1987, I GOT UP AND GOT READY FOR school, just like any average day. I was in tenth grade and had to catch a school bus that stopped at an intersection near a field behind my house. I lived in a trailer with my father, Clyde Masters, in Fort Collins, Colorado, near the corner of Landings Drive and Boardwalk. It was just the two of us living there; my mother had died a few years earlier, and my older sister had joined the U.S. Army.

I walked out my back door at 6:55 A.M.; sunrise wouldn't be until 7:00. A barbed-wire fence marked the line between our property and a vacant field. I carefully pushed down on the top wire by placing my hand between some barbs, and I stepped over and headed across the field toward my bus stop. The temperature was in the thirties that morning, but

I remember there was no snow on the ground. As I hurried across the field, I saw what looked like just another pile of trash in the middle of the field. People had been dumping trash—everything from McDonald's wrappers to used furniture—on this property ever since they had put in Landings Drive, running alongside the empty field. I kept walking in the early morning twilight; my bus would be at its stop at 7:00 sharp, and I didn't want to miss it. Then I came across a reddish-brown streak in the grass and some small furrows that ran in a line with the streak. In the dim light, it looked like brown spray paint. I slowed down and looked back to see where the streak ran. It went from the curb and out into the field toward what I had thought was the pile of trash. Whatever it was had been dragged out there the night before. I walked toward it. As I got closer, it looked like a mannequin—pale and shaped like a woman's body. *Could it be real?*

My heart was pounding. The shock was nearly paralyzing. I was suddenly very scared. The body itself has never been clear in my head, probably because of the shocking nature of the situation. What I do remember is that it was extremely pale, and it appeared to be a blonde woman with her pants pulled down. The mouth had a pained expression.

I told myself it couldn't be a dead body. Bodies don't appear in Fort Collins, Colorado. No one is that pale. Someone was playing a sick joke. They put that dummy in the field and spray painted that brown stuff to make people think that's a body. Then, when someone freaks out over it, they'd have a laugh about what suckers people are.

I was not falling for that. They wouldn't make a fool out of me. And I sure as hell wasn't going to say anything to anyone about it and have my dad, once again, tell me what a dumbass I was for falling for a prank. At that time of the morning, when the sun had not yet crested the horizon, the figure looked like a blonde-headed CPR practice doll, called a Resusci Anne Simulator doll. For the next eleven years, I would think I had seen the body of a blonde woman out in that field and would only find out so many years later that she was actually a redhead. I walked to about six feet from the figure and decided it was a CPR practice doll stolen from one of the schools. I turned around and walked on to catch my school bus, pretty sure of my opinion, and proud that I didn't fall for someone's sick joke. I had endured taunts at school, and some of the kids were relentless in their teasing of me. Would they take a dummy and dump it in the field I walked every morning to catch my bus? Were they watching me to see if I was freaked out?

But the butterflies in my stomach didn't go away with my revelation that I had seen a Resusci Anne. I caught my bus as usual, and didn't say anything to anyone, as usual. I wondered, *What if it really was a body?* And I had a more horrifying thought: *What if it really was a body, and she was still alive, and I did nothing to help her? I just walked off!* No, it was a mannequin. *But what if?*

I didn't mention what I had seen that morning to anyone. I wasn't really even sure what I had seen. The problem is that I had few friends and no one I trusted enough to confide in. If the body was real, it would still be there when I headed home, and I'd confirm what it was and call the police then.

A FEW MINUTES after I had caught my bus, a man riding his bicycle by the field on Landings Drive noticed something that caught his eye. The sun was now coming up. He stopped and walked over to the curb to get a better look. He also thought he saw a mannequin in the field. As he looked, he also wondered: *Could it be real?* As he scanned the field, he saw the brown trail from the curb to the body. At the curb, there appeared to be a dried pool of blood. He decided to go to a nearby friend's house and call the police. At 7:13, he told the police he saw "what looked like a mannequin" out in the field, but he thought it could be a body, based upon the blood he saw at the curb.

FORT COLLINS POLICE officer Michael Swihart arrived at the scene within minutes and walked out into the field to get a closer look. As he approached the body, he saw that her eyes were open and her skin was ghostly pale. She had obviously been dead for some time. A paramedic came out to Peggy's body and confirmed that she was dead. Swihart notified Fort Collins police dispatch that the matter was a homicide. Soon, more police arrived and secured the area to begin their investigation. From the amount of blood in the field, it was apparent she had been stabbed, but the knife wound was not visible at first. It was clear from the positioning of the body and clothing that one of her nipples had been sliced off. Fort Collins police soon had twenty officers at the scene. Officer Sherry Wagner was summoned at 7:40 A.M. and told to report to Boardwalk and Landings to assist with the investigation. She was assigned the job of canvassing the neighborhood to see if anyone in the nearby homes had seen or heard anything helpful. The fourth house she approached was at 401 Skysail, just a couple hundred yards from where Peggy's body was found. A young couple—Dr. Richard Hammond and his wife, Becky—answered the door. They told Wagner they had both been home all night and had gone to sleep sometime before midnight. They had not seen or heard anything suspicious or out of the ordinary. As Wagner went door-to-door, she heard the same thing over and over again. Nothing out of the ordinary had caught anyone's attention in the neighborhood the night before.

A detective named James Broderick arrived at 7:45 A.M. and wondered about the placement of Peggy's body. Obviously, her pants had been pulled down and her blouse pushed up. He thought her body had been placed in a particular manner by the killer, rather than just haphazardly dumped by someone in a hurry. He suggested the murder was a sexual homicide, possibly a "lust" murder. He later contacted the FBI's Violent Criminal Apprehension Program (VICAP), hoping for some further insight.

Out in the field, police began studying the scene. Peggy lay on her back with her arms above her head. Her eyes were open, and her purse strap was still over her arm. Her skin was white, and even a police officer would later admit she looked like a mannequin as she lay in the field. The officers approached the body carefully, trying not to disturb any footprint impressions in the dirt. The Larimer County Medical Examiner, Dr. Pat Allen, came to the scene and also went out and examined Peggy as she lay in the field. Allen agreed with Broderick that the body had been "displayed," and he also noted that someone had cleaned portions of her body, wiping blood off of her with a sponge or a cloth. Peggy's blue jeans and panties had been pulled down to just above her knees. She was wearing dark-red cowboy boots.

The roadway of Landings Drive was elevated a few feet above the field, with a small ditch near the curb. Police photographers recorded the scene and even brought in a fire truck so they could take elevated photographs of the area. In the earliest photographs, the scene is still dim as the sun was still rising. The later photographs have more sunlight in them, and onlookers can be seen gathering just beyond the crime-scene tape the Fort Collins Police Department had strung across the road.

As the police examined her body at the scene in the field, they took note of the fact that someone had cut off her left nipple and left her breast uncovered and on display. There was a long cut on her right cheek, with some odd marks that paralleled the cut. They also found two hairs on her that came from someone else. Going through her purse, they found identification. She lived nearby and worked at the Fashion Bar, a store in a nearby mall. Photographs were taken, and she was carried from the field. Later that day, Allen would conduct an autopsy.

Detective Jack Taylor attended the autopsy, along with

district attorney Terence "Terry" Gilmore. Allen determined that Peggy had suffered a punctured lung and the knife had also severed an artery and fractured a rib. She had not been sexually assaulted. He observed the injury to her breast, where someone had sliced off her nipple. After a closer examination, he noticed that a piece of her clitoris had also been sliced off. No one had noticed it in the field because the injury was difficult to see with the victim's legs together. To photograph the mutilation, two people were required to manipulate the body to expose the injury. Allen determined that the death was not instantaneous; Peggy may have lived anywhere from five to thirty minutes after she was stabbed the one time.

A LITTLE WHILE later, as I was sitting in typing class, someone phoned the teacher and asked him to send me to the school's main office. "Tim, someone wants to speak to you."

At the office I was greeted by a man I'd never seen before. He told me his name was Gonzalez and that he was a police officer. He wasn't wearing a uniform, but he had a badge hanging from his belt. "Tim," the plainclothes cop said, "my name is Officer Francis Gonzales. Do you know why I'm here?"

"Yeah," I said, "I think I saw a body."

Gonzales took me into an empty office and pulled out a yellow legal-sized notepad. He began to question me.

"If you suspected you saw a body, why on earth didn't you report it?" he asked me incredulously.

"Because the body looked just like a Resusci Anne

doll," I told him. "I thought someone was playing a prank. Like when me and my friends used to draw chalk outlines of ourselves in the street to make it look like someone had died there. That's what I thought was going on, and I wasn't going to fall for it."

"Yeah," he agreed. "I thought it looked a little like a mannequin myself when I first arrived at the crime scene."

He questioned me for probably an hour. I explained to him how I lived at home with my dad and that my mother had passed away. He asked me about everything I could remember from the night before until the next day when I arrived at school. I searched my memory and tried to tell him everything I could think of that might help with their investigation. I mentioned a broken-down car at the hardware store I'd seen on the way to the Albertson's store.

"Tim," he said, "will you come down to the police station and fill out a witness statement for me?" He asked it as if I had a choice. I would never tell authority no. I just wasn't raised that way. My father taught us to respect authority without question.

Gonzalez drove me to the Fort Collins PD, and along the way, I told him about how my father was a retired U.S. Navy man and had spent time in Vietnam. The police radio squawked with what my dad called "cross-talk" as the dispatcher sent out messages and patrol cars answered.

Outside the station, Gonzalez led me to a flight of stairs that went under the building, like we were climbing down into the cellar of the police department. He pressed a doorbell-like button and someone buzzed us in. He led me to a desk and handed me a blank witness statement. He told me to write a complete statement of everything I had told him at the school. My statement was a single page. At the school he had probably taken thirty pages of notes on his legal pad, writing down almost everything I said. So I wrote out what I knew about the case:

> *At 6:16 I woke up, got up and took a shower. At 6:20 I ate breakfast and then got dressed. At 6:55 I left to catch my school bus. I walked through the field and then seen something between the two ditches. At first I thought it was a Resusa Annie Doll, but then I seen what looked like a trail of blood. I circled around to take a closer look at the bodie. I stopped about 4-6 feet away from it and looked at it. It still looked like a doll. It had its pants pulled down. I thought that some kids were just messing around so I walked on and caught the school bus.*

Gonzales wanted more detail so I turned the statement over and drew him a map of the field where I had seen Peggy's body. While I was drawing, two men came out of another room, one of them crying uncontrollably. One man—who I later learned was officer Randall "Ray" Martinez—was trying to comfort the other. I assumed one of them was a relative of Peggy's. His reaction looked to me like he'd lost a loved one, something I could relate to. When my mother died, I had felt just like that man looked. Later, I found out the man crying at the police station was Matt Zoellner, a former boyfriend of Peggy's. Gonzales then drove me home.

2

Mom

M Y MOTHER, MARGARET, HAD DIED A FEW YEARS EAR-
lier, when I was eleven years old. She had started
feeling sick on a Sunday, but thought she merely had the
flu. On Monday morning she went to work, even though
she still felt sick. She thought she could make it through
the day but ended up coming home early, something she
never would have done if she could avoid it. I could never
remember my mom taking a sick day before. She worked
all day on an assembly line at Teledyne Water Pik and then
came home each day to cook, clean, and do the laundry
and the other household chores and still had the energy to
tend a garden in the summer. I never helped her with the
chores. I feel bad about it now, but she had never asked.

Mom stayed in bed the rest of that Monday and all day

Tuesday. My dad spent a lot of time watching after her, and I was left alone in the living room watching TV for a couple of evenings. She said she felt good enough to go back to work on Wednesday. Again, she only made it half-way through the day. She came home looking gray, feeling worse than before. This wasn't getting better like we expected if it had been the flu.

On Friday, I got in trouble at school for not having my homework done, so a teacher kept me after class to finish it. I missed my school bus as a result, and when I couldn't reach my parents by phone, the teacher had to drive me home. When I got there, my dad was upset. Although he hated doctors and hospitals, he had talked my mom into going to the hospital. Whatever she had, it clearly wasn't the flu. They had been waiting for me to get home before they left for the hospital and assumed I had been goofing off rather than just coming straight home after school. As we were walking out to the car, my mother actually told me to be careful and not to get too close to her so I wouldn't catch whatever she had. Even then, she was more concerned about us than she was about herself.

My dad drove us to a local family doctor, but we were only there for fifteen minutes before the doctor sent us to the hospital. Mom's blood pressure was way too low. It wasn't the flu.

We rushed Mom to the local hospital emergency room. It wasn't like what I'd seen on TV. Doctors and nurses weren't rushing around and yelling orders. A nurse calmly came over with a wheelchair for my mother, and they took her away. It was the last time I saw her alive.

It became clear that she was not coming home right away, so my sister, Serena, who was seventeen at the time, and her boyfriend took me home. Dad stayed at the hospital that night. On the drive home, Serena told me that Mom could die. I thought she was being dramatic. With modern medicine, what could go wrong? She was in a hospital, and the nurses and doctors seemed so calm when they came and got her. I was sure she would be fine.

They sent Dad home from the hospital around midnight, telling him my mom had stabilized. I didn't hear him come home, but he was there when I woke up. He took me over to my uncle Melvin's house for the day so he could go back to the hospital and be with Mom. It all seemed so routine. I spent the day playing board games with my cousins Travis and Rodney until my dad called, and my uncle drove me back home.

As we were leaving, he told one of my cousins to leave a note for their mother, "telling her what's happened." Again, it didn't seem terribly significant.

The drive home was quiet, but no one said anything important had happened. When we got there, my dad was waiting for us out front. As we walked up to the trailer, he said, "Come here, boy; I've got something to tell you." I walked up to him, and he spoke in a quiet voice I rarely heard him use. "Son, I've got some bad news for you. Your mother just passed away."

My mom's symptoms, which looked just like flu symptoms, were actually from a condition called myocarditis. Her heart had begun to fail when the heart muscle became inflamed from an infection. She was so focused on taking care of the rest of the family that she didn't think of complaining about how she felt.

"What?" was all I could manage. I felt the crushing weight of sadness that I would experience a few more times in my life. I started crying immediately. My little world had just been torn to hell. She couldn't die! She was safe in a hospital! She looked sick when I saw her last, but she didn't look like she was going to die. No one told me she was going to die. I never got to say good-bye to her. "Welcome to the real world," I thought. Bad things can happen to anyone. And they happen without warning.

I went and sat in my room and cried. A little while later, Serena joined me. She put her arm around me, and we cried together. Eventually, my cousins thought it would be a good idea to get me out of the house, so we all went for a walk down by the lake. We had spent many summer days playing down by "our" lake—we called it that, even though it was a few streets over from the trailer—but its shores were now lined with large houses. Now the lake was surrounded, and deemed "private." This was just another sad thing for us to lament as we walked. We hung out by the lake, talking about everything else besides my mother's death.

Uncle Melvin offered to let me stay at his place for the weekend, and my dad agreed. That night, Travis, Rodney, and I went and saw a movie called *The Entity*, starring Barbara Hershey. It was a horror movie about a woman who is terrorized by an invisible, evil spiritual force. It's the kind of movie we all loved at that age, but I couldn't get my mind off my mother. When Barbara Hershey took care of her children in the movie, all I could think of was how I no longer had a mother to take care of me.

I took the next week off from school. That Tuesday, my teacher, Ms. Cook, showed up at my house with a bag full of Valentine's Day cards. The day before had been Valentine's Day. The two sixth-grade teachers had also encouraged all of my classmates to write me sympathy letters in class. I went through all the cards and letters and cried some more. I still cried every day, but it eventually became less and less frequent.

Dad deferred to Serena and me on my mother's funeral arrangements. He felt that we knew her better. I started to see some of the guilt my dad felt for all the time he'd spent away from us while he was in the military. It wasn't his fault, but he couldn't help feeling that way. Serena and I picked out the coffin and the funeral announcements. My mother loved the mountains, and we found cards with mountains on them. Serena picked out a dress and described my mother's hairstyle to the woman who would do her hair for the funeral. We wanted her to look like herself. We also hired someone to sing "Amazing Grace," which was her favorite song from church.

At the funeral, none of us cried. Serena and I had been raised to not show emotion, and I had already spent so much time crying at home. We sat stoically through the funeral. The body in the casket did not look like my mother. They had done her hair all wrong and put on way too much makeup. She never wore all that much to begin with, and her face was puffy from the medical treatments she'd gotten at the hospital.

. . .

I HAD LOST my mother, but I soon found out I would lose much more. My mother had let me have quite a bit of freedom. She let me spend a lot of time with my friends, even staying over at their homes or having them sleep over at our place. I had a very large circle of friends while she was still alive.

My dad took over in the only way he knew how; he had spent twenty years in the Navy. As a result, my mother had done the bulk of the parenting, and for many years, we only saw him on the weekends. I remember meeting him at the airport when he came home and seeing him in his dress blues. Rows of ribbons adorned his left breast, a gold chief's insignia marked his left arm, and a long row of gold hash marks covered his left sleeve, indicating more than sixteen years of honorable service. I was proud of him then, and of the service he provided to the country. I didn't realize until later that none of it would help him with his parenting skills.

Having spent his life in the military and dealing with sailors, my father gave me the military treatment. I couldn't spend the night at other kids' homes, and they couldn't spend the night at ours. I couldn't just come and go when I felt like it. I had to account for where I had been and tell him where I was going. I soon noticed I had lost most of my friends. Who could blame them? After my mother's death, they would call and ask if I could come over and spend the night. I always had to tell them no. Eventually, they stopped asking.

3

The Investigation Begins

THE DAY THEY FOUND PEGGY HETTRICK'S BODY IN THE field, my dad had spent the better part of the day watching the police out behind our trailer. He was upset with me for not calling the police or doing something when I saw the body. After listening to my explanation, he then told me about the beehive of activity in the field behind our trailer. He told me about how a policewoman, Linda Wheeler—as I would later learn—had come by earlier that day, and he had told her that he saw me walking through the field that morning, and he thought I had stopped to look at something. When she told him there was a body in the field, they both went to the window but couldn't see it from the trailer because of the berm out back. They had both walked out back to the barbed-wire fence, and from there, they could just make out the top of the body. Later, my dad saw them pick up Peggy's body and carry it away. This explained how the police knew to come to my school and ask me about what I had seen.

At one point my dad said the police were walking from the body to the curb, retracing the steps of the killer as he made his way back to the street. It looked to my dad like the strides were quite long, indicating the person who had left the prints had been running. I had walked across the blood trail—not alongside or on top of it. I knew that I had circled back and looked briefly at the body but my footprints would not have been near the body, nor would they have been going back and forth from the body to the curb. I was only fifteen years old and wore size eight shoes. I weighed only 115 pounds. If the footprints in the field told a story, they would certainly confirm my story and clear me of any suspicion.

Officer Michael Swihart came by our trailer that evening and asked me some more questions. He also asked me about my shoes. I was wearing the same ones I had worn that morning, and I showed them to him. He took out a camera and photographed my shoes.

Later that night, the police took down the crime-scene tape and opened up Landings Drive to traffic. Once the details of the murder were made known to the general public, the field became a tourist attraction, with cars slowing down to gawk and people walking around out where Peggy's body had been left. Children on bicycles rode through the field. Seeing that people must have gotten information from somewhere, my dad wanted to see if the police had released any additional details about the murder, so he drove us down to the 7-Eleven to pick up a copy of the *Coloradoan* to see if it had any coverage of the murder that had taken place in our backyard. The paper gave details about the crime, including the fact that the victim had been stabbed in the back.

The next day I headed out my back door and through the field to the bus when I noticed a man in a car driving slowly along Landings Drive, watching me. I thought it was creepy, so I started running and he sped up, following me. As I started to head toward the homes on the other side of the field, he yelled out to me, "I'm a police officer. I'd like to ask you some questions." I approached the car cautiously. He looked like a police officer, but he wasn't wearing a uniform, and his car was unmarked. He had a little flip notebook in his hands, and he asked me why I was walking through the field. I pointed to my home and to my school bus and told him that this is how I walked every morning. With that, he let me go in time to catch my bus. He was Detective Russell, and he had been assigned to watch the field for suspicious activity.

The kids on the bus were all talking about the murder. One of my classmates—who lived about a mile away—told everyone sitting near her that she was scared, with a murder happening "so close" to her house. She must not have realized there were people who lived within a couple hundred yards of the field. Another guy on the bus speculated that the victim was probably raped after she died, "because the corpse would have been stiffer and tighter." I was disgusted by many of the comments, but then again, these kids only knew about the story from the news. I had already spent a few hours of my life discussing it with the police. And I had seen the body. Much of what was fueling the childish speculation on the bus and at school was a story from another newspaper. The *Reporter-Herald* had reported the additional detail that the *Coloradoan* had chosen to leave out—that Peggy's body had been mutilated.

4

School

SCHOOL WAS TOUGH FOR ME. NOT LONG AFTER MY MOM died, I started junior high. All my friends from my elementary school went to a different junior high than I did. As a result, I showed up with no friends on day one. Although junior high is generally pretty tough on teenagers, it's even worse for a quiet and skinny kid with no friends. I wasn't good at making friends and felt like an outsider from the start.

Adding to my difficulties, my father picked out my clothes for me, and he had a penchant for western wear. Although there are undoubtedly cowboys in Colorado, I was the only kid dressed like one in my junior high. The rest of the student body was divided neatly into the jocks and the preppy kids, and I stood out from both groups.

Standing out in junior high is dangerous. I became a target for bullies, more so because I was small for my age.

I can't blame my dad too much. He was overwhelmed after the death of my mother and didn't really know how to pick up the slack after she was gone. For example, he didn't insist I shower every day. That's the kind of thing other kids notice; it can make you a target. I was called names, spit on, and pushed around. One kid stuck gum in my hair. Another shot staples at me with a rubber band. There was no way to fight back. I was outnumbered—one against everyone else, it seemed. I withdrew.

I also discovered an outlet: I liked reading horror novels and seeing scary movies. I began drawing scenes from movies and scenes I imagined. I first read the novelization of the movie *Rambo: First Blood Part II* in the eighth grade. Rambo became my hero. He used Zen Buddhism as a defense mechanism to deal with difficulty. As a result, he could overcome anything. I started writing my own stories. It was a way to escape the very ugly reality that was my junior high existence. Reading helped me imagine what my dad had been through. He had spent time in Vietnam, and I read everything I could find on the topic. Soon, many of the stories I wrote were set in Vietnam, and they involved heroic soldiers battling against overwhelming odds—and winning.

High school was a welcome change of scenery. A lot of the kids at this school had no idea who I was, and I managed to blend in for once. There wasn't the same kind of hazing either. I was quiet and shy and didn't make a lot of friends, but there were more kids I could say hi to who would say hi back. My dad still wouldn't let me have friends over to my house, or go visit other kids after school, so my social life was nonexistent. I still managed to enjoy some of the classes. Playing flag football outdoors on a crisp morning during phys ed was always a highlight. I continued to draw pictures and write stories. It was how I dealt with the boredom of the classes and not having anyone to talk to.

IN MY TENTH-GRADE health class, I sat next to a kid named Wayne Lawson, and I often showed him the gory pictures I drew. Wayne was one of my classmates who seemed to appreciate the drawings. He liked the same kinds of movies I did, like *Nightmare on Elm Street*, and he'd often give me an approving "Cool" and nod when I showed him my latest creation. The day after Peggy's body was found, Wayne asked me if I'd heard about the murder. *Heard about it?* I told him I was the first person to see the body. Wayne asked me if I reported it to the police. I lied and said I had; I didn't want to admit I was dumb enough to not realize it was a real body. I told him how much Peggy's body looked just like a Resusci Anne doll.

"Where did you find the body?'

I tried to explain it to him, but Wayne didn't know my side of town. I sketched a map, putting in landmarks he'd know. He knew where the driver's-license bureau was, so I pointed that out to him and then drew in other things in relation to it. My trailer, the ditch, and where the body had been. I drew another map, just of the field, showing where the drag trail had been and where the intersection and the bus stop were.

I also drew a picture of someone being dragged. It had really disturbed me to see the body and I couldn't get it out of my mind. Since I was always drawing, it was only natural that I would draw what I imagined had happened. It was obvious from the trail of dried blood that the body had been dragged into the field. In fact, when the police questioned me, they referred to the "drag trail" between the body and the curb. I started drawing the person who was doing the dragging and some blood dripping. I also drew a few arrows and some other doodles and then I stopped. I never finished the drawing. The same page contained pictures of a dinosaur and a person whose tongue was being nailed to a table.

A little later that day I was in math class when the teacher's phone rang. She answered it and looked at me. After she hung up, she told me to take my things and go to the office. "Ooooh, you're in trouble," a few classmates sang out. I got up and left and found my dad and a detective named Harold "Hal" Dean waiting for me in the hallway. Dean drove us to the police station.

5

The Interrogation

Hal Dean took my father and me into an interview room and read me my Miranda rights. I was scared, but I knew I had done nothing wrong, so it couldn't hurt me to talk to the police, right? After my father and I signed the forms to say we understood what was happening, and consent forms to let the police search our home, Dean asked if it would be okay for him to interview me without my dad present. We agreed—again, being an innocent by-stander, I had nothing to hide. With the signed consents in hand, detectives went to our trailer and ransacked it while I was being questioned.

With my dad out of the room, Dean closed the door. Before he could ask me a question, I asked him one. "Are nunchakus legal?" Nunchakus are a martial-arts weapon made out of two wooden sticks held together by a piece of rope or chain. I had made a pair of them after seeing them used in Bruce Lee movies. They weren't as easy to use as they seemed in the movies. I wouldn't have been able to hurt anyone with them even if I'd wanted to.

Dean told me they were considered illegal.

I immediately told him that I had a pair of them in my dresser drawer. I knew the police would find them when they searched my room, and I was worried I would get in trouble for having them.

Dean told me not to worry. The police wouldn't be too worried about them. I was relieved. If he was telling the truth, it was the only thing I had to worry about that day.

Dean then asked me to go through the story in great detail—the same one I had detailed in the witness statement the day before. I told him I saw something in the field and doubled back to look when I crossed the drag trail. The trail looked like spray paint to me, and it led to what I thought was a Resusci Anne doll, a mannequin we practiced CPR on at school. He asked me for details, even though I told him I had only looked at the body for a moment. Did I see if her panties were pulled down? Had I noticed her breasts? I couldn't answer a lot of his questions with anything more than "I don't know." He would continue to press me for details, even after I told him that. I soon noticed that he asked me follow-up questions regardless of what my answers were. I'd say I didn't see something and he would ask me what it looked like. I'd say I didn't remember something and he would ask me for details. Was he even listening to me?

I told him I had gone to the Albertson's store the day before the killing and could put together a timeline based upon the television shows I remembered watching. I got home in time to watch the end of *Too Close for Comfort*. Later that night I watched *Carson's Comedy Classics* and *M*A*S*H*.

He asked me if I knew Peggy, and I told him no. He asked me if I had ever seen her before, and I said no. He asked if it was possible I had seen her before, and I told him that if I had—like in a crowd or something—I certainly didn't remember and never would have recognized her. I did not know who she was.

It soon became clear that Dean didn't believe anything I told him. He started one question by asking me about "this lady that you may or may not have known." I had already told him I did not know her. Dean didn't care what I said; he was convinced I was lying to him.

He then told me that Peggy had a "thing" for younger guys and that she was a "tease." Had she been teasing me and flaunting herself as she walked by my home? Dean said he remembered what it was like when he was fifteen. Maybe it was partly her fault, what had happened to her? He wanted me to say that Peggy had teased me and then I got out of control and killed her. He asked me what I thought of that.

I told him I thought someone had killed her and dumped her body there. I told him I thought she had been raped because her pants had been pulled down. He asked me if I knew anything else and I told him no. That was all I knew.

"C'mon Tim. I think there's some more there. I understand that you'd be afraid to tell me, because you're scared of what could happen. But I think there's some more there that you need to tell me and that you need to talk to me about. Can we do that? I'm trying to work through this thing with you here. Can you do that with me? Can you tell me what happened?"

I couldn't stand it anymore. He wasn't listening to a thing I was saying. "I don't know what happened!"

He asked me about my dogs. Wouldn't my dogs bark at someone out in the field? I told him they probably would. What about if it was someone the dogs knew? I told him they barked at anyone out there. They barked at my dad; they barked at me; they barked at my uncle. It didn't matter if they knew someone. He asked if I could call out to them and get them to quiet down. That I could do, and I told him so. I didn't know it at the time, but a decade later, exchanges like this would be twisted by the prosecutor to make me look guilty. At trial, they would tell the jury about the end of this part of the discussion—how I said the dogs would quiet down if I told them to be quiet—and not about the part where I said the dogs barked at everyone, even people they knew.

He then returned to his "let's-work-through-this-thing-together" angle. He asked me why I thought she was raped. He asked me why I thought she was killed. I kept telling him that I didn't know the answers to his questions. "Okay, why do you think somebody would do that?"

"Because they're *sick*!"

He asked me if it was possible that someone killed her because he was "afraid." Was that possible?

If I said no, he'd ask why I thought that. If I said yes, same thing. It was never ending. I asked him if they knew what time she was killed. I could explain where I was at any time that night, so I was curious.

Dean told me they knew, but he wanted to know what I thought. "What time do you think she was killed?"

"Probably late at night or early in the morning."

Dean wanted me to be more specific. What time did I think she was killed?

A police officer had told me the day before that she had been dead about six hours. Simple math meant that she had been killed around 1:00 A.M. if that was true. Dean claimed he hadn't heard that and wanted to know if I agreed with that time of death. I told him I didn't know.

He kept returning to the theme that it was partly Peggy's fault that she got killed. He was hoping that by doing that, I'd be more likely to admit I'd done it. The problem for him was that I kept insisting I had nothing to do with it. I didn't feel comfortable with him telling me it was her fault. I didn't even know her; how could I say such a thing? I told him, "I'm not sure if it was her fault."

Eventually, Dean just came out and told me I did it. He said they knew I did it and had found all kinds of evidence that proved I did it. He just wanted to help me and let me explain it to him before things got worse. I couldn't imagine what could be worse than being falsely accused of murder, but he kept telling me that I had done it. I kept denying it. He started yelling at me. "Tim! Don't be lying to me, now!"

"I'm not lying!" I answered.

After a couple of hours of this, Dean asked me if I would take a polygraph. Again, I had nothing to hide, so I said I would. It didn't occur to me then that all of their yelling and accusations might cause the results to come out skewed.

They led me into another room, where I met Ken Murray. He had in front of him a polygraph machine, just like you see in the movies. Before we began the test, he asked me some preliminary questions about why I might be a suspect in this crime. I had already denied having any involvement and told him I had no idea who might have killed Peggy.

He then asked the five-hundred-dollar question. "Have you ever thought about doing anything like that?"

I didn't know all the facts of the murder. All I knew was that she had been stabbed to death. I'd written hundreds of stories that contained every form of killing imaginable. Shootings, stabbings, bombings, electrocutions, drownings—you name it, I had written it. If I'd written about it, I must have thought about it, right? I had never considered doing anything like that in real life, but I had thought about it. I answered truthfully: "Yes."

Murray attached wires and sensors to me that ran into a device with needles dragging across a strip of paper like a seismograph. Murray told me the machine was infallible. I noticed that this room also had a two-way mirror in it.

While I was being tested, I was being watched by detectives on the other side of the glass. I could even hear them talking about me while I was being tested. Murray asked me some introductory questions, but they were just to make small talk while he strapped me in.

"What is your greatest ambition?"

"I want to join the Navy."

"What's the worst thing that has ever happened to you?"

"Probably my mom dying." I thought for a moment. "Or this."

"Is anything bothering you right now?"

"Yes," I told him.

"What?"

"Being falsely accused of murder."

Once the machine was up and running and I was connected to it, he asked me a series of simple questions. "Are you in Montana?" "Are you in Colorado?" "Are you in Canada?" He told me to answer one question truthfully, and then the next falsely. Does it really work the same if you're told to lie? I didn't ask; I just did as I was told. The whole time, my heart was pounding. The men who had been yelling in my face just moments ago and telling me I was a murderer were now watching me through a two-way mirror.

Murray then told me the questions he would be asking me:

"Have you told me the truth about that murdered girl?"

"Are you the one that stabbed that girl?"

"Right now can you take me to the knife used to stab that girl?"

"Yesterday did you murder that girl?"

"Yesterday do you know for sure who murdered that girl?"

"During your entire life, even once, did you ever tell an important lie?"

"Other than what you've told me, during your entire life did you ever hurt anyone?"

"Do you intend to lie to even one of my questions?"

He asked me the questions randomly and paused after each answer I gave. Adrenaline flooded my system, and I could hear my heart beating in my eardrums. When I gave him my final answer, he then told me that the first set of questions and answers didn't count. We would do it again, and this time it would be for the record. He went through the list again but this time he asked each question several times. Each time he changed the order.

After the last question, Murray came around to my side of the table and knelt in front of me. "There's no doubt about it, Tim, that you're not being completely truthful. Your chart shows you're not being completely truthful."

"On which question?" I asked.

He wouldn't tell me. He asked me to tell him what had happened between me and "that woman." Murray turned from being a polygraph operator into another inquisitor, like Dean. As he asked me this, he reached over and grabbed my hands. The way I was raised, men don't hold hands. Why was this guy touching me? It creeped me out almost as bad as the questions he had just asked me.

Still holding my hands he said, "I might as well lay it out on the line for you, Tim. They've built a pretty good case against you. But they don't have your side of the story. This isn't going to affect your career in the Navy. You need to get this taken care of now so that it doesn't come back on you at some point down the road. I don't know all the details. You can provide us with those details." His sales pitch now sounded just like the one Dean had been pitching me. Except this guy was holding my hands. I told him I didn't do it.

"Unless you're able to provide your side of things, people are going to think bad things about you. I don't want people to think bad things about you."

"I didn't do it!" I said again.

"Tim, I'm not interested in your lying at this point! That's what the polygraph is for! It's only a matter of time before they can prove you did this. Lying at this point isn't going to help you. You had terribly strong reactions to the questions."

We went around in circles like that. He kept asking me to confess and telling me I failed his test, and I kept denying that I knew anything more than I had already said. I finally got so angry I did the only defiant thing I would do at the police station: I pulled my hands away so that Murray was no longer touching me. It didn't slow him down any, though. He kept badgering me, calling me stupid, saying I was being a "baby," and telling me that if I simply admitted I had done it, I wouldn't get in very much trouble. Eventually, he got up and walked out of the room. He left me hooked up to the machine.

To this day, we don't know what the actual results of my polygraph were or if I really was tested properly. The results of the test—the "charts" drawn by the machine—have been "lost," and the way the polygraph was conducted was entirely inappropriate. For all I know, the entire exercise was a ruse to make me confess. People within the department told me later that my test was "inconclusive," which was also what the results were for Matt Zoellner, Peggy's ex-boyfriend. These same people told me that Murray wasn't really a polygrapher in the true sense of the word. He wasn't trying to find out if I was telling the truth; he was simply using the machine as a tool to try to get me to confess. Veterans of the Fort Collins legal community note that Murray never seemed to come up with results that were useful and often simply said that the results were inconclusive and that the charts had been lost. Later, the police claimed that Murray had conducted polygraph examinations on four people and that all four of us failed, showing deception. None of us knew each other, and obviously, four people weren't involved in the killing of Peggy Hettrick.

While I was sitting in the room alone with the wires and sensors still attached to me, I heard one of the detectives on the other side of the two-way mirror say, "Look at him. He's thinking about what he did."

Eventually Murray came back and disconnected his machine from me and then took me into another room to be interrogated by another detective. This one was Sherry

Wagner. I suspect she was watching me while Murray was holding my hands and saw how uncomfortable that made me. The first thing she did was sit me in the corner of the small room and pull up a chair as close as she could to me, invading my personal space. She leaned in toward me. "I need to know what happened. Did you come up behind her? Did she fall? Did she trip onto the knife? What happened, Tim? I don't know."

"Neither do I," I responded.

Wagner started off like the others, ignoring everything I said to her and everything I had said to the others. Wagner fired questions at me. "What time did you leave your house?"

I started to respond, "I didn't . . ."

"No! Shut up!" She held her hand up in front of my face like a traffic cop. She pointed her finger at me and scolded me. "I can tell by the way you look, you do know. I can tell by the way you respond, you know. You did it. What time?"

I shrugged my shoulders. No matter what I would say to her, she wouldn't believe me. All she wanted me to do was to confess to a crime I didn't commit. We went around and around, with me responding "I don't know" each time she insisted "Tell me! You *do* know!"

After a few minutes of that, she grabbed my arms. She pulled my hands forward and placed them on the table. I wasn't happy with these strangers touching me—first Murray and now Wagner. "Are you going to be like the junior high kids who come in here and deny everything they did? Or are you going to be a responsible adult? What's it going to be?"

"I don't know what happened."

At one point she asked, "What seems to be the reason you can't accept responsibility for what you did?"

I told her I didn't like being accused of something I didn't do. Wagner corrected me: "I'm not accusing you of anything. I'm telling you, you did it."

From time to time I stopped answering her questions with anything beyond a yes or no, so she changed her line of questioning. "How tall are you?"

"I'm 5' 10"."

"And how tall was she?"

"I don't know."

"You don't know?" she asked angrily.

"I never saw her standing up." I couldn't estimate how tall she was when I only saw her in the field for a moment in the predawn darkness.

Wagner stood up. "Come on. Was she shorter than me?"

"I don't know."

She jumped around from topic to topic. At one point she asked me to describe a "scenario" in which I had attacked Peggy. Each time I inserted a fact that didn't fit with the actual murder, she would yell at me to change it to fit the facts of the real murder. She asked me how I would murder someone, as if it was something that everyone had planned on doing. I told her the easiest way would be with a machete. Since Peggy hadn't been killed with a machete, she told me to use a hunting knife in the "scenario."

She asked me what kind of a souvenir I would take from a victim I killed in her "scenario." I didn't understand her question.

"Money," I replied, that being the only thing that came to mind.

"What else?" She was driving at something, and I had no idea where it was going.

"Her purse, because it might have money in it."

"You don't want the purse. The purse can be traced. You show up at home with a purse and your dad's gonna know. You don't take the purse, that's stupid."

Yes, she was now calling me stupid because I couldn't figure out what she wanted me to steal from a dead woman in an imaginary scenario.

She then told me that the "scenario" I had spelled out described the crime so perfectly that it proved I had killed Peggy. I knew she was bluffing at this point; at one point in the "scenario," I had said I would have used a pink hunting knife. Although I owned some hunting knives, I did not own a pink one, so I had purposely chosen one that made no sense. When she had yelled at me about that, I had told her "I thought this was just a scenario?" She also told me that Peggy had not been killed with a machete and that her body had not been hidden under a bridge, something else that I had thrown into her "scenario."

She then told me I had left "all kinds of things" at the crime scene. I knew she was lying because I hadn't been close enough to Peggy's body to leave anything. I couldn't argue with her though, because it was pointless. At this point, she was getting frustrated and angry and just decided to spend some time humiliating me in front of the detectives on the other side of the two-way mirror.

"Do you ever masturbate?"

Of course I did, and I told her. But what could that possibly have to do with Peggy Hettrick's murder?

She pulled out a diagram of the field. "Did you masturbate here?" She pointed to the curb where the drag trail started.

"No."

"Did you masturbate here?" She pointed to where Peggy's body had been.

"No."

She then shifted gears again and asked me if maybe I needed to see a counselor "for this."

"I would if I did that!"

She lectured me about why she thought I was having trouble admitting I had killed Peggy and then she finished. "Want to talk anymore?"

I shook my head.

She picked up her stuff and walked out of the room. I thought it was over since I had indicated I didn't want to be questioned anymore. I was wrong. Ray Martinez then came in, and we started all over again.

Martinez tried to scare me. He walked into the room and slammed a plaster cast of a footprint onto the table in front of me. The cast hit the table so hard it broke in two. He started yelling at me. I finally pointed at the cast and said it was the wrong size; it clearly wasn't from one of my shoes. Martinez insisted it was a cast of one of my footprints. It was annoying; anyone could see the cast was the wrong size. I finally got fed up with it and pulled off one of my shoes. I laid it against the cast. It was way off.

6

Broderick

Since Martinez wasn't getting anywhere, a mustachioed, dark-haired detective named James Broderick joined us, and he ratcheted up the questioning. It got to the point where he wasn't questioning me so much as he was yelling accusations at me. I kept denying them, and he'd turn up the volume. He was the officer who had gone to the trailer as soon as we had provided the signed consent forms, and he had personally torn apart my bedroom. There, he found my knives and my drawings and stories. I would find out later that Broderick wasn't alone in rifling through my stuff. Five other members of the Fort Collins police were inside my trailer, accompanied by Terence Gilmore, the district attorney.

Broderick was really hung up on the drawings and stories, and he yelled at me about them. Apparently, he had spent quite a bit of time looking at my pictures and actually reading the stories I had written. For instance, one of the stories, called "Reds vs. Recons," told the story of children at war when their parents were away. I was inspired to write it after reading William Golding's *Lord of the Flies*. Broderick thought it contained much deeper meaning and told me it proved I was guilty.

"And you're trying to tell me you're not involved? The bicyclist [who reported the body] doesn't have this stuff! I don't have this stuff! Nobody has this stuff but you. And you know why you have it? Because you're the one who did it! Tell me how this thing ends, Tim. Tell me how it ends! Be honest with yourself and be honest with me and tell me how it ends. Are you going to do it again? Was it enough? Is it over with now? Did you finally get to live it? Was it enough? Is it over with now? Did you finally get to live it? And was it everything you expected, or not? Was it not as hard as you expected? Was it easier? Are you surprised at how easy it was? Tell me! Tell me exactly how you feel now! Are you going to do it again?! Do you feel compelled to do it again?"

I said back to him, "I told you I didn't do it!"

At this point, Martinez told Broderick they had a phone call. "Jim, we got the district attorney's office on the line. We've made a decision on what we're going to do. Tim, I'm sorry . . ." His voice trailed off. Martinez and Broderick both tried to look like they felt sorry for me.

Broderick stepped it up one more notch and started suggesting that I had lost any chance I had to come clean.

"Why couldn't you just stand up and tell me? Why did you have to bring it to this? You made a mistake! Why can't you just SAY it? Why is it so hard for you to tell me? Is that what it came down to? A phone call to the D.A. because of this, because you didn't tell me? I'll never know! You'll never know now, will you. You can't come forward and tell me, I'm disappointed in you! I can't tell how disappointed I am in you! I thought anybody with this calculating of a mind and cunning would be able to come through in the end. And you can't! It's a story that never ends. It's like somebody's tried to write a book and then stopped! What do you think of a story like that, that just ends and leaves you? You're doing it to yourself! You're missing out! Are we . . . are you going to come forward? Are you going to jail? Sit over there . . . go to trial? You'll like that! All that publicity?! But you never had a chance to tell anybody! It's unfulfilled! You haven't finished yet! You knew it was going to end, and it has ended. And now you're not going to finish it. You're going to hold back? Are you still winning? Are you still winning if you go to jail? Are you still winning when they sentence you?"

He paused, so I answered his last question. "No."

He started yelling again. "You've lost! Somebody had to lose, partner! YOU lost! I don't care one way or the other! It's just that you got to admit it when it's over. People get killed in battle, right? Their friends die! A piece in you just died a minute ago when Ray told me this! It's over! You're not free anymore!"

Martinez interrupted him; he'd been holding the phone through Broderick's rant. "Jim, they're waiting on the line for a decision. Tim, it's now or never. Tell us quick. What's the deal? What's the deal? Be honest, please."

"I have been honest," I answered.

Martinez looked at the phone. "Okay."

Broderick threw in, "That's too bad."

No matter how much they yelled at me, threatened me, or tried to trick me, I just couldn't get myself to admit to something I hadn't done. Even so, it wasn't over. They simply began another line of questioning, as if the whole "D.A. phone call" had never happened.

They could yell at me all day and all night if they wanted to. I would continue denying any involvement in the crime, but they weren't going to be able to break me by simply yelling at me. They didn't know I had built up a tolerance to that kind of treatment. After my mother died, my father had a very difficult time dealing with Serena and me. One time, while visiting family, the two of them got in an argument, and Serena stormed out. My dad took me with him to look for her but told me he didn't really care if we found her. "I might just ship you off to military school then," he added. It was clear he didn't want to raise me— or so I thought. He yelled at me all the time, about not cleaning my room, about not doing my homework, about everything. He was right to be upset with me—what he was saying was true. I hadn't cleaned my room or done my homework. It's just that the yelling didn't accomplish anything other than to make me immune to outbursts like that from adults. It peaked when my dad told me he hated me. He even suggested I wasn't his son—maybe Mom had fooled around while he was in the Navy—although I knew that wasn't true. It would be years before I overcame the effects of this treatment. At the time though, it meant that an adult could scream, yell, or threaten me and wouldn't see a glint of reaction from me. And, Broderick had nothing on my father. My father's yelling made Broderick's look childish by comparison. When Broderick was finished, he sent in my dad and closed the door.

7

Dad's Questions

MY DAD AND I WERE ALONE IN THE INTERROGATION room. I was hoping he'd come in and save me from the intense questioning, but he had no idea what had been happening in there before he came in. He also had no idea what was going on with the investigation, but he seemed to think I might have somehow been involved in the murder. "Tim, if you did it buddy, you're going to have to say something so I can get some damn help."

"But I didn't do it!" They had told him there was overwhelming evidence pointing to me, but, like they had done with me, they hadn't told him what any of the evidence was. "They seem to think I snuck out at night and did it. While you were asleep."

I could tell my dad was thinking about it, whether that

made any sense. But the police had talked to him and even told him some of the same things they told me. I know, because he said one of them to me.

"You gotta help me so I can help you." He suggested a lawyer or a public defender but he wanted me to tell him what I had done.

I kept telling him I had done nothing and had nothing to do with the murder. My dad was torn: he instinctively trusted law enforcement and authority because of his life in the Navy. He also knew I'd been home all night and couldn't have climbed out and then back in my bedroom window without him knowing it.

"But they've searched your room." He probably assumed they'd found something in my room that he didn't know about, some kind of evidence. "Well, I don't know how the hell I can help you, buddy, if you won't tell me anything! I can't! And my hands are tied. So I wanna help. I wanna help them out, and I wanna help you out so we can get you the hell cleared . . . so we can get some help!" He still seemed convinced I had killed Peggy Hettrick. He took the police at their word. They had told him that his son had brutally killed and mutilated a woman right in the backyard, and he believed them, even though there was no way I could possibly have done it. He kept pressing me to cooperate, to just admit that I had done it so we could get some legal help. Even though I had the same respect for my father that he had for authority, I couldn't do it. I kept denying that I had done anything wrong or that I had anything to do with the murder.

We went around in circles like that for while. My dad

kept pushing me to tell him everything I knew, and I kept telling him I didn't know anything. They had also told him I'd failed the polygraph, even though the results were inconclusive. Eventually, my dad threw in the towel and left, and Broderick returned to the room and continued questioning me. No one ever told us that the entire time my dad was talking to me, the Fort Collins PD was surreptitiously videotaping the entire conversation. Anything I told my father when we were alone in the room would have been inadmissible in court, and taping us without our consent was illegal. And they knew it. Still, they did it anyway.

After nine hours of questioning, they decided to call it quits for the night. It was ten o'clock, but they weren't done with me yet. They asked me if they could take my shoes to examine them. I had no problem with that since I knew where my footprints were in the field. Broderick took my shoes and never offered me anything to put on my feet. I assumed he would give me something to wear, but I was wrong. They asked me to go to the hospital to give blood. I walked out of the police station and then through the hospital in my stocking feet. There, I gave them a blood sample. My evening finally ended, and I got to go home.

When I got home, I saw the mess the police had made out of my bedroom. They had ransacked it and removed all kinds of things. Not only had they taken my stories and drawings, but they had taken all my knives and even all my shoes. I had to borrow a pair of my dad's tennis shoes for school the next day. They were way too big for me, but that was the least of my worries. They also asked me to come back the next day for further questioning. As frustrating as it was—they kept accusing me of killing Peggy and then not listening to what I told them—I agreed to come back on the thirteenth at one o'clock. Since I wasn't guilty of anything, what harm could it do? It didn't matter; I really had no choice.

TWO DAYS AFTER Peggy's body was found, the police went back out to the field where her body was dumped and searched it more thoroughly for clues. Thirty people, including police officers, both on and off duty, stood shoulder to shoulder and walked slowly back and forth across the field. The group included members of the Explorer Scouts, a local organization to encourage kids who were interested in law-enforcement careers. It was strange for the police to do this now; there had been a massive amount of activity in the field after the police had taken down their crime-scene tape the day before. Was there even a possibility they could find uncontaminated evidence out there a day after the body was found?

The activity at the scene sparked rumors in the community, and soon calls were flooding the police station and the local newspapers. Had another murder taken place? Were they looking for more bodies? The police chief issued a press release to dispel the rumors; they were simply looking for clues to find out who killed Peggy Hettrick. Until this murder was solved, the community would be on edge.

. . .

THE NEXT DAY at one o'clock, I left school and showed up at the police station by myself, and once again, Martinez spoke with me. This time he tried being overly nice to see if that might help. He showed me the computers they had at the police station and demonstrated how they worked. He asked me about school and about my grades. He noticed a Navy pin I had on my jacket and told me he'd been in the Army. He asked me if I might want a police badge. I told him no.

He asked me if I had any ideas on where the police might look for evidence to try and solve the case. At least he wasn't yelling at me. I thought about it and suggested they look in the woodpiles out by a nearby lumberyard and maybe in the ditches near the road. These things seemed terribly obvious to me, but I had nothing else to offer him.

After a while, I began to wonder why I was even there so I asked him, "Do you still think I did the murder?"

He looked at me and said, "Yes, Tim, we know you did the murder."

They let me go without keeping me there all evening. As I walked home, I noticed I was being followed by an unmarked police car.

Meanwhile, Broderick followed up with the VICAP request he had made to the FBI. An agent from the FBI told Broderick that he could make some educated guesses about the perpetrator of the Peggy Hettrick murder. Murderers like this were usually involved in voyeurism and often were involved in stealing women's panties. He said that if the murderer were to strike again, it wouldn't be for at least six or eight months. Broderick had run a crazy idea by the FBI agent: he told the agent that the date of Peggy's murder coincided with the anniversary of my mother's death. It didn't—it was off by a few days—but the FBI agent didn't know that. The agent said that if that was a factor, they should watch my activity on the anniversary date of my mother's death and Peggy's murder, to see if I killed another woman on that date.

The police continued searching the neighborhood around my trailer and even fanned out a bit, searching buildings and ditches farther and farther away from my home.

On the fifteenth—four days after the body had been found—the police even brought in a canine unit to scour the area. An Officer Clingan found a credit card under the bridge over the drainage ditch not far from where Peggy was found. The credit card was lying on the surface and belonged to someone named Theo Meyer. The card had not been there previously; that ditch had been searched several times already. Near the card were men's shoe prints with a distinctive horizontal line pattern. Theo Meyer was a woman who lived on Skysail, a street with houses whose backs faced the field where Peggy's body was found.

At school, I began hearing from classmates that they had been questioned by the police. My friend Mike had the police at his house, asking him and his mother all kinds of questions about me. He and I often shot our BB guns together, but he couldn't believe that I was actually a suspect in a murder case. I told him about my marathon interrogation sessions at the police station, and he was amazed. I later heard similar questions from other kids: "Are you really a murder suspect?"

The Monday following the murder, I was sitting in art class. Peggy's body had been found on Wednesday, and on Friday, the police had come out to the field where they'd found Peggy's body and had done a line search with a whole bunch of volunteers, including some teenage Explorer Scouts. They were looking for evidence. One of the Explorer Scouts was in my art class, and she asked the group sitting at my table, "Who's Tim Masters?" Her name was Kelly, but she had no idea who I was.

"I'm Tim Masters," I said quietly. With all the attention I'd been getting recently, I knew this wasn't good.

"Oh," she replied. She might not have known I was sitting at her table. "The police told us to stay away from you because you're dangerous." She went on to explain, "I'm an Explorer Scout and I want to be a cop. I helped do the search in that field where they found that woman's body the other day. When we finished, two Fort Collins police officers told all of us to stay away from you because you were a suspect and you're dangerous."

"What?!" was all I could say. I couldn't believe they had told people I was a suspect. And to tell my classmates only guaranteed the story would spread like wildfire.

Now that Kelly had the table's attention, she continued. "You should have heard the stuff they told us to look for in the field. It was gross. That woman's nipple had been bitten off. They told us to look for it in the field." The kids were grossed out, but I knew some of them were looking at me, wondering *Did he bite her nipple off*? Still, some of my friends came to me and told me they knew the police were wrong to accuse me of this.

From time to time, I'd see the police following me. They weren't very good about being secretive, even when they used unmarked cars. I think they didn't care if I knew; they were trying to scare me, to see what I might do. On one occasion when I saw them following me, I cut behind a building and climbed through a hole in a fence and took off running. I looked back to see a couple of the cops standing at the fence, watching me get away.

Around this time, I started drinking. I had beer before, but had never been drunk. I knew some older kids who could get alcohol and it wasn't hard to get my hands on beer and whiskey. Drinking was a way for me to escape and it was how I dealt with the pressure of being accused of murder. I got drunk every chance I could. My dad got mad at me a couple of times for coming home drunk but he never knew how often I drank.

8

Peggy

PEGGY LEE HETTRICK LIVED IN AN APARTMENT IN FORT Collins about a mile from where I lived. She worked at a local clothing store, the Fashion Bar, and spent a lot of her time in and around a small area between where she worked and where she lived. Peggy did not own a car and would walk to and from work or to meet friends at local bars and restaurants. Her former boyfriend, Matt Zoellner, also lived within Peggy's walking circuit.

Peggy was outgoing, a characteristic she had probably developed as her family moved around the world with her father, who was in the U.S. Air Force. She had graduated from high school while living in North Africa and had spent time in many different states. She was thirty-seven years old, pretty, stood about five feet two, and weighed about 120 pounds, with red hair and blue eyes. Like me, she had aspirations of becoming a writer.

I never knew her and never saw her alive, but I eventually heard all about her and can now reconstruct her movements on the evening before she was found in the field on February 11, 1987, from police reports and later court testimony. When the police searched her apartment, they found diaries and an unfinished novel she had been working on. On the evening before she was killed, she had gotten off of work at 9 P.M. and gone to her apartment. When she discovered she had been locked out of her apartment, her final odyssey of wandering Fort Collins began.

When the police canvassed the local bars and restaurants, there was no shortage of people who knew and liked her. Patrons and workers all spoke kindly of her, and they told the police about how she would often be seen walking in the neighborhood. She had been dating a local used car salesman named Matt Zoellner, but the relationship had hit a rough patch. As the police began piecing together Peggy's last evening in Fort Collins, they discovered that Zoellner had seen Peggy at a bar called the Prime Minister, a place they both frequented. Earlier that evening, Zoellner had been at a bar called the Rumor, where he had met a woman, and the two had agreed to go to the Prime Minister for drinks. When he got there a short while later, Zoellner said he ran into Peggy in the parking lot. She told him that she had been locked out of her apartment by her roommate and she said she might need a ride home. She hoped to go inside the bar and call her apartment to see if she could wake up her roommate, who was sound asleep inside.

Once inside the bar, Peggy saw Zoellner with his new lady friend, and she even saw her kiss him. Zoellner found the situation awkward and went over and offered Peggy a ride home. She declined, and around closing time, they parted ways. Peggy made a phone call and then walked off into the darkness, while Zoellner went back to his apartment with his new friend.

Zoellner's date would be his only alibi. And Peggy would never be able to tell anyone what happened to her after this.

9

More Investigation

THE POLICE WERE FLOODED WITH TIPS. LATER, WHEN I was given access to the police files from the investigation, I saw how much activity Peggy's murder spurred. A waitress at a local Perkins restaurant called the police and told of how she had seen some suspicious men in the restaurant the night of the murder. They had been accosting female customers and acting suspiciously. They were driving a car with Texas license plates. Shortly after the police took statements from the waitress and the two female customers, they got word that the car was back at the Perkins. A police officer named Paul Landolt raced out to Perkins and found the car and the men who were driving it. After some brief questioning, the men agreed to let the police search the car. In it, they found a sharp boning knife hidden under the front seat, some marijuana in the ashtray, a cooler full of alcohol in the backseat, and some pornographic magazines. One of the men had no picture identification. There was also a bag in the car that contained a knife sharpener.

They decided to bring the men in for questioning. Their story quickly turned bizarre. The car they were driving was a rental, and it had been rented in someone else's name. The two men now claimed to have only known each other for a few days; one of them had picked the other up hitchhiking. At the restaurant, they had claimed to be old friends. They claimed to have spent the night Peggy was killed out drinking together. The police asked them to have the person who rented the car come in and vouch for them, and soon a man showed up to do that. Landolt and Broderick decided that their stories were consistent enough to rule them out as suspects in the Hettrick murder case. It didn't seem to bother them that one of them had a rap sheet of petty theft, grand theft, stolen vehicles, and forgery in the states of Texas, California, and Louisiana. The other man had been found guilty of battering a law officer, resisting arrest, driving while intoxicated: things he had done in Kansas and Nevada. One detective even noted his belief that the men were drunk at the time they were being questioned at the police station.

Landolt and Broderick decided to release the men. The next morning, Martinez had second thoughts. The police went to the address where the men claimed they were staying, and there was no one there. They called the rental agency and found out that the car had not been returned and that the credit card used to rent it was bad. They sent word to local law enforcement to keep an eye out for these men, but they cancelled it after a couple days. Since the men were probably out of state, the police considered it a dead end.

A few days later, a detective called the rental-car company and found out the vehicle had been impounded in Texas. The two men had been arrested on other charges and were in jail. Landolt quickly called the jail and found out that one of the men had been released, but the other was still being held. Rather than go to Texas and interview the man, Landolt asked a Texas police officer if he would ask the prisoner if he had been involved in Hettrick's murder. The police officer called him back and said that the man told him he wasn't involved. His alibi was the other man, the one who had been released from jail already. The Texas police officer told Landolt he believed the man's story, even though he didn't know how to get ahold of the alibi witness to try and confirm the story. So, despite all of the red flags raised by these odd characters, and their knife and knife sharpener, the Fort Collins Police Department closed the file on them and continued hounding me.

TWO WEEKS AFTER the murder, there was a strange incident at the Prime Minister. A woman named Terry Safris was working the door for an event that required tickets when she was confronted by a man who threatened her. Terry had red hair and was roughly the same height as Hettrick. The man came toward Safris and pulled an icicle out from behind his back. He made stabbing motions toward her with the icicle. He then disappeared. She was so shaken that she contacted the police and told them the man was built like an athlete, approximately thirty years old, and had light brown hair and a square jawline. The police didn't do much to follow up on this, however. They were too busy working on the Hettrick murder and somehow did not see the obvious connection.

Another woman reported an incident even closer to where Peggy's body had been found. Rosey Sinnett called the police on April 17 and said she had been walking on Landings Drive near the scene when a man exposed himself to her. He was partially erect and in his midtwenties, perhaps twenty-seven years old. He had a muscular build, brown hair, and a square jawline. The police made note of her report but did nothing further. Again, they had a murder to solve.

While they focused on me, other suspects seemed to come and go—suspects that most people would have stopped to wonder about. In March 1987, the police heard about a suspect in a sexual assault case in Aurora, Colorado. Robert Owen Young was being looked at for a recent assault, and his rap sheet was impressive. In the previous twenty-six years, he had been convicted of robbery, burglary, kidnapping, rape, and impersonating a police officer. It seemed Young raced out to break the law whenever he was released from prison. On at least one occasion, he escaped from prison as well. When the police came to question him about the recent sexual assault, he got in a shoot-out with them that ended when he put his .44 revolver to his own head and pulled the trigger. Detective Wheeler went through some of Young's belongings with the Aurora Police Department but found nothing linking him to the Hettrick murder. Among his things they found "numerous loaded guns" and a thousand rounds of ammunition. Out in his truck they found a rifle and more ammunition. He also had several knives, but detectives ruled Young out as a suspect because the knives they saw were too short to have been used to stab Peggy. The police seemed to be operating on the assumption that Peggy's murderer must have saved the murder weapon.

THE POLICE ALSO questioned the recent boyfriend of Peggy's, Matt Zoellner. The two had dated for some time but had recently begun seeing other people. There was some question about how "off" their on-again, off-again relationship was. It was clear that it wasn't that "off" to Peggy. Just three weeks before she was killed, she wrote in her journal about a recent date with Zoellner. "For some odd reason today I'm uncommonly happy. Matt came over the other nite and professed his love about 63 times. Oh, I hope it works out."

Clearly, it wasn't working out, though. Several witnesses told police that Peggy would sometimes hang around Matt's apartment late at night to see if he brought anyone home with him. One witness claimed Peggy would hide behind cars in Zoellner's parking lot, especially if she saw him talking to any women at the local bars. Another friend said Peggy would sit on the curb down the street from

Zoellner's apartment late at night and wait to see him drive by, to see if he was alone. A former roommate of Peggy's claimed that Peggy had gone so far as to hide inside Zoellner's apartment to see if he came home from the bar alone. She also said that she was familiar with Peggy hanging out at the Prime Minister and that on the occasions she walked home—which she did quite often—she would not have walked the Boardwalk and Landings route.

This last point seems terribly important, but the police ignored it in their investigation when they investigated this murder. The Prime Minister was about a half mile west of my trailer and Peggy lived about a mile or so north and east of where I lived. The shortest and most direct route for her to get from the Prime Minister back to her apartment would take her north on South College Avenue and then east on Horsetooth Road. Those two roads were shorter and also better lit than Boardwalk and Landings. If she had chosen to walk by my home, it would have been a much longer walk down poorly lit roads.

The day after the murder, Broderick and police officer Bob McKibben went to the car dealership where Zoellner worked to ask him about Peggy. He told them how he had seen her the night before at the Prime Minister. Broderick asked him what had happened, and Zoellner said they "had a fight." Peggy had seen a woman come up and give him a kiss. He knew Peggy wasn't happy seeing that. He spoke with her for a few minutes and heard about how she'd been locked out of the apartment. He then went and joined his friend at a table in the Prime Minister.

During his interview with Broderick, Zoellner explained how he had spent the rest of his time at the Prime Minister with "Shawn," a woman he had met the night before. In fact, he did not even know Shawn's last name. After the bar had closed, they had gone to his apartment and drank some more. Eventually, around 3:00 A.M., Shawn had left. She would be the one who would provide Zoellner with his alibi for the evening. The most interesting part of the story was that Zoellner repeatedly got the woman's name wrong when he was talking to Broderick. Her name was Dawn—not Shawn—Gilbreath. This incident would shed an amazing light on how the police focused on me during this investigation—and overlooked painfully obvious clues that pointed to others. If I had gotten such a major fact wrong—like the name of my only alibi witness—they would have spun it around and claimed it incriminated me somehow. How did Broderick react to Zoellner not even remembering the correct name of his alibi witness? He put a note in his report: "It later turned out to be Dawn Gilbreath." That's it. Zoellner also smoked Merit brand cigarettes, which is the brand of the cigarette found at the crime scene and the same as the ones Peggy smoked.

As a salesman, Zoellner had access to many of the cars on the dealership lot. Broderick asked him which car he had been driving the night before, and he pointed to one. Broderick asked if the police could search it, and Zoellner consented. Inside the car, they found a gym bag filled with soaking-wet clothes. The police report indicated the clothing had either been recently washed and not dried or

Zoellner had been swimming in them. The car was eventually taken to be processed more thoroughly by the Fort Collins PD, but they found nothing further. It never occurred to Broderick that he should have asked Zoellner's boss which car Zoellner had been driving the previous evening. With access to so many cars, how did Broderick know Zoellner was telling him the truth?

Broderick, McKibben, and an evidence technician went and searched Matt Zoellner's apartment. They collected forty-five items of evidence, including some "very large" knives with homemade handles, a razor blade, and some Merit brand cigarette butts. One of the knives had a ten-inch blade. They found a tweed sports coat hanging on the back of a chair, and Zoellner told them it was the coat he had been wearing the night before. Later, Zoellner's date from the night before would tell police that he had been wearing a leather jacket when she saw him. Also in his apartment, the police found pornography and a pair of women's pantyhose.

Over the next few days, the Fort Collins Police Department sent teletypes to other police agencies describing the murder and asking for responses from any departments that might have seen a similar crime in their jurisdiction. They described it as a "sex assault" and a homicide.

10

More Murders

ON MARCH 18, 1987, ANOTHER YOUNG WOMAN IN HER thirties was abducted and murdered in Fort Collins. Linda Holt was thirty-nine, and the police found her body in a remote location after she had been stabbed to death. The real specter of a serial killer loomed over the community when Mona Hughes was abducted from Greeley, Colorado—which is about thirty-two miles from Fort Collins—in September 1987. Another attractive woman in her thirties, she was also murdered by someone who stabbed her in the back. Strangely, both women, like Peggy, had last names beginning with *H*.

Some people within the Fort Collins PD saw the obvious connection between the three murders. One of them was Linda Wheeler, but when she mentioned the idea, she was told that I was the only suspect in the Hettrick murder. The police caught a break when someone tipped them off to a local man named Donnie Long. The police got a warrant for his arrest, and then they spread out to his known hangouts to apprehend him. Officer Troy Krenning was given one of the lower probability places, a trailer in a park that Long had been known to frequent some time earlier. Not thinking he was likely to encounter a serial killer that night, Krenning let an Explorer Scout ride along with him. When Krenning knocked on the door, the person who answered the door said, "Sure, he's right here," and pointed at a man sitting on a couch.

Krenning identified himself and said, "Donald Long, you're under arrest."

Long stood up and said, "For what?"

"Murder," Krenning responded.

Long shot back instantly, "Which one?"

Long would later confess to the Hughes and Holt murders but was never considered a suspect in the Hettrick murder. It appears no one ever asked him. When Wheeler asked about it, she was told that Long had been "cleared," but no one would ever tell her how or what had cleared him of the crime that was so oddly similar to the two he confessed to.

Also in November, the police began following up on suggestions they had gotten from the Colorado Bureau of Investigation (CBI). A profiler with the CBI had sent over a flowchart of sorts that gave likely characteristics for the detectives to look for in suspects. One of the people who seemed to fit the chart well was a coworker of Matt

Zoellner's. Detective Jack Taylor didn't indicate what it was that made this man stand out but noted in a report that he was the manager of the dealership where Zoellner worked and he knew Peggy. Taylor asked the man to come by the station for an interview; he arrived almost a half hour late. Some of his answers struck Taylor as contradictory, so Taylor asked him if he would take a polygraph. The man said he'd be happy to and left. It is not clear why they didn't just walk him into the room next door and have him take a polygraph unannounced, like they did with me.

A short while later, Taylor called the man and asked him about scheduling the polygraph. The man had a change of heart; he told Taylor he had an attorney and that any polygraphs would have to be arranged through him. Taylor tried calling the attorney but never got a return call. We don't know if the man had a good reason for not taking the polygraph or if he had simply heard that Ken Murray's polygraphs were a scam.

THE FORT COLLINS police sent a couple dozen items of evidence to the FBI crime lab in Washington for testing, along with blood and hair samples from me and a few other people they had questioned. The FBI reported back that there was nothing linking me to any of the evidence they had viewed, no blood, no fingerprints, nothing. They did report that they found a hair from someone's head on Peggy's sock and on one of her boots. The hair was not Peggy's, and it didn't match me or Matt Zoellner.

The police also sent a request to the FBI Behavioral

Science Unit (BSU) asking them to review the case with me as a suspect and to give advice on how to proceed. They did not, however, ask them to review the case and provide a profile of the killer. They told BSU to start with me and work backward. In May, an FBI agent called Martinez and told him his opinion of me, based upon videotapes of the interviews that had been sent to Washington and based upon the premise that I had killed Peggy. He said that if I was the killer, the motive was "sexual curiosity" and that Peggy's missing "body parts" were buried in a favorite hiding place of mine. He said that if I did it, I had preplanned the attack and had snuck up on her in a "combative method by low crawling into position." I guess no one told the FBI that there were no prints in the field indicating that anyone had crawled through the field in a "combative method" or that Peggy had been killed and mutilated somewhere else and simply dumped in the field. Off the record, the man told Martinez that I was "definitely dangerous."

Martinez asked the FBI profiler if he had any ideas on how the Fort Collins PD should follow up on the case, since they had no evidence against me. The FBI made a bizarre suggestion. They told Martinez that arrangements should be made to allow me to "shadow a S.W.A.T. team member who is recognized as a sniper-man." They figured if I hung out for the day with the SWAT sniper, I might confide in him that I had killed Peggy. Perhaps the idea seemed as ridiculous to Martinez's supervisors as it seems to me now. They never called me up and asked me if I wanted to shadow a "sniper-man" for career day.

Not everyone in the Fort Collins Police Department was convinced I should be the prime suspect. Police officer Troy Krenning saw the drawings I had made and thought little of them. Krenning recognized the themes of the drawings because he had a younger brother who drew a lot of similar things. Krenning's brother was a fan of Dungeons and Dragons, the fantasy role-playing game popular with junior high and high school kids around this time. As a result, Krenning thought the drawings were fairly common and dismissed them as being irrelevant to his investigation.

THE FORT COLLINS police were stymied. They had no evidence pointing to any suspects, but a couple of the detectives were simply convinced I had killed Peggy. It was at this point that they began coloring outside the lines in their investigation. Detective Jack Taylor sent my drawings and stories to the Colorado Bureau of Investigation, and from there, they were forwarded to a man in Illinois who called himself "Dr. Robert Thorud." Thorud was employed by the state of Illinois in some capacity, and after viewing my drawings and writing, he spoke with Taylor, telling him that I was "talented and crazy." Thorud was certain I was the proper suspect and even told Taylor that I needed "some sort of psychological treatment." I wonder now why the diagnosis of "crazy" didn't tip Taylor off to the fact that Thorud wasn't really a doctor. In 2004, the *Chicago Daily Herald* ran an exposé of "Dr. Bob," noting he had worked as a psychologist for the state despite not holding a license to do so in Illinois or any other state. His diploma had been granted by a diploma mill that had long since been shut down by the state of California.

THEN, ON AUGUST 31, 1987—more than six months after the murder—the Fort Collins PD thought they caught a break. A thirteen-year-old boy named Gregory Schade was playing in a drainage ditch a couple blocks from the field where Peggy's body had been found. He found a broken survival knife. He picked up the two pieces and played with the knife for a while. He stabbed it into the mud a few times and then wiped the mud off the blade. After a while, he took it home and showed it to his father. The elder Schade called the police, and soon the detectives were swarming the area, looking for clues. They came up with nothing further, but some of them became convinced that this knife was the murder weapon, even if they didn't know who had used it. The knife was about the right size to be the murder weapon, but the police couldn't locate any evidence on it.

11

The Case Goes Cold

EVEN THOUGH I HAD BEEN RUN THROUGH THE WRINGER by the Fort Collins Police Department, they did not have enough to charge me with a crime. They made it very clear that they were going to come and get me someday because they "knew" that I had killed Peggy and they had "evidence" to prove it. I tried to get back to my normal life, but it was difficult. Everyone at school knew I had been taken out of class by the police for questioning, and the police had told everyone that I was their only suspect. Some of my classmates believed I was guilty. Everyone knew I had seen Peggy's body, and they also knew I lived next to the field where she had been found. They had also heard from the Explorer Scout that the police had warned her about coming near me.

In August, Ray Martinez of the Fort Collins Police Department called me. He asked me if I would come and
meet him at the local Perkins restaurant. I was still a sucker
for authority, so I went and met with him. I was still a
minor, but my dad was not with me. Martinez did not ask
me to bring my father, so I thought nothing of it.

He told me about the knife Gregory Schade had found
and said that it was found near my house. He said it was
the murder weapon and that it looked like the knives of
mine they had taken from my bedroom.

I came right out and asked him, "Do you still think I
did the murder?"

"There's no doubt in my mind that you did it, Tim."

I told him again that I had nothing to do with the
murder. He took a couple of photographs of me. I had finally cut my hair shorter and no longer looked like a head-
banger. When we were finished with lunch, I got up and
left. As I headed home down Landings Drive I began to
wonder if this would ever end.

12

Life Goes On

FEBRUARY 11, 1988, WAS THE ONE-YEAR ANNIVERSARY OF Peggy Hettrick's murder. Some people within the Fort Collins Police Department wondered if the killer might return to the scene of the crime on that date, or perhaps to her gravesite. They decided to stake out both locations. They rented a construction trailer and placed it across the street from the field where her body had been found. The police spent more than a week taking turns sitting in the trailer and watching the field. No one suspicious showed up. One of the officers who spent his time out there was Troy Krenning, the one whose little brother made drawings like mine. He later said he thought the entire theory about me being the killer was "foolish." Another detail was assigned to watch Peggy's grave, even using night vision goggles they had borrowed from the National Guard. Again, no one showed up. Apparently, Broderick and some others thought I might show up at Peggy's grave and lie down on top of it in the middle of the night on the anniversary of her death.

I didn't realize that the date was the one-year anniversary of Peggy's death. It wasn't exactly a pleasant memory I wanted to revisit, that's for sure. It snowed that day, so I took the bus to school and then planned to catch a ride with my friend Brett to my afternoon classes at the local community college. When I got in his truck, he handed me an envelope. It had my name on it and he said he found it on the windshield of his truck when he came out of class.

The envelope contained copies of several newspaper articles about the Hettrick murder investigation and a copy of my mom's obituary. One story was headlined, "Police Closer to a Solution in Hettrick Case." In that one, an officer named O'Dell said, "I'm not bashful about saying we have interviewed several people who could be suspects and have eliminated all but one. We're closer to putting together a case on that person than we were a year ago, and we're hoping to do that." The paper also said rumors "began circulating that police had somehow 'botched' the investigation," and "that a juvenile with affection for knives had murdered the woman." Everyone in Fort Collins knew who they were talking about when it came to a "juvenile." Since there had been rumors at school about me and this case, I just assumed one of the kids had put the envelope on Brett's truck and thought nothing more of it.

I tried to act like none of this got to me, but it was eating me up inside. Whenever someone reminded me about the murder case or asked me if I was the one they'd heard about, I'd get stomachaches. I thought I might have an ulcer. I had no appetite and was underweight for my age and height. I would get such bad pains in my stomach that I would be doubled over. I would have to lie down to make them go away.

Although I had owned knives and other weapons, I just collected them. I never used them on anyone or anything. However, when the case started worrying me and I thought about being arrested and going through more rounds of questioning by people like Broderick, I started thinking about killing myself. Not just suicide, but killing myself if I got arrested. I busted the razor blades out of shaving razors and hid them in my shoes. I sometimes even carried a six-inch-long fishing knife, which I imagined using on myself if I got arrested. There were times when I was convinced there was a cop around every corner; every knock on the door could be the police coming to get me.

The rumors swirling through the halls of school ensured that most other kids steered clear of me. My senior year was no different from the other years following the murder. I didn't go to any dances, didn't go to prom. I had no dates, no invitations to parties. I had no relationships with girls at school. I was in vocational training in the morning and regular school in the afternoon. Girls might talk to me when they first met me, but they would cut it off when one of their friends told them that I was the murder and rape suspect.

All the time I was in high school, the police kept tabs on me. My dad would stand at the front window and call out to me, "Look at that, Tim; there's a cop parked out there watching our house." My uncle Lloyd worked for the city, running a snowplow in the winter and a street sweeper in the summer. He told us that he came by our house one day and saw a police officer in an unmarked car, watching our trailer through binoculars.

At the vo-tech class one day, a former convict came in and gave us the "scared straight" talk. He told us all about how horrible prison was and how we needed to stay out of trouble because we didn't want to wind up going through what he had endured. I hated it but didn't say anything. I had been accused of something I didn't do. If I was arrested and put on trial for it, there was nothing I could do about it. What good was his advice to me? Stay out of trouble? My trouble was beyond my control.

I DIDN'T HAVE much of a social life in Fort Collins, but I kept drawing and writing. I also read a lot—horror stories and military books. I had always wanted to be in the military, like my dad and Serena. I had opted for the Navy, and I began studying *The Bluejacket's Manual*, the bible of the Navy. I memorized portions of it, like the eleven general orders of the sentry. The Navy was my dream, it was the way I would escape Fort Collins. Fighting with my dad and enduring my difficulty at school inspired me to get as far away as possible. What could get me farther away than the Navy? I became obsessed with the idea.

Right before I turned seventeen, I took the Armed Services Vocational Aptitude Battery (ASVAB), the test to determine a candidate's potential for a military career. I studied for the test for a few months before taking it, and I did pretty well on it. I got a 65, while the average score was around 45. A really good score would have been above 70. (In my boot-camp company of eighty recruits, perhaps ten scored higher than I did on the test.)

After I took the ASVAB test, I got calls from recruiters. Everyone but the air force called; it turns out the air force had more than enough people looking to get in. I knew before I even took the test that I was bound for the Navy. I wanted to get out of Fort Collins in the worst way, and I knew the Navy was the best bet to see the places that sounded exotic to me, like the Philippines. Recruiters from the army and marines called me, and I blew them off. I could sense that it pissed them off, especially after I mentioned to one that the Navy hadn't called me yet but I knew they would. Looking back on it, I was probably a bit too cocky. I was still only sixteen. The Navy did call, though, and I started my enlistment paperwork. When I turned seventeen, I went to the Denver Military Entrance Processing Station (MEPS) for my physical. There, I ran into some snags. My eyesight was pretty bad. I was seeing 50/20 in one eye and 40/20 in the other. I should have been required to wear glasses to drive, but I had somehow managed to pass the eye exam for the driver's-license test.

The people at MEPS sent me down the street to an optometrist for an eye exam. I had never been to an eye doctor before, and he told me I had astigmatism and had probably had it for some time. He evaluated my eyes pretty quickly, and I was soon back at the MEPS station. It turned out that I was also underweight. I was five feet eleven but weighed only 129 pounds. For my height, I needed to weigh at least 130 to be accepted into the Navy. Missing the cutoff by a pound didn't worry the recruiters though. They gave me a waiver for being underweight, and I completed the enlistment process. By the time I left the MEPS, I had my rate—"AMH" meant that I would be trained to be an Aviation Structural Mechanic (Hydraulics)—and a departure date for boot camp. I would graduate high school on June 2 and head off to boot camp on June 9, sixteen days before my eighteenth birthday. I would turn eighteen in the Navy at the Recruit Training Center/Naval Training Center, often called RTC/NTC, in typical military fashion, in San Diego.

There was a light at the end of the tunnel now, and I looked forward to getting out of Fort Collins. Even though it had been a few years since Peggy Hettrick had been murdered, I still got questioned about it from time to time. Before I graduated, I was working a full-time job painting houses for the city under a program called "Operation Brightside/Breakthrough." One day, one of the guys on the crew said to me, "I was talking to a friend of mine, and he told me you were involved in a murder." No matter how I tried to go on with my life, it was always there.

13

The Navy

I GRADUATED HIGH SCHOOL AND BEGAN PLANNING FOR THE Navy. When I had gone through the processing, I had been given a date to show up for boot camp. The day before I was to leave, I called my recruiter to find out what time I needed to show up.

He sounded surprised to hear from me. "Be here for what? Oh, nobody told you?"

My heart sank. "Told me what?"

"Tim, can you come down here?"

My heart raced as I drove down to the recruiter's office to find out what was going on. When I got there, the chief took me into a back room and asked me to sit down. That's never a good sign, when a chief asks you to sit.

"We were informed that you are a suspect in an ongoing murder investigation. Therefore, it was decided to DEP discharge you from the Navy. I'm sorry, but there's nothing I can do." I had committed to the Navy as part of the "Delayed Entry Program"—I'd signed up long before I actually had to show up—but now the program had discharged me.

I was crestfallen. There was nothing I could do, so I went home. My dad asked me what was wrong, and I told him. I went to my room and grabbed the paperwork I had gotten when I enlisted and all the Navy pamphlets I had accumulated over the years—all the literature that told you the pros and cons of the Navy, why you should join, and how great Navy life was. I grabbed all the stuff that said "Navy! Not just a job, it's an adventure!" I had spent a lot of time reading over it all and dreaming of a future life. And now it was gone, stolen from me. It was so unfair. I took all that literature out back, put it in a metal bucket, and lit a match to it all. I watched the paper burn up in smoke and flames, just like my dreams of having a future.

The only work I could find that summer was washing dishes at the Charco Broiler, a local steakhouse. I worked the late shift. I'd work until midnight and then head home exhausted. My dad lectured me a few times about how I needed to get a decent job, but I told him that this job had been the only thing I could find with just a high school education and no training. He decided to see if there was anything he could do about getting me into the Navy.

Dad put on his chief's uniform and went down to the recruiter's office to find out what was going on. The recruiter took my dad into the same back room he'd taken me and told him, "It wasn't my call to discharge Tim. It was the young punk lieutenant who decided to discharge Tim. Now, between you and me, he was wrong to do this. Tim has every legal right to serve his country." He pointed to the thick binder that contained their recruiting guidelines and said, "There is nothing in our recruiting manuals that says being a 'suspect' disqualifies anyone from service. My advice to you and your son is to get a good lawyer and file a lawsuit."

My dad took the chief's advice to heart. He was no longer the father who hated me, and I think he was getting over the bitterness of my mom's death. He also understood my desire to be in the Navy. His own career in the Navy gave him the understanding of what I wanted to do, and he understood the value of it. He also knew I didn't kill anyone and that my being a suspect was not my fault. Even though he couldn't afford it, my dad somehow scraped up the money to hire a lawyer. A few days later, we were sitting in the office of attorney Jan Larsen for an initial consultation.

Jan couldn't believe I'd been kept out of the Navy because I was a "suspect" in an investigation and said he would make some phone calls first, to see if it really would be necessary to file suit. The phone call from the lawyer did the trick; I later found out that the phone call started a chain reaction. Jan called the lieutenant, and the lieutenant called the Navy Judge Advocate General (JAG) office in Denver. The JAG office said there was nothing on the books disqualifying a recruit from service because he or she was a "suspect." A few days later, as I was preparing to go to my job washing dishes, the phone rang.

"Hey, Tim! Do you still want to join the Navy?" the recruiter asked.

"Absolutely!" I was ecstatic. That night I gave the Charco Broiler my notice that I was quitting. I would wash dishes for one more week and then I'd be in the Navy.

The night before I left for boot camp, I barely slept. Obstacles had a way of popping up on me unexpectedly. Would anything happen between now and tomorrow? The question kept me awake for most of the night.

I grabbed a few things to take with me the next morning, but for the most part I was traveling with the clothes on my back. One thing I knew: the Navy would provide me with everything I'd need from this point forward. I went to the recruiter's office and from there, we drove south. We picked up a few more recruits along the way and then camped for the night at a Holiday Inn in Denver. This was the staging area for new recruits, who would spend their last night here before leaving for boot camp.

One of the other recruits we had picked up wound up being my roommate that night. A lot of guys wanted to get drunk or stoned this last night of freedom before the nine weeks of boot camp. I wasn't interested in that; the idea of starting the first day with a hangover didn't appeal to me. My roommate had other plans, though. He called his girlfriend and got her to agree to come to the hotel to celebrate his last night of civilian life. She turned up at the hotel at six that evening.

"Hey Tim, can you give us some time alone?" he asked me.

"Sure, no problem." I wandered around the hotel for a couple hours and finally headed back to the room around nine. I was happy to let my roommate have some alone time, but I needed my sleep. My roommate's girlfriend spent the night with him in the other bed. A few weeks later, when we were well into our training, my roommate told me that he and his girlfriend had had sex after we had all gone to bed that night. "You were in the room and you never woke up," he told me proudly. What a class act.

The next morning we had breakfast, and then a Navy sailor came and drove us to the Denver MEPS. There, we were sworn in and shown a promotional video about the Navy SEALs. The video was a recruiting tool, but it fired us up nonetheless. Then we were given instructions on how to take the bus to the airport, fly to San Diego, and get ourselves over to boot camp.

Once we landed in San Diego, there was no one there to greet us. We wandered around a bit until we found some more confused-looking young men. I asked one of them if they were Navy recruits, and he said they were. As we talked, a decrepit Navy bus rolled up in front of the terminal, and a first-class petty officer jumped out, obviously in a hurry. He was late, but he wasn't sorry about it.

"Gather your shit and get on the bus," he told us. "And I don't want to hear a goddamn word out of your pieholes. Keep your fucking mouths shut during the ride." It was our first boot-camp experience. He wasn't bad, I thought to myself. He was nothing compared to my dad. My dad could really chew someone out.

Our destination was the RTC/NTC. My uncle Johnny and my uncle Lloyd had both gone to boot camp here. Now it was my turn. The gate guard waved the bus through the entrance, and I saw rows and rows of tan stucco buildings surrounded by acres of pavement. As the bus passed through, we saw thousands of men in uniform, marching around or standing in formation. Except for the calling of cadence and the occasional order being barked by a recruit chief petty officer, the place was totally quiet. It seemed unnatural. That many people together in one place should have made so much more noise.

We drove across the complex, and eventually the bus stopped in front a building with a sign out front that said, "WELCOME ABOARD R&O [Receiving and Outfitting] DIVISION." The building looked a little more modern than some of the others we had passed. As I was soaking it all in, the driver of the bus yelled, "Get the fuck out!"

As we piled out of the bus, we were greeted by guys in navy-blue dungarees and red armbands that said "R&O." "Grab your shit and line up over there," one of them said as he pointed to a long line that wrapped all the way around the compound. We got into line, and the red armbands kept yelling at us. "Tighten the line up. Nut to butt! Keep the line tight." We were standing within inches of each other. The line slowly moved ahead. From that point forward, I got to see how regimented the Navy was. Each of us was given thirty seconds of phone time to call home and let our loved ones know we had made it safely. My dad wasn't expecting the call, but I called anyway. He had been in the Navy; I'm sure he understood. "Hey Dad, they're making us call our family to tell them we got in alright. We only have thirty seconds to talk. Bye."

The following morning, they dragged us out of bed at 4:30 A.M., fed us, and then shaved our heads and gave us our uniforms. Our first task was to stencil our names onto our new clothes. With the lack of sleep and the unfamiliar surroundings, even this simple task seemed difficult. I saw a few guys screw up their stenciling jobs, but I managed to get mine done right. I was assigned to Company 227.

They also gave everyone a drug test. I'm not terribly comfortable with urine tests, especially when they assign someone to watch you urinate to make sure you don't cheat. There were about fifteen of us who couldn't urinate on command in front of the guys assigned to observe. Eventually I managed. About a dozen guys failed that first test. At the time, the Navy had a zero-tolerance policy on drugs, but they'd go easy on you if you failed this close to the start of your military career. These guys who failed had used the drugs before they were in the Navy. This time, they'd get off with a write-up for their service record. If it happened again, they wouldn't be so lucky.

I had been borderline underweight when I joined the Navy, but I assumed the boot-camp training regimen would make me bigger. With all the exercise, I was bound to develop some muscle, right? Turns out I was wrong on this count. Although they fed us regularly, the Navy did not give us a lot of food. Nor did they give us a lot of time to eat it. It seemed like were racing to the mess hall, racing to eat, and then racing to our next assignments. Whatever calories they gave us in the mess hall, we burned off marching and doing physical training.

Boot camp was rough. It was physically demanding and mentally challenging. Every minute of my day was now owned by the Navy, and it took advantage of that fact. Even so, I was happy. I was finally starting my life, and I was away from Fort Collins. The time I'd spent there under a cloud of suspicion for Peggy Hettrick's murder began to fade into my past.

On the first day my company formed up, Senior Chief Smith and Chief Stonehocker gathered us together on the first deck of the barracks and pulled out the recruits who had gotten good ASVAB scores. There were about fifteen of us. They then asked for volunteers and ran down a list of jobs that would need to be filled for the company: Recruit Chief Petty Officer, Company Yeoman, Mail Petty Officer, Laundry Petty Officer. Each time they announced a new position, someone snapped it up. I had been told by many people to never volunteer for anything in the Navy. One common joke I heard was that Navy stood for "Never Again Volunteer Yourself." As a result, I decided to maintain a low profile and didn't volunteer for anything. Looking back on it later, I realized I had made a mistake. People who volunteered for those jobs were promoted to the next pay grade, E-2, upon graduation from boot camp. Live and learn.

The Navy also put me back in a classroom, but for once

I didn't feel the need to doodle away my time. We studied damage control, basic military courses, history, and every other Navy-related topic you could imagine. I did well on the tests. For the first few weeks of classes, I was second in my company, academically. That didn't surprise me; I had been around the Navy my whole life, and I had heard all about the Navy from my father and my uncles. And I always knew I could do well in a class when the topic interested me.

Despite keeping my head down, the company commanders noticed me and asked me to "volunteer" for Assistant Laundry PO. The Laundry POs had to take care of the laundry every day and, as a result, missed out on most of the academic classes. I had no choice in the matter; my good grades cost me the ability to stay in the classes I enjoyed! The guy who was the Laundry PO was overwhelmed and really needed help; soon I was buried in the laundry as well. I found out that the position had its perks. I no longer had to eat lunch with the rest of the company. Instead of rushing through the ten-minute lunch as before, I got to eat in the "detail" chow hall, where I could take as long as I wanted to finish.

I found out that I also got to skip some of the more difficult classes, like firefighting and the gas chamber, where recruits experienced tear gas in what some people called "the confidence chamber." Those were two I didn't mind missing. I still had to take the tests for the various academic classes, so I just studied the books in the barracks in what little free time I could manage. My academic standing fell slightly, but I was still near the top of the company.

Boot camp was more difficult than I expected in some ways but easier in others. The physical demands were less than I expected. What killed me was the attention to detail the Navy expects from its recruits. Folding clothes, making a bed, even wearing a uniform—the chiefs could find a mistake in anything you did. It would get to the point where you were convinced that it was impossible to do anything perfectly. I had never held myself to such a minute attention to detail, so it was a culture shock for me. In later years, I would look back on how difficult boot camp was for me and marvel that the police would claim I had managed to kill Peggy and somehow not leave a trace of evidence anywhere. If they had only seen me try to straighten my bunk to the point where it would pass an inspection.

On the night after graduation, in the fall of 1989, I got drunk. It was legal for eighteen-year-olds to drink alcohol on base, and I took full advantage of that. The company commanders discouraged us from drinking, but that was all they could do. Senior Chief Smith told us, "We encourage you to stick to the honor system and stay sober tonight." The following morning, more than a few of us probably wished we'd taken those words to heart. But then again, how often does an eighteen-year-old kid graduate from boot camp?

The next day, a bunch of us who were not going to Class A School marched over to the Apprentice Training side of boot camp for more work. I hadn't gotten my orders yet, and I would spend another month there before going to join the fleet. At that point, I drew orders for the USS *Constellation*, out of North Island, San Diego. Before I had to report, I was given fifteen days of leave. Although I had promised myself I would never return to Fort Collins, it was the first place I headed. I didn't really know what I was doing, so I bought bus tickets home and back. As a result, I spent four days of my leave riding on buses that stopped at every single little town between San Diego and Fort Collins. I should have flown.

14

The *Constellation*

ONCE ON BOARD THE *CONSTELLATION*, OR "CONNIE" AS WE all called her, I settled into a routine. Some of the guys from boot camp were there, including a few I got along with really well. It was nice to finally have friends who only knew me from the Navy and had no preconceived notions about me being a killer or a suspect in a murder investigation. We didn't make a lot of money back then. We were E-1s, and after they had deducted their $100 for the GI Bill, I only made about $430 a month. I often ran low on money before the next payday. We would often pool our money to buy a gallon of cheap wine. If you wanted to get drunk for $4, there were only so many options available.

One night, a friend of mine and I had polished off a

gallon and were sitting on a bench on North Island Naval Air Station, looking out over the airfield. I decided to tell him about those terrible days in high school. It would be the first time I'd complained about it to anyone since I had spoken with Ann Livingston, my old junior high school counselor.

I wasn't sure where to begin so I said, "Something happened to me when I was a kid."

Out of the blue, he said, "Did you kill someone?"

My heart leaped out of my throat. "No, but I was accused of killing someone." I broke down crying and told him the story. "I've never hurt anyone, and they blamed this murder on me." In the years to come, this scene would repeat itself, each time me crying to a friend about the ordeal the Fort Collins Police Department had put me through.

I even told a few strangers the story. I wasn't sure of any other way to deal with the pain I felt. I would drink and reflect on my life, my wasted high school days. How I had no friends in Fort Collins. Somewhere along the line, I realized I was dwelling on it. I was grieving. And I was drinking far too much. I wasn't going out and meeting anyone. I spent my spare time drinking and trying to forget about Fort Collins and the police.

The alcohol caused some problems for me. One time, another friend and I spent the day at the beach, drinking and listening to his stereo. As we walked back to the ship, some cop cars pulled up and surrounded us, with their lights flashing. With their guns drawn, the police approached cautiously. They were responding to a bank robbery and hostage situation that had just been reported. The police decided to arrest the two of us for being drunk and disorderly. They turned us over to the Military Police, and we were released to our ship.

MY FIRST JOB on the Connie was a V-1 Division Blue Shirt. I worked the flight deck of the aircraft carrier, hauling tow bars, chocks, and chains. I assisted the aircraft handlers by "walking chocks" and tying down the aircraft on the flight deck. It was a boring job, but you had to keep your head on a swivel because the flight deck is such a dangerous place. Along with the planes landing and taking off, there were jet engines everywhere that could suck a body in one end or blast you off the deck from the other. We put to sea and spent days just turning big, lazy circles in the ocean, slowly making our way south. At sea, we worked twelve-hour shifts on the flight deck and then went below to clean our spaces.

The *Constellation* stopped in Valparaiso, Chile; Rio de Janeiro, Brazil; and Saint Thomas, in the Virgin Islands. For an eighteen-year-old who enjoyed alcohol, these places were paradise. In Chile and Rio, there were beautiful women everywhere, and if you were old enough to walk into the bar, you were old enough to drink. In St. Thomas, a bottle of Jim Beam whiskey cost only $7. I was one of about a dozen underage sailors from V-1 Division who routinely spent liberty call getting drunk and rowdy in a local bar.

We arrived in the Philadelphia Naval Shipyards in April

1990. Although we had been drinking heavily in every port of call before, we were not supposed to drink here. It was actually against the rules, but not all of us thought those rules made a lot of sense. We were allowed to drink everywhere else, and we were old enough to die for our country! So a friend of mine named Tom and I decided to have a couple of beers. It wasn't such a good idea though, when the base commander walked over and busted us. He said he was sick and tired of *Constellation* sailors drinking on his base. He thought it gave sailors a bad image. We thought it was comical. Drunken sailors! Who could imagine such a thing!?

Because this was my second alcohol incident, it earned me a trip to the Level I alcohol program called the Navy Alcohol Drug and Safety Action Program, or NADSAP in Navyspeak. Despite its good intentions, the program was not all that effective or helpful.

While docked in the Philly shipyards, we were pulled out of our divisions and sent to temporary assigned duty. I was sent to Fire Watch Division, where I would stand by with a fire extinguisher and watch a welder in action. If a fire broke out, I would step in and put it out. It sounded like a plum assignment until I found out how boring it was. I could stand for seventeen hours, just watching someone else work, and not have to do anything. I hated it. But it got worse. The duty rotation called for us to stand twenty-four hours of duty once every five days. Later, we stood fire watch from 7:00 A.M. until midnight, then got the next day off. I stood watch all over the USS *Constellation*. There are very few spaces on board that ship I have not stood watch. We also stood in all kinds of weather. It could be burning hot and humid in the summer, or freezing cold in the winter. I thought Colorado was cold, but standing next to the Delaware River in the middle of the winter, I learned what cold really was. That wet cold in Philly would bite right through your jacket.

In October 1990, I earned a DUI while driving on base. I was too drunk to walk back to the ship from the parking lot where we'd been drinking, so I figured it made sense to drive back. In hindsight, this was not a good idea. The Navy could have kicked me out for having three alcohol-related incidents. Instead, they sent me to a Navy doctor, who diagnosed me as an alcohol abuser—a step or two above a casual drinker—and assigned me to Level II treatment. I had attended Level I, which was pretty low-key "alcohol-awareness" stuff. Level II was more intense, with three weeks' worth of eight-hour-per-day classes. The classes were a hassle, and they almost messed up my Navy career. I had been waiting to attend Class A School; it was just a matter of getting scheduled. I got word I had been scheduled for Class A School when I was told to attend Level II treatment. The Level II was given priority, and the Navy could have simply canceled the Class A School at that moment. I lucked out, and they agreed to reschedule Class A when I finished Level II treatment.

One of the first things Level II treatment required was that I remain sober for the entire three-week class. With the exception of boot camp and being at sea, this was the first time since before the cops accused me of being a murderer I had stayed sober for more than a week.

During the classes, we spent a lot of time discussing our lives and thinking about what kinds of things made us want to drink. I thought a lot about the ordeal with the Fort Collins police, but I also reflected on the troubled relationship I had with my father. Toward the end of the third week, they gave us a homework assignment. We had to write our own biographies. I started out with my childhood and the places I had lived and wrote about my mother's death. Then I talked about seeing the body in the field on the way to school and how the police tried to pin the blame on me. It was overwhelming. I couldn't finish the story or even talk about how I had been ostracized in high school. My autobiography stopped right after the interrogation.

When the counselors who ran the Level II read my story, it shocked them. They called me out of class the next day, and a woman counselor sat me down to talk with me about what I had written. She only knew the first half of the story, and I tried to tell her the rest. I tried to tell her everything I had gone through, but I couldn't seem to get it out; I was crying too much. I managed to tell her the story and even told her things I hadn't been able to tell my friends in my drunken rants. After we talked, she suggested I should talk with the base counselors about my experiences. She described what had happened to me as terribly traumatic and that I should be receiving counseling to deal with it. I left her office with the intention of following up, but I never did. When the class ended, I celebrated by going out with some of my friends and got drunk.

I had been calling my dad regularly while I was in the Navy. At first, the phone calls were just simple updates. As the time went by, I realized how much I looked forward to the phone calls home. Dad and I didn't get all mushy or anything, but just "shooting the shit" with him felt great. I realized that my dad had become my best friend. Who'd have thought that would happen?

In August, I got my orders for Class A School, so I hopped in my car and drove to Millington, Tennessee, for a two-month program in aircraft hydraulics. Once I graduated, I would be qualified to perform maintenance and repairs on the hydraulic systems of Navy aircraft. I did keep drinking while I was in Tennessee, even though I was still underage. One day, I borrowed someone else's ID so I could drink in a local bar, and I accidentally showed that ID when I tried to get back into the barracks. The guard on duty recognized the guy in the picture—it wasn't me— and when he asked me about it, I was belligerent. Yes, I was too drunk to realize I was showing the wrong ID to a guard or that I shouldn't be telling a guard to "Fuck off!"

Again, I got lucky. I got a counseling chit for conduct unbecoming an enlisted man. Counseling chits didn't even go into your service record, so my command never found out about this incident, which was my fourth.

When I graduated Class A School, in October, I was automatically promoted to E-4, making me a third-class petty officer. This refocused my attention on becoming a twenty-year Navy man, like my father.

IN FEBRUARY 1992, we had a routine muster. A lieutenant commander who headed the department asked for a volunteer to go down to Virginia to help work on hydraulic ground-support equipment, including a device called a "Jenny." "We prefer the volunteer to be an AMH." The "AMH" designation meant "Aviation Structural Mechanic (Hydraulics)," and I was the only AMH in the department at the time. I didn't feel like volunteering, so I didn't raise my hand.

It became apparent that I was the only one in the department who was qualified to fill this bogus request, so I went and offered to go. It turned out that I would get to stay in barracks in Virginia that were substantially nicer and roomier than the bunk space I occupied on board the ship. Once I arrived, I was happy to be there. I also got to work regular hours, instead of standing duty for twelve-hour stretches.

It seemed a little odd, though. The guys I was working with in Virginia were nice enough, but they didn't understand why I had been sent. None of the Jennys needed anything special done to them, and no one was really sure who had asked for me to be sent. Still, the Navy works in mysterious ways, so I just kept my head down and did my job. When I had free time, I enjoyed having access to a refrigerator and being able to work on my car.

Unknown to me at the time, the Fort Collins PD had contacted the Naval Investigative Service (NIS) and told them they were investigating me in relationship to the Hettrick murder. While I was off the ship, the NIS interviewed everyone who worked with me in the Navy. They questioned my classmates from Class A School and my shipmates from the *Constellation*. They asked if I ever talked about being involved in a homicide. Five years later and thousands of miles from Colorado, the Fort Collins police—stubbornly refusing to look in any direction but mine—were still tampering with my life and alienating me from people. Imagine what my shipmates thought of me after they had been pulled aside by the NIS and asked, "Did Masters ever mention being involved in a homicide? What did he say?" In a culture where most people tried to keep their heads down and avoid untoward attention, it looked like I was causing people to get sucked into something bad.

I was enjoying my stay in Virginia when I got a call from the ship. They wanted me back in Philadelphia the next day. They said it was for "finance issues," which didn't sound right to me. As an enlisted man, however, I had to keep skepticism like that to myself. Still, I couldn't make it back that quickly. Worse, I had my own finance issues: I was broke. I lived from paycheck to paycheck and didn't have money for gas. I talked to my division officer about my predicament, and he told me I could hold off for another day. That would give me enough slack to where I could float a check at the Navy Exchange and, by payday, I would have it covered. I was more disappointed to say good-bye to my roomy bunk, the shorter workdays, the TV and refrigerator, and the other luxurious comforts we didn't have on board the Connie.

15

The Philadelphia Interrogation

THE NEXT DAY, I SHOWED UP FOR MUSTER AND WAS TOLD to report to the master-at-arms (MAA) at 7:30 A.M., but I wasn't told why. I assumed someone in the division was being investigated. I reported to the MAA's office, and I heard a third-class officer ask his boss, "Should I handcuff Masters before we take him to NIS?" Now, the alarm bells went off.

"No, that's not necessary," the first-class officer told him. "He'll be fine. Just drive him over there and check in."

I was taken to the base NIS office. The ship liaison brought me into a room and introduced me to Linda Wheeler, James Broderick, and Hal Dean. I didn't recognize them. I couldn't believe that after all this time, the Fort Collins Police Department was still messing with me.

I thought my life was finally getting on track. I was stunned.

Linda started off by asking me if I remembered her. I had never met her before, so I had to tell her I couldn't remember her. They read me my rights and asked if I would be willing to talk to them. I really had no choice. I wanted this all to end, but I also knew how ugly it had gotten back in Fort Collins.

I didn't know then about what had been happening back in Fort Collins regarding the Hettrick murder investigation. In 1991, Linda Wheeler-Holloway—she had gotten married a year or so after Hettrick was killed—took over the cold case after attending a seminar on reopening cold cases. She asked if she could have six weeks to devote to the case and found that she spent much of that time simply tracking down the files and evidence, which had not been sent to records.

As she organized the files, she was told to look at me as the only suspect and do what she could to build a case against me. When she asked why I was the only suspect, they told her that I had been on the verge of confessing back in 1987. They told her that if she watched the tapes of my interrogation, she would be convinced as well. She sat down and watched them and was puzzled: all she saw was a scared fifteen-year-old kid who appeared to be honestly denying any involvement in a crime. She couldn't find any places in the questioning where I almost confessed. She decided to check the rest of the files.

She read and reread all the reports and even interviewed many of the people who'd been interviewed years earlier.

She sent items of evidence to a crime lab to see if advances in DNA testing might turn something up. She thought she was on to something when the lab told her they had found traces of blood on my pants. The blood was mine, however, and I had told investigators back then that I had cut myself with one of my knives and could have gotten a small amount of blood on my pants. Items of Peggy's clothing were tested, but nothing new emerged.

Then she talked to Wayne Lawson. Wayne mentioned that I had told him about an injury to Peggy Hettrick's breast. He wasn't certain when I had told it to him, but he remembered me telling him about it at some time. A lot of time had passed, and Wayne's memory on the subject wasn't too sharp. Still, this was a fact that Linda thought was known only to the police and the killer.

With this new piece of key evidence, Linda asked Broderick to draft an affidavit to support probable cause for arresting me in the Hettrick murder case. The affidavit ran twelve pages and is enlightening for those who are curious about how our criminal justice system works. There was still no direct evidence linking me to the killing of Peggy Hettrick. What "evidence" was contained in the affidavit to support the warrant? After recounting the details of the murder that weren't in dispute—cause of death, where her body was found—the affidavit then turned to me. My father had seen me walking through the field that morning and had seen me pause and look at something. From where he was, he couldn't see what I was looking at. I had admitted to seeing Peggy's body and not calling the police. I owned survival knives. I had a flashlight, and the window to my room didn't have a storm window. I had a copy of the newspaper with coverage of the murder. There were the drawings and stories, and adult magazines. The affidavit told of a Quonset hut in the neighborhood and pictures and bullet holes inside it I had nothing to do with. The affidavit contained a page or two of quotes taken out of context from my interrogations, and even then it doesn't look all that convincing. One lesson was quite clear: if I hadn't spoken with the police and hadn't cooperated with them, they would have had absolutely nothing to go on. Almost everything in their affidavit came from me, by way of my interviews with them or my consent to letting them search my bedroom and my locker.

Wheeler-Holloway and Broderick did not tell me they had a warrant for my arrest with them. They simply said they wanted to ask me more questions. Wheeler-Holloway took me into an interrogation room and started out being nice—a welcome change of pace from all the others who had questioned me—and didn't accuse me of anything. She simply asked questions as if she was trying to investigate a crime. She asked me all about the Navy and why I had joined so young, about my sister and my dad, and all the time her tone was relaxed. Eventually, she got around to all of the other areas Broderick and the rest had asked about, but she wasn't yelling and she still didn't accuse me of anything.

Still, she was a cop. When I told her about the DEP discharge for being a "suspect in a murder investigation," she asked if it angered me.

"Hell yeah, that pissed me off."

"Are you angry that we're here right now, questioning you?"

"Yes, it does kind of make me mad," I told her. "I know you guys are doing your job, so I can't be mad at you as individuals." I was angry, but I didn't want them to know how angry. Here we were, years later, and they were messing with me some more. I had tried so hard to put this behind me and distance myself from it, but to no avail.

Linda tried to make me feel at ease. "I don't want to make some of the same mistakes that some of the other officers who interviewed you did. Can you think of anything that they did during their interviews that you just didn't like, things that ticked you off, or things that happened, so I don't do those things?"

"Just . . . being accused of the crime itself pissed me off. Just them standing there saying 'You did it. We know you did it,' just pissed me off."

She managed to avoid accusing me of the murder, but she did go over every little thing I had ever said to the previous officers, down to the finest details. After all these years, they still expected me to remember everything as if I had a photographic memory. What did she look like in the field? How were her clothes? What did her purse look like? What color was her hair? Somewhere along the line I mentioned that a piece of Peggy's breast had been bitten off. I added that I didn't know that from my own knowledge; I had learned it from one of the teenage Explorer Scouts from my school who had helped the police search the field. Wheeler-Holloway spent some time on this. She wanted to know exactly what I had heard, who I had heard it from, and who else may have heard it. I didn't know at the time how important this was, but I knew the answers to all her questions. The Explorer Scout had told a whole bunch of us her story while we were all sitting around a table in art class.

Linda then pulled out my drawings, and we went through them one by one. It had been years since I had looked at them, and I was a little shocked by how gory they were. Since I had been in the Navy, I had been too busy to sit around and doodle, so it was kind of a flashback to look at the pictures I'd drawn as a teenager. I told Linda that I remembered drawing a lot of things as a way to deal with my emotions. If something got me really upset back then, I didn't have anyone to talk to. I would often draw the pictures as a way to get it out of my system. We went through the drawings, and on each one, Linda would ask me when I drew it, what I was thinking when I drew it, and all kinds of detail I could never possibly remember after all these years.

She asked me about a Quonset hut, but I didn't know what she was talking about. I thought she was referring to a shed that used to be on the back of our property. She said that my dad had caught me looking at *Playboy* magazines in it. I corrected her. My dad had torn down a shed that used to be back there, but it couldn't have been the hut they were talking about; the shed was torn down long before the murder. She told me that detectives had searched a Quonset hut in the neighborhood and found drawings in the shed. I had no idea what she was talking about. She had a map of the area, but she admitted she had never been in the Quonset hut, so she had no idea where it would have been on the map. The detectives had not photographed the hut or the drawings they said they found in it. They also never tracked down the owner of the Quonset hut to find out what it was used for, or if anyone might know who had made the drawings in it.

She asked me if I had seen the pool of blood by the curb, at the beginning of the drag trail. I told her I hadn't, because I hadn't walked over there and the field was higher than the curb. You couldn't see the blood pool unless you actually had walked right up to the curb. She should have known this, since my footprints were nowhere near the curb.

Linda asked me about the bullet holes in the Quonset hut. I told her it couldn't have been me. Although my father had a .22 rifle, I had never fired it. In fact, I don't think my father had ever fired it, either. That should have been easy enough for them to verify if they really wanted to look into it. I told her I had fired a .22 rifle as part of an Outdoor Recreation class and also at my uncle's place in Laporte, Colorado.

Linda seemed to be getting tired. After five hours of asking me questions, she indicated she was done. She and Broderick switched places and it became apparent: Broderick was the "bad cop" to Linda's "good cop." He started right where he left off before. He accused me of killing Peggy. His tone and attitude were the exact opposite of Linda's, and as a result, I reverted back to yes and no answers.

When my answers got shorter, it ticked Broderick off,

and his questions became longer. He would give little speeches and then pause for a second to hear my yes or no.

> "So she didn't have a car that she'd be going somewhere else. It made sense for her to walk this direction because that's where, where she was going; so not only did it happen there, was she dragged there, was last seen there, but she walks that route. It's not as though that's an unusual place for her to have been, okay? I'm just going through 'em.
>
> "Uh, trust is kind of negative; one you don't have an alibi where other people do, like her boyfriend and stuff like that. Uh the, the believability as to why you didn't report it kind of gets shot down in a few places, in that there's logical reasons you could see for some of it. It's just whether you [inaudible]. When you see a cop and you've just seen something strange, you put one and one together and you make two. I think is what you're saying. Uh, but you look at that, you look at what you've seen and in your past comments and I think we can give that to, that you were afraid of being accused of it that's worrisome. That it's possible, you know, if you've got blood on you that may not mean that you did it but that you walked through the drag trail but it's still something to think about as to how because you know nobody knows for sure how something got somewhere. You could make all kinds of a—there could be a logical explanation, you know. They could find a gun in my back yard that was used in a shooting and conclude that it's my gun but somebody could have

thrown it over the fence too, okay? So I mean there's explanations for everything is what I'm saying. Uh, we already talked about the pornography. I guess we'll put a question mark on this Quonset hut, but I think if I didn't already tell you that the inference is that you were in it, based on what your dad said and we gotta check all that out and that there were some gunshots to the breasts and the pubic area, so again that's showing some violence and some escalated violence as well as to the drawing, but actually some things that . . . that your window was in a direct line of sight and that you have access outside that window and to a large degree the believability and, tell me if I'm wrong, that you went out that window, and maybe twice, when you were in 6th grade and never since then is that right?"

Could there really be a correct answer to that question? Broderick eventually came to a list of twenty-nine things he said pointed to me as Peggy Hettrick's killer. He ran down the list one by one, and I sat there thinking the list sounded pretty bad. It didn't help that I had been stuck in this room with these interrogators for more than six hours. I stuck to my guns; I told him again I didn't do it.

Broderick continued like this for hours. We ran long after 10:00 P.M., and he hinted he might go all night. Eventually, we broke for the night. They had interrogated me for thirteen hours that day. Broderick said he wanted to talk again the next day. I told him my story wasn't going to change; I was going to continue telling them I had nothing to do with Peggy Hettrick's murder.

Richard Mebs, the local NIS liaison to the *Constellation*, told me I could return to the ship that night or even go out for a beer if I wanted. "You know, you're not under arrest or anything, don't want you to have that impression, but if they want to talk to you tomorrow, you know, to wrap things up, then we'd like you to be available."

I agreed to come back for another day of grilling. I didn't know that Wheeler-Holloway and Broderick were carrying a warrant for my arrest and had already told Navy officials they were going to arrest me when they were done interrogating me.

At least the next day, I knew what to expect. I drove myself to the NIS building and went inside. This time, both Broderick and Wheeler-Holloway were in the room at the same time. They continued with their relentless questions, the same ones over and over again. Finally, I broke down crying. I turned to Linda. "It doesn't matter what I say to you guys; you don't believe me. What's the point?"

Broderick kept asking questions, asking me to recall things I had said in the marathon interrogation in 1987. "When you were talking to Hal Dean and mentioned something about footprints and you were pretty interested in particular footprints, and my recollection of even yesterday was, it's your feeling that if—the footprints would exonerate you. Is that right?"

"That's what I thought."

"Okay, tell—go into that as to why you think those would exonerate you."

"I figured whoever did it couldn't be—couldn't have the exact same shoe size as me and be the exact same weight. So I figured once they checked the footprints, I'd be cleared." I didn't know yet that the police had gotten clear footprints from the killer, and they could even identify the brand of shoe he had been wearing.

"So you never went anywhere around the curb area where the body was and where . . . where the . . . did you even see any blood there at the . . . at the, in the gutter?"

"Not that day."

Broderick kept bringing up quotes from the 1987 interrogation. Things like, "At one point in time you said something about her being drunk. Do you remember that?" He did this with countless quotes and snippets; there was no way I could possibly remember them all. I had very little recollection of the actual conversation from 1987. It was ridiculous that he kept bringing up all these little quotes and asking me, did I "remember that?" as if I had total recall.

Linda finally ended it. "How are you feeling?"

I was all shook up and exhausted. "It's hard for me to say. You guys just keep on haunting me." This session had lasted three hours.

"Maybe someday it will get resolved," she responded. When they walked out, that was the last I saw of Linda Wheeler-Holloway and James Broderick for years. I didn't know it at the time, but Wheeler-Holloway had changed her mind about arresting me. The affidavit supporting the arrest warrant stated that I had told Wayne Lawson that Peggy's breasts had been "cut off" and that "This is a fact known only by the police and the killer." Keep in mind that Peggy's breasts weren't "cut off" and that the police said that her breasts were exposed when they first saw her body. I didn't remember seeing them, but what I had been talking about was something one of the Explorer Scouts had told me. The night after the first day of interrogation in Philadelphia, Wheeler-Holloway had called back to Fort Collins and confirmed my story about the Explorer Scout.

16

The Case Goes Cold, Again

WHEELER-HOLLOWAY FELT THE INVESTIGATION WAS at a dead end. She contacted Roy Hazelwood, a behavioral-sciences expert with the FBI, and told him about the case. He offered to have the FBI perform a complete review of the file at no cost to Fort Collins, and he would start from square one. He would not begin with me as a suspect and work backward. With the offer from Hazelwood in hand, she told her supervisor and was told she could not pursue it. The head of the Crimes against Persons Unit at Fort Collins PD at that time was a sergeant named Don Vagge, and he subscribed to the "Tim Masters killed Peggy Hettrick" school of thought. Rather than have her send the file to the FBI for the free case review, she was told to return the file to cold cases. Two years later, she left the Fort Collins PD and began working for the Colorado Bureau of Investigation.

THE DAY AFTER my second interrogation, my division officer, Lieutenant Mitchell, called me into his office. He told me to shut the door and sit down. He was the one who had been told to order me back from Virginia on short notice, and now he heard I was being questioned over at NIS. He wanted to know what the hell was going on.

So I told him the whole story. About seeing the body and being interrogated in 1987. About enlisting and then being discharged because I was a suspect. And now, about the two detectives wanting to rehash everything from before.

He looked stunned. "Frankly, you've just shocked the shit out of me," he said. I was getting used to that reaction. People who knew me were stunned that I had been questioned for such a heinous crime and thought the notion was ridiculous.

A few days later, I was sitting in the shop with some other guys, and we were just killing time, whittling on sticks with knives we'd bought in the ship's store. I had sharpened the end of my stick when the lieutenant commander came by and noticed it. He freaked out, claiming I had made a "weapon." It wasn't a weapon; it was a stick. I had a knife in my other hand and we were all sitting on a warship with unimaginable destructive power, and here he was, lecturing me about a pointed stick. He never would have even noticed it if he hadn't heard that I was suspected of brutally stabbing a woman. It now appeared to me that the Fort Collins police had done it once again; they found a way to turn my friends and acquaintances against me.

After they left, I began to get angry. At least I had avoided getting angry at them while they were there. I called my dad to talk to him, and he told me that the police had come by and questioned him some more about the murder. While we talked, he came up with the idea of talking to Jan Larsen, the attorney we had called when I had trouble getting into the Navy. My dad went to see him a little while later. Although there was nothing legal we could do, Jan suggested the media. "Think about it, Mr. Masters. The police are always using the newspaper for their benefit; why don't you talk to the media and tell your side of the story. Use the media to your advantage for a change."

My dad ran the idea by me, and we agreed it was a good idea. It was time we told the public about the police hassling me. Dad called a reporter from the *Coloradoan* named Tony Balandran, who was interested in the story. He talked to my dad, and I spoke with him over the phone. He wrote a piece entitled "Life as a Murder Suspect." The story really only scratched the surface of what it was like to be a murder suspect, and there was no way he could explain everything I had gone through. A few days later, I heard from some guys on the ship that they had seen the article. Most of them had not heard the story before and expressed surprise that I was considered a suspect in a gruesome murder.

In February 1993, the *Constellation* headed out to sea, stopping first in Mayport, Florida. After some minor work on the ship and replenishing the ship's stores, we headed for the Caribbean. After running the ship through some trials and qualifications, we stopped in Saint Thomas, Virgin Islands. I had been here before but had squandered my time getting drunk in port. This time I was determined to explore the island.

My friend Pat and I decided it would be an adventure to walk around the island. Of course, since we spent most of our time belowdecks on a boat, we weren't prepared for the hot sun. I had worn long pants and neither of us wore any sort of sunscreen. I only got sunburned on my face and arms; Pat got burned all over.

Despite our burns, the day was still a blast. We made it all the way around the island and saw some amazing things. I swam in the ocean, and then we sat at the local outdoor nightclub and relaxed. We watched the locals put on a show, with calypso music and dancing. My sharpest memory however, is of the prices on the menu and how ridiculous they were. Soup was $7, and the shrimp cocktail (with only four shrimp!) was $10. But we had enough exotic tropical drinks to take our minds off the overpriced food and the ship waiting for us back at the dock.

THE *CONSTELLATION* RETURNED to Mayport. On a previous trip there, I had met a nice woman my age, and we had spent some time together. She was a college student and had a few more years before she graduated. I met up with her again when we returned, but I had decided to reenlist. I remembered how difficult it was for my parents when my father was away, and I decided I was not ever going to get involved in a long-distance military relationship. I never spoke with her again.

On our first day at sea, June 6, 1993, I reenlisted. The Navy offers incentives to sailors who are eligible to reenlist, and I got a few of them. I was given ninety-six hours of special liberty, which I would not be able to use right away because we were at sea, thirty days duty free, and thirty days head-of-the-line privileges. The head-of-the-line privileges came in handy when battling the long chow lines. Some of the first-class petty officers didn't like it when someone like me got the treatment that was usually reserved just for them.

My duty-free days came in handy as the USS *Constellation* headed back to San Diego. We stopped in Trinidad and Tobago and then Acapulco, and I could go ashore and enjoy my visits, knowing I did not have to worry about having to stand any watches. The day after we left Mexico, the *Constellation* pulled into San Diego, and I said goodbye to the ship for the last time.

I really enjoyed my thirty-day leaves in Fort Collins. Dad and I worked together on pulling the engine out of my Nova and putting it into his old 1969 pickup. Then, I built a new engine for my car, and Dad helped me install it. Working together on those projects was a bonding experience for us. We made a great team, and it was something I truly enjoyed. It was hard to believe that this was the same guy who had constantly yelled at me and who had said he hated me just a few years before. He was such a good guy that it seemed like a waste we'd spent so much time not getting along after Mom died.

The thirty-day leaves always ended too soon. I had to report to Naval Air Station (NAS) Miramar, also in San Diego, by August 25. On the drive there, I stopped by Serena's, in Los Angeles, and met my nephew for the first time. He was already four years old. This was also the first time I'd seen Serena since I'd left for the Navy, in 1989. It was strange to be around family again. I had spent four years back east alone. Now I was only two hours away from my sister. It was strange having this little kid call me "Uncle Timmy," but I liked it a lot.

At Miramar, I attended a six-week program for E-2/ C-2 aircraft and then went to work with VAW 110, the E-2/C-2 rag squadron. Rag squadrons were pilot-training programs. Life was so easy at Miramar compared to life on the ship that I got fat. I had consistently weighed 165 pounds on the *Constellation*; soon, I weighed a dress-uniform-splitting 185 pounds. On the ship I had been quite active; now I just sat in a classroom and then drank beer when I got out. It was startling how fast the weight came on.

Despite my rapid weight gain, I found out that the days weren't any easier than they had been on ship. They certainly weren't shorter. We were putting in twelve-hour days in Miramar, just as we had done twelve-hour shifts on the *Constellation*. Was this how the Navy was going to be? I was managing the twelve-hour days, but would I be doing this for the next sixteen years? I wanted to make a career out of the Navy, but I was having my doubts.

I found out that VAW 110 was decommissioning less than a year later. The Navy had us fill out "wish lists," indicating where we would like to go if we had the choice. There was no guarantee we would get what we asked for, but it was nice of them to pretend they cared. I listed North Island, San Diego; China Lake; and Point Magu, all bases in California. I wanted to finally be able to spend some time near my sister and her family. It was 1993, and I had spent almost no time with her since she joined the Army in 1984. We spoke on the phone occasionally, but she had been stationed in Hawaii, and I was on an aircraft carrier. She was often on maneuvers, and I was often out to sea.

I drew orders for the Naval Air Weapons Station in China Lake, California, which was near the town of Ridgecrest. I hadn't known anything about it when I put it on my wish list, and on the drive there I began to wonder if I'd made a mistake. Driving on Highway 395 took me through a barren desert landscape that reminded me of Mad Max's world. There was nothing out there. "Where the hell did I just take orders to?"

I started out living in the barracks at China Lake but soon moved into my own apartment in Ridgecrest. I was miles from Colorado, but I still thought about the murder investigation all the time. Broderick and Wheeler-Holloway had followed me to Philly. Would they stalk me here? Thinking about it upset me.

I made friends with someone who didn't drink alcohol.

Cy Linsteadt became my best friend and was a great influence on me. He and I would drink Kool-Aid and hike through desert junkyards looking at all the old cars. Cy helped me with a lot of the work necessary to keep my old Nova on the road and never asked for anything in return. He was a genuinely nice guy.

At China Lake, I got promoted to E-5. After the Gulf War, the military had been scaling back a bit, and promotions like this were less common. I was the only E-4 in my shop to make E-5, and there were some in the shop who weren't happy when they found out I'd made it and they didn't.

I was thrilled to make E-5. This encouraged me in making the Navy a career, and making E-5 was a milestone; it ensured that I would not be kicked out for high-year tenure after eight years. I would now be able to finish my twenty years, even if I never earned another promotion.

But I still drank enough to get me into trouble again. I was out late drinking in September 1995 when I took a turn too fast in my Nova. When the transmission shifted into second, the rear tires broke loose, and I lost control of the car. I crashed into the desert and totaled my beloved Nova. I wasn't seriously hurt, but the police showed up. I was cited for DUI and lost my license for three months. I also had to pay the state of California $1,400, the local police $350 for emergency response, and the towing company $300 for hauling away and impounding my Nova. I lucked out, and I knew it. I hadn't hurt anyone else, and I had gotten away with nothing worse than some scrapes and bruises.

The Navy suspended my base driving privileges for a year but took no other action against me. I thought that my punishment from the state of California was harsh enough, so I ignored the Navy's prohibition against driving on base. It didn't seem fair to me that they would punish me on top of what the state had done. This was a bad move; I got picked up for this, and I was finally sent to the Captain's Mast. Captain's Mast is a non-judicial hearing held before your commanding officer, but a step below a court martial. There, I heard about how Navy personnel represent the country 24/7, and we had to hold ourselves to higher standards than civilians. It didn't matter that the crime I was charged with had happened on California soil and that they had already punished me. As a result, I would now be punished by the Navy: I would surrender half my pay for two months as punishment. It could have been worse; I could have been busted in rank.

Still, the episode upset me. I decided I didn't want to make the Navy my career if it meant that they owned me all day, every day, for the twenty years I gave them. I decided I would not reenlist when my enlistment was up.

My second DUI earned me an evaluation with the local Navy drug and alcohol counselor. I took a 150-question test and scored as an alcohol dependent. Alcohol was a problem in my life. It wasn't the root of my problems, but it sure didn't help things.

17

Doctor Hammond

O N MARCH 19, 1995, GINA BURKHARDT WAS HOUSE-
sitting for a local eye doctor and his family. The Hammonds lived at 401 Skysail, in Fort Collins, and whenever
they left town, they would hire a local girl or young
woman to stay in their home while they were away. The
Hammonds had children who went on these trips, so the
women they hired were not babysitting. They were just
house-sitting. Gina was a thirty-year-old college student,
and she had seen a posting at the employment office of her
campus advertising the need for a house sitter.

The house was a trilevel, and the Hammonds allowed
the house sitters to use the guest bedroom in the basement.
There was a guest bathroom as well, which Dr. Richard
Hammond, or his wife, Becky Hammond, showed to the

house sitters; it contained a shower and clean towels for the women to use. Becky Hammond had been the one who had contacted Gina and made all the arrangements for her to stay at the house. Gina had another friend who would be keeping her company during the stay, and the Hammonds had no problem with that.

On the nineteenth, Gina went to use the bathroom, and something seemed odd to her. The lights in the bathroom were terribly bright, and as she sat on the toilet she could hear a strange noise coming from a heating vent that faced the toilet. The vent itself seemed strange. It was larger than other vents in the home and it was higher from the floor. From the vent, she could hear a slight mechanical whirring noise. As she leaned forward to look at it, the noise grew louder. It sounded to her like the autofocus mechanism of a video camera. It was.

Gina panicked. She called for her friend and showed her the camera in the vent. It could be seen by getting up close to the vent and looking through the slots. Gina's ex-boy-friend had been a police officer, so she called him and told him about it. When he arrived, he quickly figured out that there was a room behind the wall with the vent. They forced the door open and found an elaborate videotape setup. A camera sat on a tripod, aiming through a false vent into the bathroom. The camera was wired into the light switch; when someone came in and turned on the bathroom light, the camera began recording. Cables ran from the camera to another recording deck. Even though there was a tape in the camera, the system recorded a backup tape. They removed the tapes—someone had written the date and Gina's initials on them—and destroyed them. They looked at the contents of the secret room, and amid the jumble of electronics and wires, they found a list of names, followed by ages. Gina's ex-boyfriend suggested they call the police when he saw that the ages ranged as low as thirteen and fourteen. They called the police.

Patrol officers arrived and soon realized they had stumbled upon something huge. They called for a detective, and Anthony Sanchez, a law-enforcement veteran of more than eight years with the Fort Collins PD, arrived. After making a quick review of the secret video-recording room and hearing Gina's story, he got a search warrant and began investigating. Soon, there were ten Fort Collins police officers and detectives at the scene, including James Broderick. Of the ten, five had been involved in the Hettrick investigation. They soon found three hidden video cameras in the house. There was the one pointed at the toilet. There was another—also stuffed into the wall of the bathroom—aimed at the shower. There was a third hidden inside a fake speaker in the guest bedroom, aimed at the bed. The two in the bathroom were easy to see, and the police were all struck by how bright the lights in the bathroom were.

In the secret control room, there were hundreds of videotapes, labeled with names of victims. Gina told the officers that the tape she had pulled out of the camera had her name on it. The detectives also found detailed lists of the tapes. The lists contained the names and ages of the females on the tapes. After that, there were descriptions of what was on the tape—was she filmed on the toilet or in the shower?—and a rating system of how "good" each film was.

On one tape, they found Dr. Hammond adjusting the camera, playing with the focus adjustments and tinkering with the tripod to make sure it was aimed properly. He set an aerosol can on the toilet and then left for a moment. The focus on the can became so sharp and clear that the officers could read the fine print on the can. Hammond had gone into the video room and was fine-tuning the focus of the camera. He also panned the camera shot in, so that it would take a close up of a person as she was sitting on the toilet. The shot was in so tight that it even cropped out the subject's face unless she leaned back. Later, an officer testified that you could see "the girls' insides" as they sat on the toilet. The police had no doubt that Dr. Hammond was the man who had set this scheme up. They just did not know who else knew about it. They also did not understand the level of Dr. Hammond's perversity.

James Broderick—the detective who had interrogated me in Fort Collins and in Philadelphia—was the supervisor in charge of the Hammond investigation. He decided to arrest the doctor as soon as he returned from his family vacation. The detectives hauled everything out of the house—after photographing it in place—and left a search warrant behind to indicate that they had done everything by the book.

While Sanchez and the other police officers and detectives were gathering evidence from the Hammond residence, at 401 Skysail, it occurred to them that there was another significant aspect to this case. The back of the Hammond house faced the field where Peggy Hettrick's body was found. In fact, the house was so close to the field that it was one of the first ones canvassed by officers the morning Peggy's body was discovered. Officer Sherry Wagner had knocked on the door before 9:00 A.M. that morning to see if anyone there had seen or heard anything unusual the previous night. Both Dr. and Mrs. Hammond answered the door and spoke with Wagner that morning. Later, Becky Hammond said police officers had come into the home and gone up into the Hammonds' bedroom to get a better view of the field. The house was within two-hundred yards of Hettrick's body and her body would have been visible from the bedroom window. Becky also said that a year after the murder, police officers staked out the field to see if the killer might return to the scene; they staked out the field from the Hammonds' bedroom.

Dr. Hammond and his family returned from vacation to find Gina gone and a search warrant in her place. Dr. Hammond raced downstairs to his secret room and found it empty. Dr. Hammond's explanation to his wife was, "I've always been interested in pornography."

Probably realizing that the police wouldn't have emptied out the doctor's secret room simply because it contained pornography, she asked him if he had any more secrets. He admitted to her that he had had an affair as well. She asked him if it had been with a man or a woman. The doctor told her it had been with a woman. Still, the police wouldn't tear the house apart over an affair and some pornography. What wasn't he telling her?

At the police station, Sanchez and some others began combing through the videotapes. They knew it had been a crime for Dr. Hammond to have set up the camera to tape Gina Burkhardt, but since Burkhardt had destroyed that tape, it would have been a hard case to prove. They didn't have to look for very long to realize they would have no problem finding evidence of other crimes and other victims. In all, they had recovered more than three hundred videotapes from Dr. Hammond's secret room. Pulling out tapes at random, they soon found dozens and dozens of people being surreptitiously videotaped while using the bathroom or shower at the Hammond residence. On the tapes, they found children as young as thirteen. The Hammonds' daughter was on tape. A niece of the Hammonds was on another. Sanchez believed there was evidence to support charging Dr. Hammond with dozens of counts of exploitation of a child. Each incident of taping would constitute a separate count; each individual taped was a distinct victim. Further, the adult victims constituted further crimes with which Dr. Hammond could be charged. Some of the victims were simply visitors to the house who had been directed to that bathroom. Sanchez duly reported all of this to his supervisor, James Broderick.

Hammond was charged with three crimes: the felonies of sexual exploitation of children and eavesdropping and the misdemeanor of third-degree sexual assault.

One officer who was on the scene at the Hammond house was a veteran named David Mickelson. Mickelson was struck by how close Hammond's house was to where Peggy Hettrick's body had been found and knew that

Peggy could have walked by the house on her trips between the Prime Minister and her apartment. He noticed that someone looking out of the upstairs windows of Hammond's house would have been able to see the field where Peggy Hettrick's body had been found. Mickelson wanted to go through all three hundred tapes recovered to see if Hettrick was on any of them.

On March 22, Sanchez received a phone call from a woman in Fort Collins who said that her daughter often house sat for the Hammonds. Her daughter had discovered the video cameras herself and had dealt with them by draping a towel over the vent when she wanted privacy. Other calls began pouring in from women who'd house-sat for the Hammonds, and mothers of girls who had as well. One woman called and told the police how she and her husband had been friends with the Hammonds. They had visited the Hammond home on many occasions; Dr. Hammond had videotaped their daughters. One of the daughters had seen the video camera in the heating duct but assumed it was a security camera. The detectives found a list of names and phone numbers that appeared to be people who had responded to an ad the Hammonds had placed for house sitters. One name was of a young man; when the police called him, he said he had called about the job, but Mrs. Hammond told him the job had been filled. It made some people wonder: was Becky Hammond helping her husband find subjects to film?

Dr. Hammond retained an attorney and called a neighbor who was a psychiatrist and made arrangements to turn himself in. First, though, he told a few people he was going to kill himself. By doing that, he ensured that he would not be held in jail but would be sent for a psychiatric examination. Sanchez soon found out that Dr. Hammond would not be treated like an ordinary criminal. First, Hammond's attorney called Sanchez and told him that what Hammond had done didn't constitute a felony—he wanted the charges reduced to a misdemeanor. Sanchez paid little heed to the request from the attorney and told him to bring Hammond in. Hammond showed up at the police station with his attorney and psychiatrist, and Sanchez soon found out that Hammond had managed to find some friends within the police department. Sanchez was told that Hammond would be booked but then released on a personal-recognizance bond. Furthermore, Hammond would be charged with just one count: sexual exploitation of a child.

Somehow, Hammond had gotten the whole process shortened. He was not handcuffed, and he never had to appear before a judge. At the time he was booked, Hammond was five feet ten inches tall. He weighed 190 pounds and had a muscular build. District Attorney Terry Gilmore was at the station at the time of Hammond's booking. Mickelson was there, too, and he was shocked by Hammond's physical appearance and behavior. It looked to him like Hammond was so depressed that he was a legitimate suicide risk. Mickelson went and found Hammond's attorney and told him that something needed to be done to keep him from killing himself. The attorney assured Mickelson that Hammond would be getting whatever help he needed when he was sent to the psychiatric facility. The attorney also said that under no circumstances was Hammond going to speak to them at this time, even with his attorney present. Mickelson suggested that they should hold him in the jail, but the attorney noted that Hammond was going to be released on a personal-recognizance bond and would be fine at the hospital.

Shortly after presenting himself at the station, he was headed back out. Hammond's only concession to the police was that he would check into the local Mountain Crest psychiatric hospital to have his "problem" checked out. No one told Sanchez at the time that the doctor who had accompanied Hammond to the station and said he should be taken to the hospital was a neighbor of Hammond's.

Sanchez was also informed that the charges against the doctor were going to be misdemeanors and not felonies. Charges are a matter for the district attorney, so Sanchez—though puzzled—continued his investigation. Meanwhile, District Attorney Gilmore announced that he had to disqualify himself from handling the Hammond case. In a statement to the press, Stuart VanMeveren, of Gilmore's office, said that a family member of someone in his office was either a witness or a victim in the matter. The statement was intentionally vague but drew obvious questions. It would later become known that Terry Gilmore and his wife were friends with the Hammonds. Recently, they had gone to dinner at the Hammond house and then the two couples had gone out to the Fort Collins Lincoln Center.

As a result of the disqualification of his office, the court ordered the appointment of a special prosecutor on March

21. Gilmore sent the file over to the special prosecutor, one from a neighboring county. Todd Taylor routinely received requests like this when conflicts arose in neighboring counties. He got a copy of the appointment order and the police report and expected he would be soon getting more materials so he could prepare the case and prosecute Dr. Hammond.

Becky Hammond informed the police that she had also hired an attorney. She would be willing to speak with them in a few days. On March 24, five days after the police had carted off the contents of the secret room downstairs, Becky finally spoke with detectives. Sanchez was informed that Becky had been granted immunity by the Larimer County District Attorney, the same district attorney who had been conflicted off of the case. She was free to tell the police anything she knew, but she could not be charged with any crimes for anything that had happened in her house. Sanchez found this puzzling as well: so little time had elapsed that no one could know for sure the extent of what had happened in the Hammond house or who had been involved. Further, she was claiming to have no knowledge of anything that happened in her home. If she was not a party to any crimes, why would she need immunity? Perhaps the most interesting twist here was that it was Gilmore's office that granted her immunity. Gilmore had already disqualified his office from involvement in the case. If anyone was going to grant her immunity, it should have been Todd Taylor, the special prosecutor who had been assigned the case when Gilmore's office was disqualified.

The transcripts of Becky Hammond's interview with the police are quite interesting. When they interviewed me, they videotaped it and later transcribed the questions and answers, word for word. For some reason, major portions of Mrs. Hammond's interview are missing. Sometimes, the missing portions were noted with a series of slashes. Other times, they were noted with vague descriptions of the missing material, such as "several sentences." Someone wanting to know what Becky Hammond said about her house being searched by the police would read this: "The police have been here and found this stuff. / / / He said, 'did you anything about it' . . . and I said, 'no' . . . you know . . . this is just a horror show here. And what are we / / / (several sentences) I don't remember exactly where it was." One particularly rambling answer of hers contained more than thirty slash-mark deletions and at least two "several sentences" deletions. Without question, her statement had not been taken in a way that would be worthwhile to investigators or prosecutors.

Still, she was clearly distraught. She told them how her marriage to the doctor had deteriorated over the years. He made weekly trips out of town that he claimed were necessary to clear his mind. She knew now he was having affairs during this time. He apparently picked up women at bars and at his gym. She said he suffered insomnia, which caused him to be up at all hours of the night, and he made and received phone calls at strange times. She showed the detectives phone bills containing calls to strange countries at all hours, and calls at 3:00 or 4:00 A.M. to California.

She had no idea who he was calling in the Netherlands, Bangladesh, and Hong Kong. The detectives dialed some of the numbers to find out who they might belong to; the calls were answered by the telltale squealing of computer modems and fax machines. Mrs. Hammond denied knowing what Dr. Hammond may have been transmitting out of his secret room in the basement when he couldn't sleep.

As Becky's story unfolded, she confided in the detectives that she found her husband "weird," and she was "scared" of him. The detectives finally asked her about the videotapes. How could she not know this was happening in her own home? At first, she pleaded ignorance, but then she made a shocking admission. A year or two earlier, their daughter had confronted her father and asked him if he was secretly videotaping people using the toilet in the guest bathroom. Becky claimed she had just found this out now. Dr. Hammond told his daughter that he wasn't taping anyone in the bathroom. Sanchez would soon realize that not only had Hammond lied to his daughter— the tapes continued to pile up—but his daughter knew it. He found tapes where the daughter walked into the bathroom and just before she used the toilet, she turned off the lights. The daughter also was not the only person who figured out about the taping system. As previously mentioned, Sanchez found a couple of tapes where someone came into the bathroom, turned on the light, and then draped a towel over the vent while she or he used the toilet.

As her story unfolded she claimed to be remembering things she hadn't thought much of before. In 1993, the

Hammonds had gone out of state for vacation and left behind a house sitter, who called them and said that the basement had flooded. Should she call a plumber? The doctor had panicked and told the house sitter to not call anyone. They would come home and take care of it. The Hammonds raced home, and when they got there, Dr. Hammond ran into his secret office and retrieved a couple Tupperware storage containers and placed them in the trunk of his car. He then called a plumber and the family got in the car and drove away. Becky said that as she thought about it now, it seemed suspicious. At the time, she said she just thought her husband had been worried about some of his valuable electronic equipment. She admitted that she had gone into the secret room on that occasion and had helped her husband haul out the containers, but she had not asked what they contained. She also apparently walked right past the camera pointing into the bathroom without noticing it.

Becky had also found out that the doctor had credit cards she did not know about—even though they had promised each other to get their spending under control because of financial troubles the family had been having. Dr. Hammond had even borrowed quite a bit of money from Becky's father and had not repaid the loan during the time he was running up the balances on these new, secret credit cards. He also had a storage locker she had not known about before; she said she found out about it just now, while going through the bills and trying to unravel their financial mess.

The detectives went to the storage locker and could not

believe what they found there. In a highly organized, almost library-like unit, the doctor had stored thousands of pornographic videotapes, adult magazines, sex toys, and other items. Everything was sorted and catalogued. Big tubs and containers held smaller containers or bags. Many of the tapes were stored with their receipts. Someone totaled up the receipts they found that matched the trove of pornography and came to the conclusion that the materials in the storage locker cost the doctor more than $13,000 to assemble. They also discovered that Hammond mail-ordered things under the name of "Richard Hamitton."

Sanchez began to feel sorry for Becky Hammond, and he would later testify that he believed everything she was telling him. Still, he never bothered to ask what her husband was doing in February 1987, the night Peggy Hettrick was murdered and her body dumped two hundred yards from the Hammond house. Likewise, he did not bother to ask why the doctor was at home the day the police canvassed the neighborhood—on a weekday, when his busy surgical practice normally had him at work at 7:00 A.M. Sanchez also never said if he told Becky that she was actually on at least one tape secretly recorded in the bathroom.

Although the police managed to haul quite a bit of material out of the Hammond house, they didn't bother to seize the doctor's computer or any of the floppy disks sitting next to it. They had someone look at the computer, but it was apparent that the Fort Collins Police Department did not have anyone on its staff versed in computer forensics. Later, investigators noticed that photographs of the doctor's hidden room showed an entire shelf of floppy disks for the computer that no one ever bothered to look at. What had the doctor saved onto them?

All of the homemade tapes were brought to the police station, and a couple of officers were given the job of going through to see what was on them. They found tape after tape of girls and women sitting on the toilet in the Hammonds' bathroom. The camera was focused so tightly that it amounted to a close up of the subject's vagina. Many of the tapes had been edited. Dr. Hammond had gone through and created compilation tapes of victims who had been to the house more than once. A couple girls had been to the house over a period of years and could be seen aging between shots.

They also found video of Richard Hammond having sex with a woman at a location that was not his house. It was later discovered that he had rented an apartment in Denver, and the woman in the film was a prostitute. Troy Krenning, who was going through the tapes, could hear Hammond and the woman making small talk, discussing how long it had been since the last time they were together. It was obvious to Krenning that the woman did not know she was being filmed.

At some point in his investigation into the Hammond matter, Sanchez made a checklist of tasks he needed to complete. On the list he wrote: "Check into Hettrick." As he investigated, he eventually checked off every item on the list, except for "Check into Hettrick." Apparently, no one ever checked into Hettrick.

On March 24, the police were told that Dr. Hammond would be released from the psychiatric facility. Someone had heard that Hammond intended to commit suicide when he got out, by injecting himself with drugs he had access to, and told the police about it. Since he had driven himself to the hospital, the police got permission from Becky to search the Hammonds' vehicle, which was in the parking lot of the psychiatric hospital. An officer, armed with the consent form, went through the vehicle from top to bottom, looking for any drugs that could be used to commit suicide. While the search was taking place, Hammond's psychiatrist came out and asked the police officers what they were doing. When they told him, he said he had treated Hammond and prescribed drugs to him that minimized the risk of suicide. He also said that when Hammond had checked in, his staff had searched the car and removed a hypodermic needle they had found, just to be on the safe side. The police continued their search but found no obvious poisons in the car.

At 3:00 that afternoon, Hammond left the hospital and checked himself into a La Quinta Inn hotel in Boulder, Colorado, and wrote a letter to Terry Gilmore. In it, he blamed the police department and the media for destroying his family. He "implored" Gilmore to not show the videotapes he had made to anyone. He referred to the women and children on the tapes as "victims," putting quotation marks around the word whenever he used it. He asked Gilmore to stop his investigation and not contact any more of the "victims." He also handwrote a consent form, to release his medical records to his wife and Gilmore. He then managed to get his statement notarized. The document was dated and even had a "Time" listed next to his signature: 11:55 P.M. It is unclear where he found a notary that close to midnight. He made a phone call a few minutes before 4:00 A.M. and then injected himself with cyanide. When a maid found his body, he was wearing a Leatherman knife on his hip. The knife had a serrated edge. His autopsy indicated he had shaved his legs, chest, abdomen, and pubic area. He had only been out of the hospital about twelve hours when he died.

Gina Burkhardt heard about Hammond's suicide and sent Becky a sympathy card. She said she was sorry for their loss but that she still felt she had no choice but to do what she had done. Gina was surprised shortly after when she received a phone call from Becky Hammond. Becky didn't seem angry with her, and she noted that things could have turned out worse. She told Gina that the doctor had a whole collection of guns and knives, and he very easily could have taken his family "with him" when he killed himself.

Even though Hammond was dead, the police continued to study the evidence and follow up on leads. One was a private mailbox he had rented where he received mail that Becky said she knew nothing about. When the detectives went through the box, they found cell-phone bills and paperwork from a medical supply company. Hammond had ordered items from the company—anesthetic, calipers, rubber gloves—and no one understood why he couldn't have simply ordered these items and had them delivered to his practice.

. . .

SANCHEZ CONTINUED TO wonder if Hammond could have been connected with the Hettrick murder. He spoke with Broderick about it. Broderick told him to look at the videotapes made by Hammond and see if they contained any violence. If there was no violence on any of the tapes, Broderick told Sanchez he couldn't see any further reason to link Hammond to Hettrick. It is not clear why Broderick thought a lack of violence in Hammond's perverse video collection should clear him in the Hettrick murder.

Mickelson wanted to examine all of the tapes to see if Peggy Hettrick was on any of them. Now that Hammond was dead, Sanchez told Mickelson the matter was closed. Mickelson was upset. It appeared to him that Hammond fit the profile of who they should be looking for in the Hettrick murder. Mickelson also thought that Hammond's reaction to being arrested for a misdemeanor charge was too much. He was convinced there was much more to the doctor than what they had uncovered so far. He wanted to keep digging.

Mickelson suggested they get a search warrant for the Hammond home, this time to look for blood or any other evidence on the Hettrick murder. Maybe they should look for knives in the house, or perhaps surgical scalpels. Sanchez pointed out to Mickelson that he was not currently assigned to the department handling crimes against persons and, as such, the Hettrick murder was none of his business.

In May 1995, Broderick decided to destroy all of the Hammond evidence. He told Sanchez to go to the Fort Collins City Attorney and seek a court order for the destruction. If there had been any prosecutions arising from the materials, it would have been the Larimer County District Attorney's Office handling the matter. Sanchez and Broderick went and found John Duval, assistant city attorney for Fort Collins, and told him they needed to destroy the evidence from a single file. Duval had never handled such a request before.

One of the reasons they may have gone to the city attorney instead of the district attorney is that the state of Colorado has a "record retention policy" regarding everything the district attorneys of the state handle. Under the policy at the time, district attorneys were required to keep all felony case files for two years after the case was closed. Even if Hammond's charges had been reduced to a misdemeanor—which they never were officially—those case files were required to be retained for one year after the case was closed. Here, Broderick sought destruction of the evidence less than half a year after the case was closed.

The detectives gave Duval copies of the police reports but did not show him any of the videotapes. He had no idea how many tapes or victims there were. The two detectives simply told him it was a dead-end case and that the evidence was embarrassing to the victims. They did not tell him that there were victims who wanted to file lawsuits over the tapes and that the tapes were critical evidence in such cases. They also did not tell him that there might be a connection between Hammond and Hettrick. Duval would testify later that he was told all of the victims the police spoke to wanted the tapes destroyed.

Duval looked at the statute governing the destruction of evidence and told the detectives he could go to court and probably get a court order allowing it. He was concerned, however, about other possible uses for the material. He wondered if some of the victims might be looking to sue the estate of Dr. Hammond—perhaps some of the victims who had not heard about the matter yet. Duval found out that Becky had opened up an estate for her late husband and had been appointed representative of the estate. Under Colorado law, creditors of an estate have one hundred and twenty days to file claims. Duval suggested they wait out the one-hundred-and-twenty-day period to see if any of the victims filed their claims within that window. None did. It hadn't occurred to Duval that some of the victims might have wanted to sue Becky Hammond; after all, the one-hundred-and-twenty-day period did not apply to her personally.

Mickelson heard that the Hammond materials were going to be destroyed, and he went ballistic. He found Sanchez and asked why they were not going to preserve the evidence. Sanchez told him that they had decided to close the Hammond matter and that no one thought there was any connection between Hammond and Hettrick. The argument became heated, and Sanchez told Mickelson to stay out of it. Krenning heard about the dispute and agreed with Mickelson; Hammond should have been looked at, and the evidence should not be destroyed. Krenning later told people that Mickelson had been livid about the destruction and that everyone "in earshot" knew it.

Later, when I was arrested, Mickelson was upset that Hammond wasn't being investigated for the Hettrick murder. I didn't know it at the time—I would find this out twelve years later—but Mickelson risked his career by trying to tip off my attorneys about Hammond. Unfortunately, he assumed my attorneys were going to come from the public defender's office. He called the public defender's office anonymously and told them about Hammond. I have no idea what they did with the information, but it was never passed along to my attorneys.

No one ever called Gina to tell her that the Hammond evidence was going to be destroyed. No one ever sent a letter or contacted Todd Taylor—the special prosecutor who had been assigned to handle the case when Gilmore's office had been conflicted off the case—about the proposed destruction of all the evidence. In legal jargon, the case to destroy the evidence in the Hammond matter was filed, and the court designated it *The City of Fort Collins versus Controlled Substance and Contraband Personal Property Owned by the Estate of Richard Hammond*. The judge signed the order to destroy the evidence on August 15, 1995. Later, when he was asked about the destruction of the evidence without his input, Taylor expressed surprise. Evidence that might play a role in a murder case should be kept, he testified, "for extended periods of time, many

many years typically." He also testified that he believed that law enforcement should have notified every single person Hammond had photographed, to let them know. He assumed that the Fort Collins Police Department would handle the matter appropriately. He was wrong.

In his request, Duval noted how Larimer County's district attorney had no need for the Hammond materials. At the time, the Larimer County district attorney had been conflicted off the case, and it was a special prosecutor—Todd Taylor—who should have been making that decision. The court did not catch the problem with the conflict, and Duval secured the court order. The materials were burned on August 15, 1995—only five months after they'd even been discovered and before anyone had a chance to detail what was contained on the tapes and disks. Duval later testified that he had never seen materials from a case file destroyed as quickly as this. That is, quickly when measured from the time of the material being seized to it being burned. The actual burning of the material took a remarkably long time. The boxes of evidence from the Hammond home and the storage locker took nine hours to burn.

MICKELSON HAD RAISED some complaints about the destruction of the files, but they had fallen on deaf ears. One of his complaints centered on the thousands of "store-bought" pornographic videos Hammond had stockpiled in his storage locker. No one ever bothered to look at any of them to see if the recordings matched the box covers. For all anyone knew, Hammond had transferred his own home-made videos onto those tapes and was simply hiding them in plain sight. Not one single store-bought tape was ever viewed by anyone at the Fort Collins Police Department.

18

The File Is Reopened

IN 1994, AN ARREST WAS MADE IN THE ONLY OTHER UN-solved murder case in Fort Collins. With that arrest and conviction, only one murder case remained unsolved on the books in Fort Collins: the Peggy Hettrick murder. Several Fort Collins officers and detectives had gone to arrest the suspect in the Dahl case, and afterward they went out for drinks to celebrate. Broderick told those around him that they now had one last piece of unfinished business. He wanted to resolve the Hettrick matter, and he wanted me convicted of it. Troy Krenning, who was there at the bar, expressed his disbelief in that approach, but Broderick brushed him off. Krenning had no problem with the idea of solving the murder, but he thought the police should approach the case with an open mind. Go where the evidence leads. Broderick disagreed; assume I was guilty and simply build a case against me.

When they returned to Fort Collins from Pennsylvania in August 1992, Broderick commandeered an old conference room at the police station and set up a "war room." The sole purpose of his project was to convict me of the Hettrick murder, regardless of what the evidence showed. Police officer Marsha Reed moved her desk into the war room, and Broderick limited who else had access to it. The two of them acted so secretively that other police officers wondered what was going on in there. Some assumed it was an internal affairs matter, with Broderick and Reed investigating other police officers, and the whole "reopening" of the Hettrick cold case was just a ruse so the rest of the department wouldn't get suspicious.

For reasons no one could ever really explain, Broderick contacted Peggy Hettrick's grandmother around this time and asked her if she would like some of Peggy's personal belongings, things she was wearing when she was murdered. Broderick gave the grandmother a bracelet Peggy was wearing and her purse. But then a few years later, Broderick thought the purse might be important, so he went and got it back from the grandmother. Both items were evidence, of course, and there was a strong likelihood that DNA evidence could have been recovered from the bracelet. It didn't matter; Broderick just decided to give the evidence away, and it would take a judge's court order more than ten years later to recover it.

Over two days in October 1995, Broderick attended a seminar entitled "Sexually Violent Offenders and Their

Victims," presented by a former FBI agent named Roy Hazelwood. Broderick attended another Hazelwood seminar the next year, this one entitled "Behavioral Analysis of Sexually Related Deaths." After the seminar, Broderick approached Hazelwood and told him about the Hettrick case, starting with the premise that I had killed Peggy. He described my drawings and writings to Hazelwood and asked if someone with psychiatric expertise might be able to somehow tie the case together—that is, conjure evidence linking me to the murder, the evidence that was lacking in the case so far. Hazelwood was optimistic and agreed to look at the evidence—for a fee.

Broderick mailed Hazelwood a pile of documents about me and asked him if he could profile me into the crime. Hazelwood went along with it, but he didn't completely convict me. He couched some of his answers tentatively. In response to Broderick's question, "Does Masters fit the profile of a Lust Murderer?" Hazelwood responded, "YES THE CRIME BEHAVIOR IS DISORGANIZED AND MASTERS' PERSONALITY IS CONSISTENT WITH DISORGANIZED BUT THAT DOESN'T MAKE HIM A KILLER. OTHER PEOPLE ALSO HAVE THE SAME CHARACTERISTICS." Broderick asked him if he would be willing to testify; Hazelwood repeated that question, followed by his answer. "What factors would make me feel comfortable that Masters is the subject in this case? SAME THING THAT WOULD MAKE YOU FEEL COMFORTABLE, FORENSIC EVIDENCE OR WITNESS. HOWEVER, THE CRIME BEHAVIOR IS CONSISTENT WITH THE PERSONALITY OF

MASTERS AND THE CIRCUMSTANCES OF THE CASE (PROXIMITY OF RESIDENCE, PERSONALITY, POST-OFFENSE BEHAVIOR, COLLECTIONS, ETC.)." Broderick would not call Hazelwood to testify at my trial; he would go with Reid Meloy, a psychologist much more willing to come right out and say that he thought I had killed Peggy Hettrick.

19

Dad

IN LATE 1995, MY FATHER SOLD THE PROPERTY IN FORT Collins. The taxes on that little place had been crushing him; they had been charging him $2,000 a year for a piece of property he had bought for only $500. When he looked into getting utilities run out to his property, he was quoted exorbitant prices, and the local inspectors would not let him do any of the work himself. Installing a septic system or running utility lines were the kind of things he had done many times before. Now they wanted him to hire expensive contractors. I could hear the stress in his voice when we spoke on the phone, and I told him he should consider moving to Ridgecrest. At the time, it was a buyer's market: A $150,000 home in Fort Collins would be the equivalent of an $80,000 home in Ridgecrest.

After he had sold his property and moved the trailer to Loma, Colorado, Dad came out to visit, and we drove around and looked at real estate. He even found a few places that he liked, and he put in offers. He was in great spirits, and my sister and nephew came for a visit. On Tuesday, I came home and found my dad sitting at the kitchen table with his head in his hands. He hadn't dressed and was sitting there in his underwear, which was very unusual for him.

"What's wrong?" I asked him.

"I don't feel good," he replied. He looked like hell. I suggested we go to the hospital, but he waved me off. He hated doctors and hospitals.

The next day he felt a little better. He showered and shaved, and later on, the two of us stayed up late and watched Buddy Hackett on television.

The day after that, though, Dad looked worse. He told me he had been sweeping and cleaning up a bit around the house—he hated to sit around doing nothing—and had suddenly felt like hell again. He said he felt a pain in his chest.

I tried arguing with him: he needed to go to the hospital! He told me, "I'm not giving my money to a damn hospital."

What good would his money do him if he died? I tried to reason with him, but it was no use. I hoped I could get him to change his mind if I kept at it.

The next day he told me that when he opened his mouth he could hear air hissing, like a leaking air hose. Still, he refused to go to the hospital. When I became adamant, he finally gave me the real reason he didn't want to go: "I don't want to go to the hospital. Your mother died in a hospital."

I was so worried and upset that I went to see a Navy counselor. I told him I was worried I'd come home and find my father dead at the kitchen table. The counselor suggested I could call 911 and simply have an ambulance come and get him.

Maybe that would have worked for the counselor's father but not my dad. He wouldn't have gone with an ambulance, even if I did call one. I also respected my dad too much to put him through such a pointless exercise. Still, sometimes I feel like if I hadn't respected my father so much, he might still be alive.

On Sunday night, I went to bed. Dad slept on the couch in the living room. Around 4:00 A.M. I was startled awake; my father called out my name and I heard him kick the glass top of the coffee table next to the couch. The tone of his voice let me know instantly: this was an emergency. I ran into the living room and found my dad clutching his chest. I grabbed a phone and called 911. The operator calmly asked me her questions as I panicked. My dad was dying, and she wanted to know how old he was, how long he'd been having symptoms. While she was quizzing me, Dad stopped breathing.

"Dad," I hollered, "you've got to keep breathing!" I dropped the phone and pulled my father onto the floor. I had been trained in CPR endlessly in the Navy, but it all became a blur as I looked down and saw my father dying in front of me. I began doing chest compressions and giving him mouth-to-mouth. I heard a rib break as I compressed; it was the most horrific sound and it made me want to stop. I didn't want to hurt my father by breaking his ribs. But I couldn't stop: if I stopped, he'd certainly die.

A few minutes later, the fire department arrived, and they took over the CPR. Then an ambulance arrived, and they hooked Dad up to all kinds of monitors and gadgets. They used a defibrillator on him a couple of times. I leaned in and said, "Hang in there, you old son of a bitch." It was the most sentimental I could get with the old guy. We loved each other and we knew it, but we never used terms of endearment or ever actually said that we loved each other. They loaded him into the ambulance, and I called Serena to tell her that Dad had a heart attack and she had better get up here quickly. I then raced after the ambulance in my car.

Dad was pronounced dead shortly after arriving at the hospital.

Without question, this was the worst day of my life.

A few minutes later, a doctor came into the waiting room and told me, "Your father had a massive heart attack. He was just too far gone to save."

I was numb. I found a phone and called my aunt Bridget. I held it together until she started to cry. Then I lost it. I broke down crying.

I drove home and walked into my empty house. I was all alone. I stood in my living room and let out a blood-curdling scream of grief.

Then I called my sister on her cell phone to tell her. She was driving so I told her to pull over.

"What?! No, just tell me what's going on. How's Dad?"

"Serena, Dad just died."

I heard the phone drop, and her husband, Mario, picked it up. I explained what had happened to him. Mario had loved my father, too.

We made arrangements to fly Dad back to Colorado so we could bury him next to Mom. The four of us—Serena; Mario; their son, Little Mario; and I—drove back to Colorado in Dad's pickup. It was the only reliable transportation we had, but it still felt funny to drive it. It was Dad's truck; he should have been driving it.

In April 1996, after my father died, an obituary ran in a Fort Collins newspaper, and—I didn't know it at the time—it caught the attention of Broderick. My father was my only alibi witness since the two of us lived alone in the trailer at the time of Peggy's murder. Broderick had been made supervisor of the Crimes against Persons Unit of the Fort Collins Police Department in January 1995, and he now found himself swamped. There were half a dozen homicides in 1996. When he saw that my father died, he decided to renew his attempts to pin the crime on me. Maybe without my sole alibi witness, he would have a better chance.

In February 1997, Broderick was willing to try anything in his pursuit of me. Someone told Broderick about an IRS agent who was skilled at detecting deception in written transcripts. In other words, this tax man didn't need to meet witnesses or see them talk to determine if they were lying. He claimed he could do it by merely reading what someone had said. He used this "skill" to find people cheating on their taxes, and sometimes he offered his services to police departments to catch other types of criminals. Broderick sent him the transcript of my interrogations from 1987 but didn't bother to send him the videotapes or the audiotapes. After all, this man didn't need them! A few months later, the agent called Broderick and confirmed Broderick's suspicions. There were a "variety of areas" in which I was deceptive, according to him. The report was "informal" however, and Broderick never called the man as a witness. He found someone a step above the tax man—a psychologist.

In November 1997, Broderick decided to hire Reid Meloy to help with my prosecution. He would be the People's "forensic psychology consultant in regard to the homicide of Peggy Hettrick." He would be paid $300 an hour for his work, and he would wind up charging the state of Colorado tens of thousands of dollars for his work.

In May 1998, the police got permission to exhume Peggy's body. It had occurred to someone that a piece of a knife blade might have broken off when it struck Peggy's rib, and something like that might only be found with an X-ray. Her body was taken to the McKee Medical Center, where it was x-rayed. Nothing new was found, there were no metal fragments, and she was returned to her resting place.

20

Life as a Civilian

I FINISHED MY LAST TWO YEARS OF SERVICE FOR THE NAVY and got out in June 1997. I was happy to become a civilian again. It was like I'd been released from prison. In the Navy, it felt like they controlled my every move, twenty-four hours a day, seven days a week. I vowed to never let anyone have that much control over my life again.

I looked around for work in the Ridgecrest area, but there wasn't much, so I collected unemployment. My mortgage was only $375 a month, so I could get by on nothing more than the unemployment benefits. In my last couple years in the Navy, I had been working up to sixteen-hour shifts, stressing out trying to get planes repaired to meet a flight schedule and worrying that I or someone under me might make a mistake and get a pilot killed. Now, I was sitting at home without a care in the world. That is, until my unemployment was about to run out. Then, I got serious and started sending out résumés to aircraft companies around the country.

One day, I hammered out fifty résumés to potential employers, and my phone rang—that same day. A contract company that furnished workers for Learjet called me. "I've looked over your résumé, and you are qualified for the job. Can you be in Wichita next Monday?"

I was taken aback. I hadn't expected a response this fast and had assumed I'd have a little more time to get my act together. They didn't even bother with an interview; he wanted me to start right away.

"The job pays $21.50 an hour," he continued, "and right now our guys there are getting between fifty-six and seventy-eight hours of work a week." He probably thought he was scaring me with the workload, but I had worked many seventy-two-hour weeks, and I hadn't been paid anything extra for the overtime. This was a huge wage for me. I would be making in a week what I had earned in a month in the Navy. The only problem was that I could not be there in a week. I had three dogs and a cat, and had to make arrangements with my house and get my truck ready for the drive to Kansas. I explained this to the contractor, and he said they would work around my schedule.

With a huge assist from my sister, I organized everything and moved to Wichita, Kansas, to work for Learjet. There, I helped with manufacturing their model 45 intermediate business jet.

The increase in wages was a game changer for me. I had gotten used to living on Navy wages, so the $21.50 an hour, especially with the long hours I was working, seemed like a windfall. Even spending some of the money frivolously, I managed to save $2,000 a month. I found out that a lot of the workers in my position chose to work teachers' schedules. That is, they would work the length of a contract—six or nine months—and then just take three or four months off before looking for the next job. I thought it was great. The freedom was exhilarating.

I was making more money than I ever had before. I was renting one house, paying the mortgage on another, driving a brand-new Trans Am, and still putting money in the bank. The one problem I still had was my drinking. I could now afford to drink the "good stuff," so I polished off two big bottles of whiskey a week. I didn't have much time to make friends.

In July I decided to take a vacation. I gave my contractor notice that I would be leaving at the end of the month. The day before I left, my supervisor at Learjet gave me his business card and wrote his mother's phone number on the back. He told me I could always get a job with him, and if he wasn't at Learjet when I called, I should call his mother because she would always know where to find him. That made me feel pretty good.

My plan was to eventually go work for Boeing. They paid as much as Lear, but they were in Washington State, and I really wanted a change of scenery after living in Kansas and the California desert. First, I would take a couple of months off and relax, and spend some time with Serena and her family back in California. So, in July 1998, I headed west.

21

Broderick Returns

IN 1998, AFTER REID MELOY HAD GOTTEN HEAVILY IN-volved in the Hettrick murder investigation, Broderick decided to arrest me for the murder of Peggy Hettrick. Of course, I had no idea about it at the time, but I heard about it later. To arrest someone in a case like this, they needed to get an arrest warrant signed by a judge; the warrant would have to lay out the case and describe enough evidence against me to convince a judge there was probable cause to arrest me. Broderick worked with Terry Gilmore, the district attorney, and an assistant prosecuting attorney named Jolene Blair on drafting the necessary documents to obtain the warrant. After they were happy with the language, they sent it to Roy Hazelwood, at the FBI, and Reid Meloy to get their approval. We wouldn't find out until much later, but Meloy took a very major role in my prosecution. Although he would present himself to the court and the jury as a man of science, he was really just bent on putting me in jail to validate his work. Meloy looked over the draft sent to him and edited major portions of it. My attorneys later said they had never seen such a thing.

Broderick bolstered his case against me in his affidavit. For example, he wrote that Detective Wheeler-Holloway had found spray-painted drawings of a "very sexual nature" under one of the bridges near the field and that they had been done in orange spray paint. This was an important fact, because the knife found by Gregory Schade had orange spray paint on its handle. By tying the knife to the drawings, Broderick could claim that it was mine, since I also drew quite a bit (even though I had not been the one to draw the stick figures under the bridge). But Wheeler-Holloway never said the paint under the bridge was orange; it wasn't. Broderick used this to get me arrested.

By this time, Broderick had spent countless hours studying my doodles and my stories. Keep in mind that these were the work of a fifteen-year-old boy, and I wouldn't try and tell you that I was an art or a literary prodigy. Broderick placed a great importance on them and had immersed himself in them. He got to the point where he confused my writing with my actual life. In the affidavit he submitted to show probable cause, he wrote, "In another narrative Masters is represented by the character 'Mace' who is part of a gang," Broderick quoted. A few sentences later, he actually wrote, "Mace, a.k.a. Masters talks of . . ."

Again, this was writing, not talking, and it was a character I wrote about, not me.

Somehow, this everything-but-the-kitchen-sink affidavit convinced a judge to sign the warrant for my arrest. I always wondered if the judge read the entire thing: it was thirty pages long and mostly single-spaced.

Broderick and Reed were tracking me, preparing to arrest me. Broderick had been making arrangements to have me arrested in Wichita, but I moved back to Ridgecrest before he pulled the trigger. On August 4, Broderick called the Ridgecrest Police Department and asked them to case my new location. They duly reported back to Broderick that I was moving into my house in Ridgecrest and even described to them what my truck and trailer looked like.

22

The Arrest

I T WAS AROUND NINE IN THE MORNING ON AUGUST 19, 1998, when I heard a pounding knock at my front door. I wasn't even going to answer it, but the bastard kept knocking. My rottweiler Misty got up off the floor and ran out into the living room barking. So I went into the living room and found a man with a badge on his belt pushing my front door partway open and Misty holding him at bay with an angry growl. I could see a police car parked across the street, and I was wondering what the hell the guy thought he was doing trying to come into my house.

"Get your dog back, or I'll mace him," the man said.

I could see that there were several more cops standing behind him.

What the hell does he think he's doing? I thought. He must have the wrong house, like the time when two cops came to my door with an arrest warrant for someone who used to live in the duplex I was renting in Ridgecrest.

"I said get your dog back, or I'll have to mace him."

"It's a her," I said, as I grabbed Misty and put her into a bedroom.

"Tim Masters?" the cop asked when I returned to the living room.

"Yeah."

"You're under arrest."

"For what?"

"I can't tell you that."

This just had to be some sort of mistake. I hadn't done anything wrong. I hadn't broken any laws.

I had just gotten out of bed, so I was in green shorts and no shirt. He let me put on the first shirt he found, a dirty white T-shirt, and then handcuffed me. He wouldn't even let me put on decent clothes. They almost took me out without letting me get my glasses until I protested about not being able to see without them. Then the bastard put them on my face for me. As I was being led out of the house, a dark-haired man with a Hitler mustache met me at the door.

"Tim Masters," he told me, "you're under arrest for the murder of Peggy Hettrick." The man in the suit was actually happy—he looked happy to be there as I stood in handcuffs, about to be taken to God only knew where. He was proud and happy; he was enjoying this. It was like he was there to gloat, as if my arrest was a personal victory of some sort. I shook my head in disbelief. *This can't be happening. I've never killed anyone*, I thought.

Then it hit me; the body I'd seen as a child in Fort Collins, Colorado. Oh my god! I couldn't believe this. That Hitler look-alike was from Fort Collins. I was being arrested for that murder. They still thought I did it!

They led me away from my own house in handcuffs. It was when I got outside that I saw there were about twenty cops surrounding my house and police vehicles parked all along the street. My neighbors were in their front yards watching me being led away in handcuffs, green shorts, and a dirty white T-shirt.

THEY TOOK ME to the local police station, which just happened to be right behind my house. I had always felt a little safer living there, because the police station was so close. I didn't feel so safe anymore. The people who were supposed to protect me and my stuff were now hurting me.

The cop driving me there started chatting with me, and asked, "Don't I know you? You look familiar. Have you ever been arrested here before?" I had been inside that police station once before.

"I wrecked my car in 1995 and got a DUI."

"Maybe that's why you look familiar to me."

This was all in a day's work for him. But then, he hadn't just been kidnapped from his home.

He took me to the detention area and placed me in a holding cell. This cell was about fifteen feet long and eight feet wide, with a concrete bench along one wall and a toilet and sink on the other. The toilet had no toilet seat—it was just a stainless-steel bowl—and the last person who'd used it hadn't flushed. I remember thinking, "There's no way I'm sitting on that toilet."

There was nothing to do in that holding cell but think. Think about what was going on, and wonder what was going to happen next.

They took me into an interrogation room, and the Hitler look-alike was waiting for me. He had a couple of three-ring binders. One of them was open on the desk, and I could see photos of footprints in it. For all I knew, it could be the same binders they had brought to Philly in 1992.

"Tim, I'd like to talk to you about Peggy Hettrick's murder," he said to me.

"I'm not saying anything until I've seen a lawyer," I told him. The arrogant bastard actually seemed surprised and angered that I wouldn't talk to him. Even though I had given the Fort Collins police endless hours of interviews, he was angry because now that I was wrongfully under arrest, I wouldn't talk to him.

"Will you sign this consent to search your house?" he asked.

"I'm not signing anything until I've spoken to an attorney," I told him. They had thoroughly searched my home in 1987 and taken anything they wanted. They had no right to do that again. I didn't even own my current home in 1987, so nothing there had any relation to what they were accusing me of.

"Fine," he said smugly, "I'll just get a search warrant."

Sitting in the holding cell, wondering what the hell was going on and not being able to get any answers, was maddening. There were no phones in there. There were no cops nearby to ask. My world was being ripped from me, and I could do nothing about it.

It seemed like longer, but I was at the Ridgecrest police station for about an hour. A local detective came up to me and told me, "Look, I'm on your side, Tim. If you have any information you want to give me, just give me a call, and we can work this out." He gave me his card, and then they got me ready to be transported to the local sheriffs. I left his card sitting on the bench. He was just another cop. He was another enemy. They transported me to the local sheriff's station, and I was allowed to make my one phone call. I called Serena.

"Serena," I said, "they just arrested me for murder."

Apparently, a cop had showed up at Serena's house that morning and had been questioning her for some time when I called. Serena said he had told her he just wanted information and had said nothing about me being arrested. In the middle of that questioning, I called and told her I was under arrest. Serena was furious. She said no more to the cop.

"I need you to come up to Ridgecrest and get my money out of the bank, sell my Trans Am, sell my truck, the 1979 Camaro, and Dad's 1946 Harley, so that I can hire an attorney."

"Okay," she agreed.

That was it, my time was up.

After the phone call, they took me into a holding cell, where five other guys were waiting. They were waiting to be transported to the Kern County Jail in Bakersfield, and I was going to be with them on the next bus there.

"So what did you do?" one young guy asked me. I was still so overwhelmed by what was going on that all I could do was shake my head. I never did answer him. He had probably been in and out of county jail several times, so this was all routine for him, but I had just been arrested for murder. I was out of my element. I didn't feel like talking to anybody.

One of the youngsters in that holding cell could dislocate his wrist and slip out of his handcuffs, which he did several times for the amusement of the other inmates. He would always put his hand back in the cuffs before the guards came back.

There were a few women locked in the cell next to us, and the guys were having short conversations with them filled with sexual innuendos.

The guards came by about an hour later and fed us sack lunches. Those lunches were difficult to eat because they left us all shackled and handcuffed. The handcuffs were secured to a chain around our waists, so I had to double over to put the food in my mouth. I was running on pure adrenaline, so I had no appetite. I didn't eat more than a couple of bites from that lunch.

A few hours later, a large Greyhound-style bus with bars covering the windows showed up, and they loaded us on it. We were headed through the hell of the desert to Bakersfield. My world was over. I was going to jail. I had no idea what to expect. I couldn't even imagine what kind of a case they thought they had against me. I did not know how the system worked or what was in store for me. The bus took us to the Kern County Jail Lerdo complex. This county jail was the size of most state prisons; it housed around thirteen hundred inmates at one facility. That place was huge. There was razor wire all around the facility. The complex reminded me of World War II concentration camps I had seen on TV. We pulled up to the sally port, and I watched the guards put their weapons into a locker.

It took forever to get processed into jail. We got there around 4:00 P.M., and I did not get into a cell until after midnight. I spent most of that time in a tiny holding cell crammed full of men. There were bench seats along two walls, a toilet, and a pay phone. The benches held about fifteen men, and another fifteen were stuck standing.

They periodically called us out of the holding cell for various things: to be photographed, to be fingerprinted, and so on. It was about 11:30 P.M. when I was taken out of the holding cell with nine other guys and taken into an open room to be strip-searched and dressed out. We all stripped down to our birthday suits, and one guard walked by us and checked us each in turn. That was the first time I had a prison guard tell me to bend over and "spread 'em." It is not a dignified experience having another man look up the crack of your butt for contraband as you are bending over.

They put a plastic wristband on each of us. I noticed mine was different from everyone else's. I had a solid red band, while everyone else's were white. Someone later explained to me that people who were accused of violent crimes got "red-tag" status.

The inmate workers tossed us prison tops and bottoms to change into. None of the clothing fit. Kern County Jail dressed us in brown tops and bottoms with yellow *P*s on them. I was given a blanket, two sheets, and a pillowcase and put in a cell. I wondered what the pillowcase was for, since they didn't have any pillows. I was only there for about an hour when, for some reason, they pulled me out and brought me to a different pod. I was put in another cell, this one with a "bunky," Kern County Jail slang for roommate, already there.

23

Bakersfield

Serena, Mario, and Little Mario came to visit me once at the Kern County Jail. I didn't know what the hell was going on, because they didn't tell me I had visitors; they just pulled me out of the pod. Out in the hall, I was standing around looking like an idiot when a guard got on the intercom and told me, "Pick up a phone off the wall and go in that room."

I looked at the wall, where there were several phone sets with cords hanging from them. So I grabbed the best-looking phone from the bundle of eight that were hanging, and walked into the jail visiting room. A thick sheet of Plexiglas separated the inmates from their visitors. The glass was so thick that the only way to talk to your visitor was with the phone. It was one phone per visitor, so only one of your visitors could talk to you at a time.

I plugged in and talked to Serena.

We pretended like her seeing me in jail didn't kill her, or me seeing her from inside didn't kill me. We talked like normal. We didn't talk much about the situation except for Serena saying, "I know what they are doing. They are using profiling to prosecute you." Serena had read several books on police profiling and discovered there was some scary stuff going on in the system. People were being convicted without any real evidence because they matched a "profile."

Serena said there were cops all over my property in Ridgecrest, going through my house. "They tore that place apart. There was stuff strewn everywhere. They had pulled the drawers open and emptied the contents onto your kitchen and living room floors. They wouldn't even let me in to get your checkbook. I had to wait until they left."

My nine-year-old nephew Little Mario got on the phone and asked me, "Why are they doing this to you, Uncle Timmy?"

That killed me. How could I explain this to a nine-year-old?

"I don't know," was all I could honestly tell him.

I had my suspicions, though.

"I didn't know I could put money on your books; otherwise, I would have brought more cash," Serena said. She smiled, held up a Kern County receipt, and told me, "I did have six dollars and forty-three cents in my purse that I put on your books."

That one made me laugh.

All too soon, the visit was over. Serena almost managed

not to cry as she left the visiting room. She then headed back to Colorado to meet with our family. She said later that when she stopped at Dad's old trailer, which he had moved to Loma, Colorado, the cops had broken the living-room window to get in. It was trashed also. They had no respect or consideration for my property. Serena said Broderick broke into my home in Ridgecrest the second time they went into it. So he ransacked it and the trailer in Colorado. Like a thief in the night, he went in through the windows of both homes, breaking the glass on one of them. His job description is to protect and serve; and this is the guy breaking into my home and just taking everything. It felt to me like he was stealing my possessions.

My arrest was all over the local papers in Colorado. If you went by nothing more than the articles you read there, they already had me tried and convicted before my arraignment. All the papers said the police were able to make an arrest because of "advances in forensics." It sounded like there was DNA evidence, or some kind of real evidence against me, rather than just the opinions of some forensic psychologist trying to match my war and horror drawings and writings to the homicide. This was my first taste of how the local media operated, and it would not be a good experience.

All my aunts, uncles, and cousins were getting together to discuss our plan. They all knew there was no way I could have committed that murder, and it pissed them off that the police had arrested me. One day I called Aunt Betty's and got ahold of Serena there. She told me, "Tim, don't worry; we're going to get you the best lawyer. We've managed to raise more than $120,000. Uncle Charlie cashed in his 401k for $60,000. You won't even have to sell your car and Dad's Harley."

I walked away from that phone call with tears in my eyes. My family had donated a small fortune to help me fight these bullshit charges. I was floored. I think, in the long run, that made so much difference having so many people support me. It meant the world to me that my family had gotten together and was standing behind me.

We had several conversations on the phone that first week about how the case was entirely based on profiling.

I started reading the Bible for the first time in my life while I was in Bakersfield. I borrowed it from an inmate in the pod. The pod I was in was a thirty-two-man pod. There were six of us white guys, four were black, and the rest were Mexican. That place was seriously segregated. White guys ate at one table, the black guys at theirs, and the Mexicans had the rest. I didn't eat much there. The food was terrible, and I wasn't hungry. My world had just been destroyed. The roof could have come crashing down on me, crushing me to death then and there, and I wouldn't have cared. I had no appetite. The first morning there, I went to the front of the pod and picked up my breakfast tray of slop and walked over to the large table and sat down. I just happened to have sat down at the table full of Southsiders, members of a large Hispanic gang.

The Southsiders were surprisingly polite.

"Hey, buddy," one of the guys said to me. "This is a Southsider table. You shouldn't sit here."

I looked around and realized I was the only white guy at the table. Everyone at the table was looking at me like I was crazy. I picked up my tray and moved to a smaller table, where the only white guys in the pod were sitting.

"Hey, man, you shouldn't sit with those Mexicans," one of my new tablemates told me. "You sit here with us from now on."

In California, the whites stuck together, the blacks stuck together, and the Mexicans stuck together. You could talk to each other, but you only hung out with your own color. That was foreign to me. The Navy had been full of people of all races from all over the country. I had hung around people of all ethnicities. I realized I knew very little about prison politics and the unwritten rules among the inmates.

I barely ate anything off my tray at any meals there. I ended up giving most of my food away. When my table-mates saw how little I ate, they were glad I was sitting with them. They tried to tell me to eat something—that I would starve—but I didn't care about starving. My world was over.

We got two hot meals and one sack lunch a day at the Kern County Jail. There was never much food on the hot trays, and even less in the sack lunches. A hot breakfast would normally consist of a couple spoonfuls of eggs, a spot of oatmeal or farina, and a piece of bread. A hot dinner tray would be something like a hamburger patty—usually a really bad quality of meat—with a little gravy, mixed vegetables, and a couple rolls. The sack lunches were always the same; a piece of mystery meat, four slices of bread, and an orange. We were probably getting around 1,200 calories a day. Before, I had enjoyed a diet of around 3,000 to 3,500 calories a day.

The water in the jail stank. It smelled like sulfur and tasted worse. I tried to dilute it by squeezing orange juice into it from my sack-lunch orange, but that was just a waste of a good orange. Fortunately, the air-conditioning worked alright there. It was around 115 degrees outside but remained a constant 80 inside.

I watched *The Jerry Springer Show* and *Ricki Lake* for the first time in that county jail. For some reason, the inmates liked watching those shows. They got a kick out of people jumping up on Springer and trying to beat the shit out of another guest. I didn't really care for those shows, but there was nothing else to do. You could read, watch TV, play cards, or talk on the phone.

The shower was at the very end on the first tier. It was never any problem getting into the shower, unlike some of the places I went later. It had a solid door you could close with an open window. I took my first shower with that door closed but the window uncovered. Everyone could see me showering. Later, I noticed that other inmates would cover that window with their towel so that they could shower in private. Some of those guys took full advantage of a little private time.

I met a lot of people in that jail. They weren't like what I expected to meet in prison. There wasn't one fight in that pod during the weeks I was there. I would have gotten along fine with most of those guys if I had met them on the streets.

It was hard to believe some of the time they were facing. My bunky was looking at twelve years for assault. Another guy was being offered a plea bargain of six years because he smacked his old lady in the head with a metal coat hanger. The one that really surprised me was a guy named Chino, who was facing six years for gang affiliation. I didn't know you could go to jail just for affiliating with a gang. At that time, the idea of spending six years in prison was an absolute horror to me. I'd only been locked up a week or so, and I was ready to die. Six years? My bunky was probably going to get into the California firefighter program to get out sooner . . . that is, if he could get the stabbings in his case dropped. Somehow, none of this fazed me; all I could think about was how I'd been arrested for a murder I had nothing to do with.

I had never been a part of the system, so I had no idea of how things worked. I was surprised when one day they called me out of the pod for a court trip; I didn't even know it was a court trip at first. They took about twenty of us to a good-sized holding cell and strip-searched us. Then they shackled and handcuffed us, and we waited. Eventually, they loaded us all on a bus. The bus was Greyhound style, like the one that had brought me over from Ridgecrest. It had wire cages welded inside it, separating the interior into compartments so that they could keep certain inmates separate. Most of the cages held anywhere from six to ten people. In the cage in front of mine were four young women going to court for drug-related charges. The guy sitting in front of me knew the girls and held a conversation with them the whole trip. One girl had her hair up just like Princess Leia from *Star Wars*. The guy in front of me asked her, "What's up with your hair?"

"I'm Princess Lay-me," she responded.

We were off to court, but none of these people seemed to take it all that seriously. It was a normal part of life to them to be going to court and possibly facing prison time. On the way to court, they laughed and joked around with each other. They talked about friends they had and crimes they had committed. The way they acted, they could have been friends on a public bus rather than a county-jail transport.

The bus weaved its way through Bakersfield streets to the courthouse downtown. After we had pulled to a stop, sheriffs' deputies got out of the bus and walked a little ways in either direction of the bus. There were deputies everywhere, toting shotguns. Many looked like they would really enjoy shooting any of us who tried to make a break for it, or anyone who tried to help us escape.

Didn't they realize that I had spent the last eight years of my life trying to protect them? Was that eight years of busting my ass in the Navy worth nothing? Weren't we all on the same side? We were all trying to keep America safe. But we weren't on the same side. They were cops, and I was an accused murderer.

We were directed into the courthouse and into a small holding cell. There was not enough room for everyone to sit. I was one of the first into the holding cell, so I got a spot on the bench, but others behind me were stuck standing for God only knew how long.

Eventually, a deputy stood in front of our holding cell

and called off a bunch of names, including mine. We waddled out of the cell, our leg irons and handcuff chains jingling, and made our way into a courtroom. I was sitting in between a girl and a young guy. The guy must have been barely eighteen, and he could have passed for sixteen years old. He told me he was charged with first-degree murder for a drive-by shooting that he had nothing to do with. He was in a gang, but not the gang that had done the drive-by. He met his lawyer for the first time that day in court. The district attorneys in his case wanted to set a trial date within the month, but his lawyer argued that she hadn't even been given any discovery in the case, so she couldn't go to trial. It all sounded crazy to me. The guy was facing life in prison and they hadn't given his lawyer any discovery!

One by one they went through us inmates, granting a continuance in this case or setting a trial date in that one; accepting a plea bargain from this or that inmate and setting a sentence date. In due course, they finally got to me, and a deputy asked me to come with him into a room in the back of the court.

"I'm asking you to waive your extradition hearing," he told me. "If you don't waive it, all that's going to happen is that we will have a hearing to determine whether or not you really are Tim Masters, and if you are, they will extradite you to Colorado. Bakersfield is a shithole, and you don't want to stay in that jail any longer than you have to. Once you sign these papers, Colorado will have thirty days to come and get you."

I think he was stretching it a little there, but one thing

was certain—they were going to extradite me eventually anyway, so I might as well get the hell out of the Bakersfield jail. The only reason I didn't sign the papers before was because that Hitler look-alike cop who'd been so happy to see me arrested was asking me to.

You would have thought I had just signed over my first-born or a million dollars to the deputies. They were practically high-fiving each other. One pumped his fist in a sign of success to another. *Wow, what jerks*, was all I could think.

Back at the Kern County Jail, they strip-searched us and sent us back to population.

A little over a week later, Larimer County deputies showed up to get me. I had been hoping they would come to their senses and realize I wasn't the murderer, but that wasn't going to happen. So when they called me out because "Colorado" was there to pick me up, my heart sank. I was put back into the same holding cell I had waited in for endless hours the day they booked me into Kern County Jail. Once again, I hunkered down for the long wait. They had no idea when Larimer County would arrive to get me. All they could tell me was that Colorado would be coming by to pick me up some time that day.

They took their brown jail-issue clothing from me and gave me back my street clothes, which consisted of green shorts, a white T-shirt, socks, and shoes. They had not been laundered.

I don't know how long it took for Larimer deputies to arrive; time gets a little skewed when you're sitting in a jail cell with nothing to do, but they finally did show up. It was a short, heavyset guy and an average-sized guy. I didn't look closely at their patches, so I thought they were Fort Collins police officers picking me up. The short, fat one put a chain around my waist that held the handcuffs, shackles, and a black box.

"This is a shock belt," he explained to me, pointing to the black box he had put around my waist. "If you try to run from us, I'll press this button and send 50,000 volts through your body to incapacitate you. Do you understand?"

I nodded my head. Try to run? In shackles and handcuffs? In those restraints a toddler could outrun me.

On the way to the Los Angeles International Airport (LAX), the deputies dropped me off in an airport holding cell while they went out to have dinner. I ate my sack lunch, imagining the deputies eating a steak dinner. As I sat there in that cell, bored out of my mind, waiting for our flight to leave, an LAX security guard in uniform was making his rounds. He stopped in front of my cell and read the tag.

"Mr. Timothy Masters . . . Murder one? Mr. Big Time, huh?" he said, smiling at me like he'd just made some kind of joke, like the whole situation was somehow funny or amusing. He went on about his rounds.

They transported me through LAX in the same clothes I'd slept in the night before I was arrested. It was so degrading. Not only was I brought through the airport in pajamas, but in handcuffs. The only saving grace was that Paulson, the taller of the two deputies, had brought a light jacket with him. He wrapped that jacket around my waist, covering up the chain and handcuffs as much as possible, to cause me less embarrassment and make less of a scene as we walked through the terminal. He also took the leg shackles off me to make walking through the airport a little easier. In hindsight, Paulson was actually a decent guy.

We arrived at our departure gate, and I took a seat next to Paulson. There was a little girl sitting near me who must have been about seven years old. She saw my restraints under the jacket and asked her father, "Why is that man in handcuffs?"

"He must have done something very bad. He's a bad man, so stay away from him," her father told her quietly.

We were the first to board the plane, and we took the seats way in the back. As we lifted off the ground, I watched the lights of Los Angeles move below us, and I contemplated the time I would have to spend in jail and the trial that was to come. I wished more than anything that we would have catastrophic engine failure and crash to our deaths. I didn't know how I could prove my innocence when all anyone wanted to do was convict me.

I made my first trip through the newly built Denver International Airport with handcuffs, a shock belt, and a police escort.

24

Larimer County

I REMEMBERED WHEN THEY BUILT THE BRAND-NEW LAR-
imer County Detention Center, back in 1983. That was
a big deal for Fort Collins. We had even taken a tour of it
during my sixth-grade class. I remember quite well walking through those corridors as a kid and peeking into the
various pods at all the bad men who were locked up there.
I never imagined I would be a guest at that jail. I never
thought I'd be one of those "bad men" locked up in there.

I was half expecting a media circus at the county jail
when they brought me in. I could picture in my head the
camera flashes going off and the crowd of reporters asking
me questions as they led me inside in shackles, cuffs, and
the white T-shirt and green shorts. I could imagine them
taking my picture just as I opened my mouth to answer a

question, making me look like some kind of crazed psycho killer with my mouth half open. They love to print the most unflattering photos of people who have been arrested, and a shot of me in those green shorts and dirty white T-shirt would have been very unflattering. Luckily, that didn't happen. The media didn't know I was coming in that night.

It was late when we finally pulled into the parking lot of the Larimer County Detention Center, the LCDC, as it is often lovingly referred to. They led me around the building and into the booking area, where they took my shoes, and then placed me in another holding cell. The guard insisted on holding my arm pinned behind my back in a restraint position as he led me back there. I guess he felt he couldn't be too cautious. He released me after I stepped into the cell and the large steel door slammed shut.

In Bakersfield, I had almost no contact with the guards. They didn't tell me anything there. I didn't know what time the meals were. I didn't know what any of the rules were. LCDC was different. They sat me down in a conference room that was in between the three pods. There, the deputy explained to me all the jail rules, when each meal was, and answered any questions I had. He let me grab two books and a Bible off the book cart and sent me into my cell. They almost coddled us there in comparison to California.

There was even a pillow in the cell.

I found it odd that Bakersfield had stuck me in General Population (GP), even with a red tag on my wrist, while

Fort Collins segregated me from other inmates until they assessed what kind of risk I would pose to them. It was a "kinder, gentler jail"—except for the fights among inmates that broke out about once a week. That part was odd; there hadn't been a single fight the whole time I was in Bakersfield, and Bakersfield was a dump. In Fort Collins, where the jail was a little nicer, there were always fights.

When they threw me right into solitary confinement, it was not because I had disciplinary problems, but because of my charges. They couldn't risk having me in population because they thought I might hurt someone. That was a dark month up there in the hole. There was nothing to do to occupy my time. I could sleep, read, and, during the single hour out of my cell each day, I could call people. God, the boredom wore on me. I must have run up all my family members' phone bills exponentially with so many collect calls. I know I ran up Serena's bill. She told me she averaged $300 a month because we talked every day I was locked up in county.

I was so hungry there; I was always hungry. My body would no longer listen to my brain's refusal to eat like it had at Bakersfield. I started eating everything off the tray, including desserts, which I usually never ate. I even ate the broccoli stems—and I hated broccoli. But anything to help thwart the hunger pains a bit longer.

My family had put some money on my books when I first arrived at LCDC, but up in the hole, you could not order any food. I could only buy stamps, paper, and envelopes. I dreamed of food all the time, especially late at night, when it was twelve hours between meals. I also dreamed of getting the heck out of there. I was not used to having my movements so restricted. As a free man, I was always traveling somewhere. I had spent eight years in the Navy, visited both coasts and many states in between, I drove to Los Angeles to visit my sister at least once a month, went out into the desert to ride my dirt bike, and more. I was never in one place for long. Now, I was stuck in a six by ten cell. Normally, when I got hungry, I ate. No matter where I was or what the time of day was. Now, when I got hungry, I waited. I waited for my captors to feed me. I had no control over anything except my thoughts.

I kept waiting for them to admit they'd made a mistake and let me out. It was so obvious to me that I didn't kill Peggy that I couldn't understand why they didn't realize it.

For outdoor recreation, we could go into an open—and I use that word loosely—area between the buildings. It was triangular shaped and about twenty by twenty by fifteen feet. It had three brick walls and a chain-link cage over the top to keep inmates from climbing out. The only thing to do out there was talk to other inmates; two could go out at one time. I could only get sunlight at certain times of the day.

I could watch the office buildings across the street from the jail through the windows of the pod I was in. I saw the people out there in the real world, coming and going daily. They were still living their lives. Life was still going on out there. But for me, stuck there in jail, there was no life. My life had stopped. All I had left was the daily boredom of the same routine over and over. Oh, man did I feel sorry for myself. I wondered how my monsters—my dogs and cats—were doing at my sister's house.

After I was in LCDC for a couple of days, they brought me out in handcuffs and shackles and walked me down to video court. Basically, they set up video cameras and monitors in the courtroom downtown, and at the jail. This saves a bunch of money in transportation of inmates.

I was already sitting comfortably in my chair waiting my turn at video court when the deputies took me out of the room and paraded me down the hall and right back into the waiting room, just so that the local newspapers could get some photos of me. One of those photos was on the front page of the local paper the next day. The guard who escorted me that day was quite a bit shorter than me, so next to him I looked quite imposing in LCDC oranges, handcuffs, and shackles. I looked like someone capable of murder. That really worked to the prosecutors' favor, my being a full-grown man as opposed to the skinny fifteen-year-old I had been when Peggy Hettrick was killed.

They brought me back to the video court, and the judge ruled that I was a flight risk and said, "No bail would be set at this time."

BEFORE I'D EVEN left California, my family had done their homework in finding me a lawyer. They had asked around about who were the best attorneys in town and made lists of potential lawyers. By the time I was extradited to Colorado, they had narrowed it down to three. They decided that I needed to be the one who made the final decision on who would represent me.

One by one I met with the three potential attorneys. There was Duane Cole, who immediately was shoved to the bottom of my list because he kept talking about seeing what kind of plea bargain the prosecutors would offer me. I didn't want to hear any of that kind of talk. Plea bargains?! I'd never take a plea bargain for something I didn't do, ever! I didn't give a damn what kind of plea the state offered me; this case was going to trial! Then there was Linda Miller, who I liked, but I couldn't hire her because, unknown to Linda, she was representing a person who was suing one of my aunts. The last lawyer I met was Erik Fischer. I liked Erik, and he seemed to be very intelligent, so I thought he was the obvious choice. Erik didn't have any of those speeches about seeing what kind of plea bargain the state would offer me. He had been a deputy district attorney for the city and county of Denver and had prosecuted murder cases. He was an excellent attorney and obviously knew his way around a courtroom in a murder trial. To assist him, I also hired Nathan Chambers. Chambers was no stranger to difficult murder cases either. He had defended Timothy McVeigh when his trial venue was moved to Denver from Oklahoma City.

Cost was also a big factor in my decision of who I would pick. Fischer would take the case with only a $20,000 retainer. The others wanted $50,000. In hindsight, I should have gone with a public defender because they have more funds than my family and I could come up with, but I had heard so many horror stories on TV and while in Bakersfield about public defenders not doing their job that I didn't trust them. The Fort Collins public defenders could have actually done better than a private lawyer because a private lawyer is limited by the client's funds. Theoretically, the public defender can spend as much as the police and district attorneys to try a case. And they would have loved to have taken my case because it was so ridiculous what the police and district attorneys were trying to do—prosecute without any real evidence.

I tried to keep the lack of physical evidence in front of everyone's minds. I still thought that Kelly said Peggy's nipple had been bitten off. During one of those first attorney meetings, I'd asked Erik why they didn't just test the breast that had been bitten off for DNA. Surely there would be DNA from the assailant's saliva there. Erik hadn't even been given the arrest warrant yet, so he knew nothing about the case. All he could do was shake his head and say, "I don't know. You would think they already did that."

He asked me to write, in my own words, everything I could remember from 1987. Erik brought me a copy of my arrest warrant shortly after taking the case. This was the first official piece of paper I'd seen concerning the case. I found it disconcerting that it said "The People of the State of Colorado versus" me. This was a revolting feeling, having the people of the entire state against me.

Until that point in time, I had not known they had obtained an arrest warrant for me in 1992. I thought they had just come out to reinterrogate me. I wouldn't find out until later about the close call: they didn't arrest me when Linda Wheeler-Holloway confirmed my story about hearing details of the crime scene from one of the Explorer Scouts.

Erik explained to me the process of a criminal trial. First I would have an arraignment, where I would plead guilty or not guilty. Then I would have a preliminary hearing to see if there was enough evidence to go to trial, and finally we would have several motion hearings, followed by a trial. Erik told me, "You drew Judge Dressel. He is the judge who signed your arrest warrant in 1992, your arrest warrant in 1998, and now he is your trial judge. There is no way he is not going to remand this to trial." Great—so we were literally just going through the motions by having a preliminary hearing.

I was both ill and angry after reading the warrant. I was sickened that they were accusing me of this crime. I had known since 1987 that it was a heinous crime, but I'd never known the full extent until after reading the warrant. Peggy had been sexually mutilated. Her nipple wasn't bitten off but cut off. Also, just as disturbing, her vagina had the clitoris and surrounding skin excised. How could they accuse me of mutilating a woman's breast and vagina at only fifteen years old? It was crazy! And in the warrant they were twisting around every story or drawing I'd created to try to create a link to this case. They hadn't been lying when they read me my Miranda rights and told me, "Anything you say can and will be used against you." What they didn't tell me was that the things I said would be twisted around so much.

I was angry that they brought my mother, who I'd loved very much, into this. They were calling Peggy's murder a "displaced matricide." They had hired a forensic psychologist to "interpret" my stories and drawings and find a link between them and the crime. It was hocus-pocus bullshit. They claimed my drawings and stories showed hatred toward older women, and that was the motive for this murder. I was dumbfounded; almost all of the examples from my drawings and stories used in the search warrant were acts of violence against boys and men. How could they claim that I specifically showed hatred toward women?

It seemed like Broderick was blaming me for every little incident that happened within about a mile radius from my house. There had been sexually graphic stick-figure graffiti painted under a bridge by my house. I've never spray-painted graffiti on anything, but according to Broderick, that was my handiwork. There was a Quonset hut about a half mile south of my house with female figures drawn on a wall and bullet holes through the breasts. Broderick implied I had done this and added that during the 1992 interview, I had admitted to being in this Quonset hut. I had admitted to taking carpet samples out of a camper that Peterson's Carpet used for storage. It was not the same as the Quonset hut. I had no idea where this so-called Quonset hut was.

The psychological parts of the warrant were just flat-out wrong. How could they be so wrong? How could all these seemingly intelligent people get it so wrong? I was just starting to see that people see what they want to see. Broderick never wanted to look at this case with an open mind and convinced those around him to do the same.

Broderick wrote, "It is the opinion of Dr. Meloy that the sexual homicide of a woman was planned and rehearsed in the obsessive fantasies of Masters as evidenced by the following excerpts from his fantasy productions drawings and narratives."

He listed dozens of violent excerpts from my work. He chose the most graphic, violent excerpts he could find. Yet there was never an instance of a sexual homicide. I didn't understand how they could claim I had obsessive fantasies about a sexual homicide, and had planned and rehearsed this murder in my writings and drawings, when I had never written about anything close to a sexual homicide.

So now I knew who the Hitler look-alike was. It was James Broderick, the same cop who had interrogated me in 1987 and again in 1992. Now I knew that this arrest had been a personal vendetta of his. That's why he had looked so pleased when he told me I was under arrest for the murder of Peggy Hettrick. He had been spending long hours coming up with the crazy, twisted theories he put forth in my arrest warrant.

Serena was right: this was going to be a profile case. They were going to claim that I was the killer because I fit the profile as evidenced by my stories and drawings.

THERE WERE TWO pods in the Larimer County "Hole." I was in one pod for about a week. Then, for reasons unknown to me, they moved me to the other pod.

Those days were so long. I was almost always hungry. I would eat everything off my tray and be starving by

9:00 P.M. The boredom of being in that cage all the time nearly drove me insane. You could almost feel the walls crushing down on your soul. I had only been locked up for a few weeks, and I was already losing it.

I was in the new pod for about a week when some of the inmates tore it up a little bit. Inmates were allowed out two at a time. Someone drew on the tables and scratched ink pictures off of newspaper articles onto them, which was kind of cool. There would be these assorted newspaper photographs on the table. They threw the trash around, and they busted the security cover off the outlet to light a cigarette that someone's lawyer had brought in. Of course, when they brought us out one at a time to interrogate us about the vandalism, I said I didn't see who did it because I was always in my cell reading. But I had actually seen most of it happen. Everyone knows, though, you don't rat on fellow inmates in jail. They probably knew that I at least had an idea of who did it, but they also knew I spent most of my time in the cell reading, and not socializing with other inmates. They decided to just split up that pod by moving us all around. So they moved three of us back to the other pod, where I stayed for a couple more weeks.

When they finally moved me to GP, it was such a joy to be able to watch TV and go to the library, the little things that you take for granted. I went to the library within a few days of moving to GP and got to listen to music. To be able to listen to music after so many days in a cold, empty, quiet cell was amazing. The music sounded so fantastic. The sensory deprivation you experience alone in a cell is unbelievable.

In GP, I was finally able to order commissary. God, the stuff was expensive. I had done my own shopping for years, so I knew the cost of things. Larimer County charged inmates sixty cents for a bag of ramen noodles. Ramen noodles did not cost sixty cents. They were ten for a dollar then. But the county jail marked them up 600 percent. My family helped to keep me fed. They would drop off twenty bucks here, forty bucks there—enough to buy some commissary each week.

After moving to General Population, even with a little commissary each week, I still continued to lose weight. I was so stressed over what was happening that I couldn't sleep at night. I would be awake until four in the morning many nights. So, when breakfast rolled around, I would get up, close my door, and try to sleep through all the noise in the pod. Most inmates went back to bed after breakfast, but many would be out in the pod watching TV or playing cards. I never understood why people felt the need to slam their cards on the table as they played. That was not very pleasant, trying to sleep and hearing the sound of cards being slammed on a metal table. Later, I learned I was in the "medicated pod." Most of the guys in my pod were on meds, but I wasn't. I guess that's why my pod had so few fights.

My family visited me all the time. Every day that we were allowed visitors, someone was there. They were such a strong support group. We were in constant communication. I called a different family member every day, and they all gave me words of encouragement. We all knew the allegations against me were so ridiculous that the state didn't have a chance of winning. I just had to endure the hell of county jail long enough to win my trial.

Each morning, the guards set out the *Rocky Mountain News* for us. Inmates would rip out photos of pretty girls for jerk-off material, so you had to get the paper early if you wanted to see it before it was torn to pieces. It's a little annoying to come to an interesting news article and not be able to read it because half the thing is cut out for the pretty girl on the other side. The tables were too small, and that placed inmates too close together for chow. Many inmates were very depressed and did not care enough to take care of their oral hygiene while waiting for trial, or a plea, or whatever. I can't remember how many times during lunch or dinner I was stuck sitting near someone whose breath reeked because he hadn't brushed his teeth for however long he'd been locked up.

General Population in Fort Collins was much different than Bakersfield had been. For one thing, it was almost entirely white guys. I didn't feel the racial tension I had felt in Bakersfield. For another, the guards treated us like children. They had rules for everything. One rule was that inmates could not trade or give away food. So if you didn't feel like eating what was on your tray, you were supposed to throw it away rather than give it to someone who wanted it. They said they did that to keep the bullying down.

Inmate movement throughout the jail was also very

controlled. You had to stay on the right side of the hall, in single file, and with no talking.

Outside of my pod, there were a lot of fights in the county jail in Fort Collins. I would estimate that we had at least one fight every week. Each time, I would hear them call, "Lock down, lock down!" over the pod intercom. We would all go to our cells and close our doors. If the fight was in the pod across from me, I would see a whole herd of about twenty deputies come running into the pod to break up a fight between two guys.

THROUGHOUT MY TIME in prison, I encountered lots of wannabe drummers—or maybe just guys trying to vent their frustrations on everything around them. The first time I got a drum-playing wannabe in the cell above me, I couldn't believe my ears. I was lying on my bunk after lockdown, and all of a sudden, I heard this annoying combination of banging noises from the cell above mine. Whoever was up there was playing the drums on the wall, his metal desk, and the floor—and not even thinking that the wonderfully obnoxious noise he was making was being heard by all of his neighbors.

That combination of beating on the desk and floor drove me crazy. I couldn't get to the guy to tell him in person, because he was in the pod above me, and he wouldn't have been able to hear me yell "Shut up" through the thick floor. Voices don't carry through concrete like banging on a metal desk does. I had to settle for slamming my shampoo bottle into the ceiling until he stopped.

. . .

MY FIRST CELLY was Tom. I knew I was in for it when I walked into the pod with my property and people whispered, "They're putting someone in the cell with Tom?" Tom was not very old, but he had serious medical problems. He had suffered from a stroke and had a bad limp. Tom was no neat freak. When I moved in, the cell smelled like urine. Tom never wiped up the toilet after using it, and he had terrible aim. He also never cleaned the cell, and he had been there for almost three months by then.

Tom was serving a three-month sentence for stealing someone's tax return check for about $2,000 and cashing it. He bitched to me a bit about this. He didn't think three months was fair. He thought he should have gotten probation. How funny—he was serving three months for something he did and was bitching; I was going to be there for at least six months waiting to go to trial for something I didn't even do. But I agreed with him that the system sure wasn't fair.

I was often offended when people would use the expression, "You're gonna 'get off.'" There was nothing to "get off" from: I didn't do anything wrong. To me, that expression always implied guilt.

Most of the time, Tom and I got along alright. I only got into one argument with Tom. It was on the day he was getting out, and he was mad because he had the notion that they would release him first thing in the morning. They didn't. County jails are in no hurry to do paperwork, so they processed him out at their leisure. I said something along the lines of, "It's funny how they're in such a hurry to put you in but so slow letting you out."

I was trying to make a joke to lighten Tom's mood. But Tom was too upset to realize I was joking. Tom went left when I said that. "It ain't fucking funny, god damn it. They're supposed to let me out this morning and I'm still here. Fuck you!"

I don't like to fight people, and I especially didn't want to hurt someone with disabilities like Tom had, but his going left on me pissed me off. Here the guy was, guilty of the crime, and getting out before me, yet bitching because he was being detained for a couple more hours. That made me mad, but I kept it in check and calmly told Tom, "I haven't wanted to beat the shit out of someone like I want to hurt you right now in a long time. Do you want to take this to the next level?" He didn't say anything. I'm sure he didn't want to fight any more than I did. He was just upset about being in that place a second longer than he had to be.

My second celly at LCDC was Rick. Rick said he was bipolar and a compulsive thief. He told me he had stolen three or four PlayStations from various stores and that he couldn't help himself. He didn't need them; he just had to take them. I liked Rick; he seemed like a nice-enough guy. I was searching for a religion I could believe in, and Rick turned me on to Christian Science. I thought, *This is something I can believe in. This makes sense.* That's also what I thought when I started studying the Book of Mormon, a Seventh-Day Adventist Bible, and Pentecostal paraphernalia. During my stay at the county, I studied many different religions. I kept trying to find something I could believe in, something that would prove to me that all this bad stuff that was happening to me was happening for a reason and not just because the world is out of control. I wanted to know that there was someone or something in control out there that would make sure everything would turn out alright. Because if no one was in control, I could easily be wrongly convicted and spend the rest of my life in prison for something I didn't do.

From time to time, Erik would come to the prison to visit me and update me on what was going on. During an early visit, he informed me that the state "doesn't have shit on you." By this time Erik had finished his initial review of all of the discovery, and he was very confident that we would win. The only wild cards were whether or not my stories and drawings would come in, whether or not the forensic psychologist would come in, and how a jury would take it if those items did come in. All of us were well aware of how the productions might prejudice the jury. There was such a strong possibility that they would see these productions and, despite the fact that I've never hurt anyone, assume I have a propensity for violence because I'd created such violent works. Juries tend to forget all about the many people who create violent things—horror movies, video games, thriller novels—and never so much as lift a finger in violence themselves.

They set my bond at $200,000 at a hearing in October. That was great. We could come up with enough property to cover that.

I asked Fischer if I would be able to see everything in

the case if I got out on bail. We didn't want me keeping a copy of the discovery in my prison cell because there was a danger of another inmate reading it and having enough information to make up a believable but bogus confession story and getting a reduced sentence to testify against me. He told me if I got out on bail, I could have a desk in his office and come over every day if I wanted to and that he had an entire banker's box full of case discovery for me to go through.

But the family couldn't put up their property. Unlikely though it might be, if I ran and didn't make my court date, they would lose their homes. I called Serena shortly after that, begging her to get me out of there. I never break down in front of other people, but I broke down on the phone with my sister. I didn't think I could handle staying in there any longer. Poor Serena couldn't do a thing to help me. I imagine she felt so helpless.

In October, I was moved to the second tier, where all the cells were single bunked. What a relief it was to be in a room by myself. This was when I learned of a California man named Wayne Ford who turned himself in to the Humboldt County sheriffs for murdering and mutilating women. He walked into the police station with a severed breast in a plastic bag. He was a trucker, and he said he had killed women in several states.

After reading about him in the paper, I immediately called Erik and told him about Ford. Erik promised to have him looked into. I thought there was a strong possibility that Ford could have killed Peggy Hettrick. I recall sitting on my bunk in that second-tier cell watching the snow fall, illuminated by the million-candle-watt lights that always surround jails and prisons. I thought there was no way in the world a jury would ever convict me for a murder I did not commit—especially since there was no physical evidence against me. I just could not believe that any group of jurors would buy into Broderick's bullshit.

DURING A ROUTINE motion hearing, Erik asked Jolene Blair, the assistant prosecutor, "What are you guys doing? You know you have a weak case here, right?"

"Those stories and drawings just aren't right," Jolene told Erik.

I'd never had any ill feelings toward the prosecutors until Jolene Blair uttered those words. Until then, I'd thought the prosecutors were not taking this case personally, that they were just doing their job. After she said that, I realized this was personal for her. She thought and still thinks I am a bad person who needs to be locked up so that good people like her will be safe from people like me.

After a few months in the county jail, I was so out of shape that I would get winded climbing the short staircase to the second floor. Handball was about the only physical activity to do, and I never liked handball, so that was out. All that most of us did was sit around watching TV or playing cards or board games. It was the longest eight months of my life—up to that point, anyway.

I had my first Thanksgiving in custody that year. We had sliced turkey, mashed potatoes, gravy, and stuffing for dinner. It sucked compared to Thanksgiving on the outside, but it was fantastic for county-jail food. Between Thanksgiving and Christmas, the county jail sort of emptied out somehow. We were down to so few inmates in the pod that some of the first-tier cells were empty, and the ones that were occupied had only a single inmate in them. I liked it that way. It was much quieter with fewer inmates.

The other thing I remember about that winter is that sometimes it was so hot in the cells that I would have to soak my sheets in cold water and wrap them around me just to cool off enough to sleep. It was ridiculous. In the summertime, the cells were fine, but in the winter, they turned up the heat so high that we cooked on the second tier. I would spend the next few months in this jail, waiting for my trial to finally begin.

25

Pretrial

A S WE PREPARED MY DEFENSE, MY ATTORNEYS GAVE ME some advice that—looking back on it now—I disagree with. They told me not to speak with the media and gave the same instructions to my family and friends. I understand that attorneys worry about their clients saying the wrong thing to a reporter, but the result hurt me. The police spoke to the press throughout the case and painted a picture of me that was not flattering. Since my side was silent, their accusations went unanswered in the court of public opinion. The other piece of advice was for me to grow my hair out from my military cut. I had worn it short and neat for years. Growing it long not only made me look different, but it made me feel different. While police officers took the stand with their clean-cut hair, I sat at the defense table, looking and feeling like a hippie.

Eventually, I got to see all of the documents and evidence the prosecution had to work with in preparing their side of the trial. Some of it was given to us as required by Colorado law; some of it wasn't given to me until long after I had gone to prison. Among the thousands of pages of documents, I found Broderick's handwritten notes. It gave me some insight into the man who was hell-bent on putting me in jail for a crime I didn't commit. For example, on his "Things to do" list for 1999, he wrote "Consider demonstrating evidence showing what he fantasizes about happens in reality." In other words, he wanted to ask the judge to allow the prosecution to act out some of my drawings for the jury. This never happened, and the subject never came up in court so all we can assume is that the prosecutors told Broderick the judge would never allow it.

We knew the prosecutors were going to use my drawings and stories to show me in a bad light to the jury. We didn't think a judge would allow it. Under Colorado law, evidence of a person's character is usually not admissible. If it was, a defendant could trot out his friends to tell the jury what a nice guy he was, and the prosecutor would go and find everyone who didn't like the person to say what a bad person the defendant was. None of that is evidence though, which is why it's not admissible. Why would a drawing I had made long before Peggy Hettrick was murdered be considered as evidence? The prosecutor said that they didn't want to bring it in to show that I was a bad person; they claimed it was to show the jury how I had planned my attack on Peggy and how I had carried out the murder. They pointed to a couple of drawings of knives and of violent themes and said they ought to be admissible because they fell outside the realm of character evidence.

The judge held a hearing on this and we spent a day in court arguing about it. We also spent a day in court arguing about whether Reid Meloy would be allowed to testify to the jury about his opinions of me and how he believed, after seeing my drawings but never talking to me, I was a cold-blooded killer. The judge's wife was a psychologist, and he seemed to hold the profession in high esteem. He said he would allow Meloy to testify but that he would have to be careful how he phrased his testimony in front of the jury. He couldn't tell the jury I had killed Peggy; he could only tell them that my drawings showed how I planned on killing her.

As for the drawings, the judge said pretty much the same thing. They could be introduced into evidence but not to prove that I had done the things in the drawings and stories. They just showed my motive for killing Peggy and my plan and "scheme" for carrying out the attack.

26

The Trial: Day One

ON THURSDAY, MARCH 18, 1999, *THE PEOPLE OF THE State of Colorado versus Timothy Masters* began, presided over by Judge William F. Dressel. A deputy from the jail came and brought me to booking so I could change into a suit. My lawyers had brought my suit and some shirts and ties so I could get out of my orange prison uniform. It had been so long since I had worn civilian clothes that I had trouble tying my tie. The deputy tied it for me. I took off my jail sandals and put on dress shoes. I couldn't believe how comfortable they were, once I got to walk in them. You lose track of little things like that when you're locked up for a few months.

I rode to the courthouse in a police van, sitting in the back and watching everyone on the streets gawk at me as I passed by. I was proud of the fact that I had lived my life well. I didn't steal, didn't lie, and didn't use illegal drugs. I had served honorably in the military. I never killed anyone and never raped anyone. And here I was, being carted around in the back of a jail van, just like a common criminal.

Serena drove out for the trial with my nephew Mario. Little Mario was only nine years old, so he was not allowed to attend the trial. I did not want him subjected to all that bull crap. Serena attended every day of the trial, sitting with my family in the first two rows behind the defense table.

Before we went into the courtroom, my attorneys, Erik Fischer and Nathan Chambers, met me in the hallway and asked the deputy if they could speak to me before entering the courtroom. He stepped aside and Fischer leaned in and whispered to me. "I know what you're going to say, but as your lawyer I have to tell you this. The prosecution has offered you a deal, a plea bargain. If you plead guilty to second-degree murder, they'll agree to a twenty-year sentence, max."

"No way," I told him, without really waiting for him to finish. "I didn't do this, and I'll never take a plea bargain for it."

"Fair enough," he said with a smile. He knew how I felt about this. "I had a feeling you'd say no, but you know—I have to convey the offers they make. We came here to have a trial, and that's what we're going to do."

We met with the judge in his chambers first and ran

through preliminary matters. It is amazing how seemingly little things can become quite important in a trial like this. The attorneys—mine and the ones from the prosecutor's office, Terence Gilmore and Jolene Blair—had drafted a "Statement of the Case" that would be read by the judge to the jury to let them know what the case was all about. We agreed on most of it, but the prosecution was pushing on one point: they wanted to tell the jury that Peggy had been stabbed and mutilated in the field where her body was found. Fisher argued to the judge that such detail was inappropriate—why not just say her body was found in the field? The judge agreed with us, and that is what the jury was told. We had never believed that she was stabbed or mutilated in the field, and it turns out that some of the prosecution's own experts didn't think so either. They had wanted the language to promote their theory, knowing that if Peggy had been stabbed or mutilated elsewhere, I couldn't have done it because I didn't have a car at the time.

We went out and sat in the courtroom as a large group of potential jurors was brought in. We would be questioning potential jurors drawn from a random pool of people who had gotten notices to appear at the court today for jury duty. Having only heard about trials in the news, I was surprised at how quickly we picked our jury. I was also surprised at some of the people who showed up in the pool of potential jurors. Right off the bat, two deputies from the Larimer County detention center were disqualified. One woman told the court she couldn't be impartial. She told the court, "I thought he was guilty based upon the paper." Suddenly, I realized the error of not speaking with the media about my side of the case.

Thirteen jurors were selected: twelve plus an alternate. We finished the selection in the afternoon, and the jury was sworn. Opening statements began at 4:00. Gilmore began for the prosecution. He told the jury about how Peggy Hettrick's body was found on February 11, 1987, and that the man who found it first thought it was a mannequin. He walked the jury through the last evening of Peggy's life, her trip to the Prime Minister, and her encounter with her ex-boyfriend. He then turned the story to me. He told the jury about how I lived in the lot next to the field where Peggy's body was found. I had seen Peggy's body but had gone to school. He jumped to the next day—February 12—and told the jury that when my room was searched, they found my "collection" of knives on "display." I had pulled the knives out the night of the eleventh after my father had gone to vo-tech and left me alone in the house. He didn't mention that I had consented to let them search my room because I felt I had nothing to hide.

He told the jury they had found thousands of pages of drawings of "cruel and grotesque images, drawings of killing, dismemberment." He then told the jury that I had been brought in for questioning on the twelfth. To the jury, it sounded like this was the first day I had been questioned. It may have seemed a small detail, but I began to notice that the prosecution played fast and loose with the facts and details in my case, always painting the picture a little worse for me.

Gilmore admitted to the jury that I denied any involvement in the murder. He quickly jumped to 1992—he didn't mention how there was absolutely no physical evidence that tied me to the crime—and simply said that the case had been brought back up for review by the police. He mentioned that I had been reinterrogated and had again denied all involvement. Then he told the jury about Broderick attending the seminars in 1995 and 1996 where he learned about the "developing area of investigation, attempting to understand sexual homicides."

Gilmore told the jury that Broderick was directed to Reid Meloy. Meloy had explained to Broderick that the "frightening view into the private fantasy life of Mr. Masters" would explain the Hettrick homicide. According to Gilmore, Meloy could interpret my drawings and, from them, explain how I picked Peggy as a victim, climbed out my bedroom window with a survival knife, scalpel, and a "red-covered flashlight to surprise her," snuck up and killed her by thrusting the knife into her back, lowering her to the curb, dragged her into the field, partially disrobed her, and then cut off her nipple and "vaginal skin." According to Gilmore, Meloy could testify to that based upon nothing but having looked at my drawings. He didn't mention that Meloy had never met or spoken with me.

He started to argue to the jury about how the evidence was going to show I was acting out my fantasy life when the judge cut him off for arguing during an opening statement. "Please get back to what the evidence will be, please."

Gilmore ended by saying the evidence would show I was guilty of first-degree murder. Erik Fischer gave my opening statement and showed the jury a picture of me taken at the time I was questioned by police. It was important for the jury to remember that they were accusing me of committing this crime a decade earlier, when I was fifteen years old and weighed only 115 pounds. He told the jury about how I had gotten up that morning and headed out to catch my bus and had seen the body in the field. I had thought it was a mannequin—just like the other witness would testify to—and had gone to school. I hadn't responded to the body because I thought someone was playing a joke on me. He then told the jury about how a detective had come to school, and when he asked me about it, I immediately told him the truth. He told them how I was interrogated at the police station for ten hours and how I had steadfastly proclaimed my innocence.

He explained how the police had tried everything to get me to confess. In a marathon interrogation, they told me they had evidence that didn't exist. Most important, Fischer told them what Gilmore had not: there was no physical evidence that pointed to me or connected me to the murder in any way. He pointed out to the jury that the drawings did not contain any images of a woman being stabbed in the back. They depicted Rambo, and Freddy Krueger, and Army men. He ended by pointing out to the jury that all the prosecution had was "an opinion from a psychologist regarding fantasy. What they don't have is any evidence to back up that opinion."

The judge gave the jury some final instructions, and we ended the first day of the trial. The opening statements had taken only a half hour. After court, I headed back to the Larimer County Detention Center, my home for the duration of the trial.

27

The Trial: Day Two

THE TRIAL'S FIRST WITNESSES TOOK THE STAND THE next day. Linwood Hodgdon was the man who spotted Peggy's body in the field as he was out riding his bicycle that morning. Hodgdon worked for Hewlett-Packard and often rode his bicycle to work. He passed by the field just a few minutes after I caught my bus. Something caught his attention in the field: "[T]here was a mannequin laying in the field." He testified that he stopped to take a look and then thought it might be a real body. He knew someone who lived within a few blocks and pedaled over to that house and called 911. On cross-examination by my attorney, Nate Chambers, Hodgdon repeated his initial belief that the body was a mannequin. What made him change his mind was a pool of blood he saw by the curb where he had stopped his bike. I had not seen the pool of blood. As is typical of anyone giving testimony, Hodgdon made a few minor errors. He said that Peggy had "long" hair and was wearing "shoes."

MICHAEL SWIHART TESTIFIED next. He was the first police officer to arrive at the scene after Hodgdon called. He then showed the jury a diagram of the field where Peggy was found, carefully noting that my home was on one edge of the field. Swihart testified that he walked out into the field and checked Peggy for a pulse; when he felt her skin, she had obviously been dead for a while. The prosecutor then handed him a series of photographs of Peggy's body as it appeared in the field and photographs of the field. Soon, other officers arrived, the scene was secured, and the coroner arrived.

Swihart testified that there were a number of footprints at the scene, and he was directed to photograph them. He focused on one footprint, which was mine: Footprint Number Two. I had told the police that I had walked up to the body, so there was an explanation for why a footprint of mine was there. However, the footprint testimony provided by Swihart and the others became so convoluted I'm not sure anyone understood it.

Swihart then told the jury about how he had come to my house to get a written statement from me on the eleventh. He noticed that my shoe looked like it matched one of the footprints he found in the field—again, this shouldn't have been a surprise to anyone since I had already told him I had walked through the field that morning. He photographed my shoe. He testified that I had not told him I had been interviewed already by a police officer. It looked like he was trying to tell the jury I had been deceptive.

He told the court that he had come back on the thirteenth to continue looking for evidence and that he had searched an abandoned house near the field and found "artwork" that he found interesting. He thought it looked similar to the drawings I had made, and that he had seen on the twelfth.

On cross-examination, my attorney asked him about whether I had told him I spoke previously to Officer Gonzalez. After checking his notes, he admitted he "was in error" when he said I had failed to mention it. His notes reflected I had told him of my previous conversation with the police. Even so, he tried to make it sound like I was somehow being evasive or uncooperative, even though I spoke with him and every other officer every time they asked to speak to me.

Regarding the footprints, Swihart admitted that the department could have used numbered markers to keep track of where various footprints were found, but they had not done so at the Hettrick crime scene. He also did not note in his report where any of the photographs of the footprints were taken. In essence, he had a lot of photographs of footprints but couldn't tell where they were taken or which way the footprints pointed; all he could tell is that they came from somewhere in the field that day. After Nate got him to admit that he couldn't tell where a couple footprints were photographed, the judge interrupted him and said he was wasting the court's time. I wondered if the judge would have the same objection for the prosecution when they started introducing my drawings one at a time for the jury.

I had told the police that I had walked up to the body and then walked away from it. If someone was dragging the body into the field from the curb, their footprints would have pointed toward the curb and have been in roughly the same path as the body had been dragged. The prosecution would tap dance around this issue the entire trial.

Swihart's memory wasn't all that good though, after all these years. He also testified there was a sidewalk along the west side of Landings, when there wasn't. We took a break, and as the deputies walked me to where I had to wait out the breaks, I couldn't contain myself. "I can't believe they didn't do a proper job collecting footprint evidence."

One of the deputies stopped me. "Mr. Masters, you need to know that anything you say to us we are obligated to repeat to the prosecution." At that point, I realized I was surrounded by people who had already convicted me in their own minds and would treat me as a murderer.

AN OFFICER NAMED Jack Taylor testified next. He told the jury about coming to the scene that morning and seeing the body, and a pool of blood by the curb with a Merit cigarette sitting on top of the blood. Merit was the brand that both Peggy and her ex-boyfriend, Matt Zoellner, smoked. They also called the fire department to use their boom to take overhead photos of the field. Taylor noted that the previous witness was wrong about the sidewalk; there was not a sidewalk there at that time.

Taylor noted that the bloody trail between Peggy's body and the curb—it was often called the "drag trail" in court—was not unbroken. There were spots where there was no blood at all and then the trail would continue. The trail was one hundred and three feet long. Most important, though, Taylor testified to finding a single print in the drag trail, a print that was clear and that they had taken a cast of. The print was mine, exactly where I had said it would be.

During Taylor's testimony, the prosecution flashed pictures of Peggy Hettrick up on the screen in the courtroom. They showed pictures of her as she lay in the field and as she lay on an autopsy table. This was the first time I'd seen these pictures, which showed the mutilations. They were shocking. In the field, her body looked pale, and her eyes were open. Her nipple had been sliced off. When she was rolled over, there was a huge knife wound to her back, and her clothing was drenched in her blood. The autopsy photos were even more gruesome. I couldn't imagine who could do such a thing. I found it shocking I was being accused of it—and when I was only fifteen years old, no less.

The prosecutor handed Taylor a bag containing the pants Peggy was wearing when she was killed. He pulled out the pants and showed them to the jury. They were soaked in blood and soiled; holes had been cut in them for testing by the police. He also showed Peggy's boots, bra, panties, socks, coat, purse, and necklace to the jury. He mentioned that she was wearing other jewelry when she died—including the bracelet—but those items were not shown to the jury. We found out later that some of the items of evidence weren't available because they had been inexplicably given to Peggy's grandmother. He testified about the contents of Peggy's purse, and he mentioned to the jury that it contained a note she had written to Matt Zoellner, the ex-boyfriend she had seen that night, before she was murdered. Taylor had also attended the autopsy; the coroner had pointed out to him that Peggy's vagina also had skin excised from it.

Taylor told the jury about how he had searched my house the next day, and they had found photocopies of my mother's death certificate on the kitchen table. They would later point to this to suggest there was a connection between the date of my mother's death and the date Peggy was killed. And although I certainly missed my mother, they wanted the jury to believe that I was fixated upon her death; they would argue I had killed Peggy out of anger and frustration I felt as a result.

On cross-examination, my attorney asked Taylor if it had seemed to him that Peggy had been dragged into the field with her pants down. This was important; the prosecution's theory was that Peggy was stabbed in the street, dragged into the field, and then someone pulled down her pants and pushed up her shirt to mutilate her body. If these things were done elsewhere, it would have required the use of a car and would have destroyed the prosecutor's case. At first Taylor denied it, but then he admitted that he had written in his report—shortly after the autopsy—

that Peggy's pants "may have been down when she was dragged."

Taylor admitted that the lone footprint in the drag trail was pointing toward the body and that there were many other footprints that straddled the drag trail. For some reason that he could not explain, the footprints straddling the trail were never cast. He also admitted that when he first saw the body, with the coroner present—they both came to the conclusion that she had been dragged by her hands out into the field.

My attorney asked Taylor if there was any physical evidence linking me to the crime. He admitted there was none but only after hemming and hawing and letting Blair object that the question lacked foundation. Fischer walked Taylor through the details of his own report and asked him point blank, "In fact, I believe you wrote in your report that—in June that year—that you had no physical evidence linking Mr. Masters to this crime; isn't that correct?"

"That's correct, sir."

My attorney then asked Taylor if it was true that another man had confessed to killing Peggy. Taylor admitted that this was true, but before he could elaborate, Blair objected on hearsay grounds. Even though such a statement should have been admissible, the court sustained the objection. What the jury never got to hear was that there were other, much better, suspects out there. There were people who had even claimed to have killed Peggy that the jury just didn't hear about.

.   .   .

THE NEXT WITNESS they called was of the sort people are only familiar with nowadays because of the plethora of crime shows—fictional and documentary—on television. Tom Bevel was a blood-spatter expert. There was a break before he took the stand, and I was left alone at the defense table. I could hear Gilmore coaching Bevel. "Couldn't you just say you wouldn't expect to find a lot of blood at the crime scene?" They looked over, noticed I was sitting there, and Gilmore suggested they "go outside for a minute." They continued their conversation in the hallway. When Bevel took the stand, he explained how he was given photographs of the crime scene and had concluded that Peggy was murdered at the curb. He somehow could also determine from what he had been shown that Peggy's killer would not have gotten any blood on himself or herself because stab wounds seal themselves "to a certain extent." Considering how much blood was on the ground at the curb, all over and soaked through her clothing, and how much was in the field where she had been dragged, it was hard to believe that anyone could accept that notion as true. However, the prosecution knew that none of her blood had been found on me, so they had to make that argument.

On cross-examination, Bevel admitted that blood-spatter analysis is not an exact science, but he defended that by claiming "most science is not exact."

PATRICK ALLEN, THE coroner for Larimer County, testified next. He described Peggy's injuries and how her nipple had been removed. He said it had been done with a scalpel or a razor. Likewise, he talked about the injuries to Peggy's genitalia in scientific terms. He noted that both mutilations took place after Peggy had died. He said he'd seen nothing like it in his twenty-one years of being a coroner. He said the knife wound to Peggy's back appeared to have been caused by a knife that could have had an irregular back, like a saw edge. It could also have been caused by twisting. The prosecutor showed Allen one of my knives and asked him if that knife "could account" for the injury to Peggy, and he said it could.

Allen then described the wound that killed Peggy. Her killer had stabbed her with a large knife that had penetrated far enough to slice into her left lung. The attack was so forceful, the knife had broken one of her ribs. About a quart and a half of blood was still in her chest at the time of the autopsy, an amount the doctor found significant because Peggy had bled to death, mostly through internal bleeding. He went back and forth though, on whether she had lost more blood internally or externally. The prosecutor would try and argue that Peggy hadn't lost much blood outside of her body—the only way they could claim I killed her without getting any blood on me—but he admitted he did not know how much she bled. "So the part that we will never know is how much blood is outside of the body at the scene into the environment; in other words, at the curb or on the dirt and the grass along the drag trail. That's impossible to measure because it can't be quantitated." Allen was also working from the assumption that Peggy had been stabbed at Landings, right where the

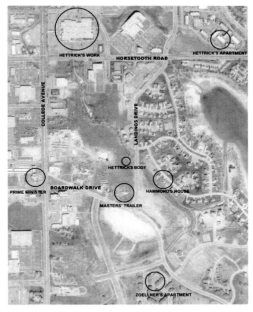

An aerial map of Fort Collins in 1987 showing the important locations in the Peggy Hettrick case, including my trailer and its proximity to where Peggy's body was found.

Photo taken of the drag marks leading from the road to Peggy's body (on the far right).

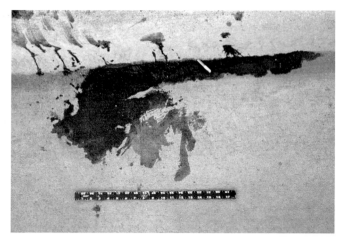

The pool of blood and cigarette butt on Landings Drive.

A section of the drag trail. My shoeprints—with toes oriented toward the body and clearly on top of the drag trail rather than beside it—are circled.

The mug shot taken of me when I was interrogated by the Fort Collins Police Department in 1987.

This photo of me at a promotion ceremony in 1995 shows the contrast between how I looked at the time of the murders and when I was arrested in 1998.

Peggy Hettrick

Most of the relevant shoeprints in the field where Peggy was found were made by Thom McAn shoes. The fact I never owned a pair of these shoes was conveniently overlooked.

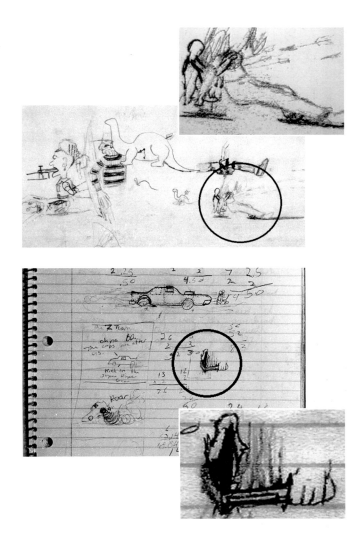

TOP: The infamous drawing that I made of a body being dragged was one of the main pieces of evidence used by the prosecution to get me convicted.

BOTTOM: The other drawing that held so much significance for the prosecution. It's a doodle of a hand stabbing a knife through the paper, which Broderick chose to describe as a knife cutting into a vagina.

Me with my mother, Margaret, my father, Clyde, and my sister, Serena, in 1982.

My mother, Margaret Masters.

Me at boot camp in 1989.

Receiving my Certificate of Reinlistment in 1993.

Richard Eikelenboom, Me, Selma Eikelenboom, Maria Liu, Barie Goetz, Linda Wheeler-Holloway, and Josh Hoban after I was released.

Me with Selma and Richard Eikelenboom.
Photo by Steve Lehto

"blood pool" had been found by the curb. He never considered she may have been stabbed somewhere else and then brought to Landings and dumped.

Allen mentioned that they had tested Peggy to see what her blood-alcohol level had been. Although the testing was subject to some variation, he said she was probably slightly over the legal limit to drive in Colorado at the time. Of course, Peggy was walking the last time anyone saw her, so we don't know what, if any, effect the alcohol had on her that night. The coroner had tried to determine her time of death, but the results were all over the board. One test came back with a window of ten hours—6:30 in the evening to 4:30 in the morning. Since everyone knew that Peggy was alive well past midnight—when she was last seen leaving the Prime Minister—Allen had simply gone off the facts he had been told about Peggy's activities. He placed her time of death at "early on the morning of February 11th, 1987." It was a pretty vague answer, considering he wrote in the autopsy report that he fixed her time of death to be between 12:31 and 3:30 A.M.

Dr. Allen was one of the witnesses who apparently wanted to please the prosecution, even though he was simply a government official, testifying about his job. After he told the prosecution it was "impossible" to measure how much blood Peggy had lost outside of her body, the prosecutor pushed him for a more exact statement. Could he tell what percentage of blood she had lost outside of her body? He then claimed "half to two thirds of her blood volume was probably accounted for." If it was impossible to "quantitate," then how could he do that math? Erik

Fischer made it his first question: Didn't he just say it was impossible? The doctor admitted, "That's correct."

"So you really can't make a percentage determination because you don't know how much blood was lost to the outside environment?"

"That's correct."

Allen left out some of his observations that would have helped my case. During the autopsy, he had been the one to remove Peggy's clothing. As he examined her pants, he noted that where the pants had been bunched up around her knees, there was no dirt between the folds. This led him to tell the police officers present that her pants had been down while she was being dragged through the field. This, of course, would have gone a long way toward proving I hadn't killed Peggy; the prosecution's theory was that I dragged her into the field and then pulled her pants down. The dirt patterns on her pants meant she had been attacked elsewhere and then just dumped near my home.

Fischer then asked the coroner about the knife that had been shown to him. No one had mentioned this to the jury yet, but Peggy's body had been exhumed after the knife had been found, to see if a piece of the knife had broken off when it hit her rib. When they x-rayed her body, they found no pieces of a knife. The coroner had been there for the exhumation as well, and he said they had found nothing new at that time.

THE NEXT WITNESS was Leslie Gaines, who had been driving home the evening before Peggy was murdered. Gaines had lived on Landings and said she saw a woman who looked like Peggy walking down the street around midnight. When the police canvassed the neighborhood the next day, she had told them that she may have seen Peggy Hettrick walking along Landings the night before.

When we broke for lunch, the attorneys, witnesses, and spectators all got up and walked out of the courtroom. I went through a routine I would become very familiar with during my time in court. A deputy shackled my feet and handcuffed me. He led me down into the basement of the building and then out the back to a county transport van. We drove back to the county jail and I was put into a small holding cell by myself. The cell had a sink, a toilet, and a bench. They gave me a sack lunch, and I sat in there for the hour and ate it by myself. At the end of the hour, they came and got me and took me back to court.

DAWN GILBREATH TESTIFIED next. She was a friend of Matt Zoellner, Peggy's ex-boyfriend, and the two had met up at a bar called Rumors the night before Peggy was killed. They decided to leave and meet up later at the Prime Minister. They drove separately, and when she got to the bar, Zoellner was talking to Peggy at the bar. Gilbreath walked up to Zoellner, kissed him on the cheek, and then went and sat at a table. Gilbreath noticed that Zoellner didn't like that she had kissed him in front of Peggy. Eventually, Zoellner left Peggy at the bar and joined Gilbreath at her table. Gilbreath and Zoellner watched Peggy speak to another man at the bar—Gilbreath testified that Zoellner "was watching her pretty close"—while they drank and talked until the bar closed. They then decided to go to Zoellner's apartment. There, they kissed, but Gilbreath denied doing anything further. She left around 3:00 A.M.

Gilbreath provided Zoellner his alibi for the time of Peggy's murder. When Zoellner was interviewed by the police on the morning of the eleventh, Zoellner had repeatedly referred to her as "Shawn."

THE PROSECUTOR THEN called James Broderick to the stand. He was a lieutenant when he testified, and he would become the foundation of the prosecutor's case. In fact, he would testify several times during the trial; this time, he was simply called to retrace Peggy's movements before she was killed. We didn't dispute anything he was going to testify to regarding Peggy's known whereabouts that night, so we stipulated to let him simply tell the jury what the police had learned about it. Peggy worked at a store called Fashion Bar, located in the Fashion Square Shopping Center in south Fort Collins. She lived in the Aspenleaf Apartments, which were located a block and a half east of the mall. She left the store at 9:01 P.M. on the tenth. She went home but couldn't get into her apartment, so she went over to the Laughing Dog Saloon. She told friends at the saloon she had been locked out of her apartment by a friend who had keys to her apartment. She had hoped her friend might be at the bar but she wasn't.

She then went to the Prime Minister, arriving around

9:30 P.M. After trying unsuccessfully to call her friend—she thought the friend might be drunk or asleep inside the apartment—Peggy left the Prime Minister. Broderick said he thought Peggy then went to Matt Zoellner's because they found a note in Peggy's purse addressed to him. No one ever explained why the note would still be in her purse if she had actually made it to Zoellner's place, however. The note said she was locked out of her apartment and she hoped Zoellner wouldn't get "grumpy" with her for seeking his help. Broderick said police had found cigarette butts of Peggy's brand of cigarettes near where Zoellner parked his car, but no witnesses placed her at the apartment that night. Broderick did not mention to the jury that Zoellner also smoked Merit cigarettes. Broderick's testimony was based upon his own reconstruction of Peggy's movements and actions the night in question. Much of it was based upon his conjecture and assumptions and it was very confusing the way he presented it to the jury.

A neighbor of Peggy's told the police that later on Peggy showed up and pounded on her apartment door until the roommate finally let her in. He wasn't sure of the exact time of this incident but it was after midnight. Apparently, she went into the apartment and changed out of her work clothes. Broderick then said the next person to see her was Leslie Gaines, who said she saw a woman walking down the street around midnight. Broderick believed the woman Gaines had seen was Peggy, but Gaines had never said that. In fact, Gaines had said the woman she saw had light-blonde hair, and she placed the blonde on Landings at the same time that Peggy's neighbor said she was at her apartment.

Broderick had spoken with Zoellner, who told him that Peggy showed up at the Prime Minister again around 12:30. According to Broderick, thirty-five or forty people were interviewed, and many of them remembered Peggy and Zoellner being there at this time. Around 1:20 that morning, witnesses saw Peggy leave the bar. Zoellner said he offered her a ride, but she declined.

On cross-examination, Broderick mentioned a few things he had left out of his testimony when being questioned by the prosecutor. When Peggy saw Zoellner at the bar, they had gotten into an argument. Zoellner had called it a "fight." Peggy was angry that Zoellner was apparently seeing someone else. Their "on-again, off-again" relationship wasn't as "off" for Peggy as it was for Zoellner.

Zoellner also had Peggy leaving the bar at 1:00 A.M., much earlier than the other witnesses.

Broderick was the last witness of the second day of the trial. The jury was excused for the weekend. I went back and sat in jail.

28

The Trial: Day Three

O N MONDAY MORNING, THE PROSECUTION BEGAN BY calling Francis Gonzalez to the stand. Gonzalez was the police officer who been sent to my school to talk to me and see if I had seen anything that morning when I walked through the field to catch my bus. He came to school and got the principal to pull me from class. In an empty office, he asked me if I knew why he was there. I told him I did and that it had been bothering me all day. I told him I saw the blood trail and then I walked back to look at the body before I headed over to the bus stop. I told him that I thought it was a Resusci Anne doll, a mannequin like the ones we used in first aid to learn CPR. He then took me to the police station and had me fill out a witness statement.

He then left me and returned to the scene, where he

was told to go and take a look around Matt Zoellner's apartment. There, he found some cigarette packages of the same brand Peggy smoked and some cigarette butts. He found and photographed some footprints that he thought matched Peggy's boots.

They then jumped ahead to August 31, 1987, when Gonzalez received a call to pick up a knife that had been found near Spinnaker Lane and Skysail. The knife had been found by a teenager, and the teen's father turned it over to the police.

On cross-examination, Gonzalez admitted that I had been cooperative with him and readily told him everything about that morning. Gonzalez also spoke about a footprint he looked at near the curb. The print was so clear that it was photographed from several angles, and the police were certain they could distinguish the pattern in the sole of the shoe. It even had a logo. After Gonzalez visited a shoe store, it was confirmed: the shoe was a Thom McAn, a brand of shoe I had never owned. Gonzalez asked the shoe salesman if they could borrow the shoe; when he was told no, he came back and photographed the shoe. The salesman told Gonzalez that the particular tread pattern of that shoe had been discontinued. Gonzalez hadn't mentioned any of this to the jury during his testimony and had only admitted it when forced to in cross-examination.

MATT ZOELLNER WAS called next. He had been selling cars back when Peggy was murdered; now he was selling floor coverings. He had known Peggy for the three years before she was killed, and the two had dated. The last six months had been "on and off." He had been to dinner at her apartment a week before the murder. The night of the murder, he went to Rumors and then to the Prime Minister. He had expected to meet Gilbreath at the Prime Minister but ran into Peggy in the parking lot. She had been drinking and they went into the bar together and had some more drinks while Peggy told him about being locked out of her apartment that evening. He offered her a ride home but she declined. He said he made the offer more than once, but Peggy went to the door and headed out. Instead of going after her, he returned to his table with Gilbreath. The prosecutor showed Zoellner a photo of Peggy and asked him to identify it; "Do you recognize the woman depicted in that photograph?"

"Yeah." He suddenly sobbed, as if he might begin bawling.

"Can you tell the jury who it is?"

"That's Peggy Hettrick." His attack of sorrow vanished as quickly as it had appeared. He then told the jury they had dated for three years but he had not seen her for a week before running into her at the Prime Minister.

On cross-examination, my attorney, Erik Fischer, got Zoellner to point a few things out to the jury the prosecution had failed to ask him. He had been contacted by the police after Peggy's murder. The police had seized the car he claimed to have been driving the night Peggy was murdered and some knives and razor blades from his apartment. Strangely, the police did not find this terribly suspicious.

. . .

THE NEXT WITNESS was Paul Landolt, a police officer who helped Jack Taylor investigate buildings around the field where Peggy's body had been found. He told about a Quonset hut he searched that had drawings of women on the interior walls. Although he noted them in his police report, he did not bother to photograph them. He said there were gunshot holes in the walls where the drawings were. There were .22 cartridges on the floor, which he picked up and gave to Jack Taylor. There was no evidence linking any of this to me, so my attorneys simply chose to not ask him any further questions on cross-examination. Although aerial photographs and diagrams were shown to the jury that indicated where the Quonset hut was situated, it was never made clear how far the Quonset hut was from my house: it was half a mile away and belonged to someone else. The drawings inside it were not mine or related to me in any way.

The .22 caliber rifle was another issue that the prosecution threw at the jury to confuse things. I did not own a .22. My father did, but I never fired it. In fact, when the police tested the rifle to see if the cartridges found in the hut came from the gun—the tests proved they didn't—it was the first time the gun had ever been fired. Later, Broderick would claim I had told him I had fired the gun. In fact, I told him I had only fired a gun at school in a class where we went to a firing range to learn gun safety.

Fort Collins police officer Wes Haynes testified next. He found some footprints along Boardwalk he thought were similar to Peggy's, but they were nowhere near the field where she had been found. He also saw drawings inside the Quonset hut. He couldn't remember if the drawings were in pencil or paint. He did think that someone had stabbed the drawings and shot them with a gun.

THE NEXT WITNESS the prosecution called was Wayne Lawson, the former classmate of mine from back in 1987. I had spoken with Wayne on February 12—the day after I had been pulled out of school by the police—and told him about seeing the body in the field. Wayne remembered that I had told him I thought it was a Resusci Anne doll. Wayne couldn't remember if I'd mentioned her being undressed; he just remembered that I said the body looked fake.

When I was telling the story to Wayne, I had drawn a sketch of the field showing where the body was. Wayne wasn't familiar with the area so I drew him a more detailed map. Wayne didn't recall a whole lot about the incident, but he did remember the police calling him the night of the twelfth and then coming over to his house and asking him about the sketch and the map. The prosecutor kept asking Wayne if he remembered telling the police that I had told him I had reported the body, but he didn't remember ever saying it—even when they said he had told Linda Wheeler-Holloway the same thing in 1992.

One point of confusion here is that the discussion I had with Wayne was on the twelfth, the day after I had spoken with the police. I told him all about being taken out of class—the whole school knew anyway—and then being dragged to the police station. If Wayne told the police that he knew I had spoken with the police, it shouldn't have been all that surprising. However, the story would look like I had spoken with Wayne about seeing Peggy's body the same day I saw it and before I spoke with the police—which was not the case.

Another point they tried to get Wayne to make was whether I had told him about Peggy's body and wanted him to keep it a secret. Had I acted like I wanted him to keep it secret? Wayne said no, I didn't want "the teacher to hear us talking or get in trouble, as far as just talking to each other in class." Wayne admitted he didn't know if I was pulling his leg or not about having seen a body—he thought I was full of "hot air."

Nate Chambers showed Wayne one of the pictures taken the day I was brought into the police station and asked him if that is what I looked like then. Wayne agreed that I was a small kid and not very strong. Wayne told the jury that he and I had rented and watched horror movies together. Wayne had seen many of my drawings and had also drawn pictures like I had during school. Wayne knew about my knives; his father had a knife collection, too.

THEY CALLED ANOTHER police officer next, Bob McKibben. McKibben had been one of the men who had searched my house on February 12. He said he saw a scalpel blade on a table in my living room but didn't bother to take it into evidence. The prosecutor showed him photographs of another scalpel blade—he also hadn't photographed the one he claimed he saw in my house—and he said the photos looked like the one he saw. McKibben was either lying or mistaken. There were no surgical scalpel blades in my house when they searched it. The only scalpel in the house was one in the sheath of one of my hunting knives, which is something included in the handle of many survival-style hunting knives. Still, none of the ones I owned were lying out on a table in the living room.

THEY NEXT CALLED Ken Murray, the detective who had administered the polygraph when I was brought into the station on the twelfth. Murray jumped right in and said that he had told me I was being questioned because I was the first to see the body, and that when he asked me if I had ever thought about doing something like this, I had said I had. He was twisting what I had actually said. I had said I had thought about killing people before based on the fact I had written many stories where characters had killed each other. When Murray asked me specifically if I had ever thought about doing something like this, I had told him no. Murray didn't tell the jury that.

On the stand, Murray looked frail. He had aged considerably since I had seen him last. He no longer looked like the man who had yelled at me and implored me to confess. We were worried the jury would react badly if we were too rough on him during cross-examination. Fischer simply asked Murray if I had denied being involved with the murder, and Murray agreed that I had.

. . .

Randall "Ray" Martinez testified next. He was one of the ones who interrogated me on the twelfth. He told the court about how he had showed me a footprint cast and that I had immediately denied it as being mine. He tried to make it sound like I was acting guilty, but he told the court I had said, "But you know it wasn't my footprint," when he said it had been found along the blood trail. He told the court I sounded "defensive" when I said it—as if I shouldn't have been defensive when I was being wrongly accused of murder. He admitted to the court that when I asked if the interview was being recorded, he had said it wasn't. He called this an "interview technique."

He said that he kept telling me that the footprint cast was mine and that I was "defensive" when I said that it couldn't be mine. He then spoke about how I had come back to the police station on the thirteenth so he could interrogate me more. He said that he started by talking about other things, and that I was the one who brought up the murder. When I asked him if he still thought I had done it, he told me that he had no doubt at all about it. When I didn't argue with him any further, he noted that I "didn't deny it any further." Again, it didn't matter how I responded: if I denied it, I was being defensive. If I didn't deny it, I must have been guilty.

Martinez claimed to find guilty behavior in everything I did at the police station. He claimed that he received a phone call while he was interrogating me and that I had tilted my head as if trying to listen in on the conversation.

Does that seem so terribly odd for a fifteen-year-old kid, being questioned about a murder he didn't commit, to wonder what the police officer was talking about on the phone?

He asked me if I had any suggestions as to where they should look for evidence. I suggested a ditch nearby and maybe underneath a bridge near the scene. He wondered why I was so familiar with a bridge and a ditch that ran right next to my yard. The prosecution was purposely vague on this issue. A knife was found under a bridge later, but it was not this bridge.

Martinez had interviewed me a couple more times, once at the station and once at a Perkins restaurant in August 1988. Martinez thought it was suspicious when I told him at Perkins that I was trying to get this case out of my mind.

When Martinez was cross-examined, one of the recurring themes of the trial became readily apparent. The police officers all suffered from selective memory loss. Martinez remembered details of his discussion with me from the police station on the things the prosecutor wanted him to say, but he forgot the answers to any of the questions my attorney asked him. He didn't know how long I'd been at the station when he spoke with me, and he didn't know if I'd already been grilled by another officer before. Was he the fourth or fifth police officer to interrogate me? He wasn't sure. Likewise, he did not know if Gonzalez had interviewed me the day before, or Murray, or Dean. He did remember Broderick, but he qualified the answer with the phrase "I think" twice. "It's been a number of years. I'm sorry."

When confronted with a question he knew the answer to, he couldn't pretend to have forgotten so he gave vague answers. Fischer asked him if it was true that Martinez misled me when he said they had evidence against me twelve years ago. "But it's true at this time you had absolutely no physical evidence against him, correct?"

"I personally didn't," he responded—as if someone else might have had some evidence.

My attorney pushed. There was no blood evidence linking me to the crime? "Not that I know of," he said, again as if there might have been some evidence out there that another police officer had failed to mention to him.

No fingerprints? "Not that I know of." He admitted he had made up some facts, including his claim to me that a "forensic scientologist" had indicated I was guilty. My attorney asked him if that was untruthful, to lie to me about this and whether or not I was being surreptitiously recorded.

"I wouldn't call it being untruthful. It's a test of the truth."

He admitted I had been cooperative and had never wavered in my protests of innocence.

Harold "Hal" Dean testified next. He came to the scene and drew diagrams to be used in the investigation. He testified that Peggy's body was found one hundred to one hundred and fifty yards from my house. He was the one who took an inventory of Peggy's purse and found the note to Matt Zoellner. Dean read the note into evidence:

"Matt, I need your help. Sharon has got my keys and isn't home. No answer. If I have to knock on your door at 2, please don't be a grump. I don't want to spend the night sleeping in the hall. Peg."

One of the few favorable rulings we received in the trial came next. Jolene Blair asked the court about something my father had said to Dean. My father passed away, and Dean had just told the jury that. When Blair asked him what my father had told him, my attorney objected on hearsay grounds. Blair tried to argue that an exception to the hearsay rule allowed sometimes for testimony like this to be heard. My attorney pointed out to the court that the rule she was referring to specifically said that there needed to be advance notice on an issue like this, and the judge agreed. Dean did not get to testify to something my father supposedly told him more than a decade earlier.

Dean told the court about how he had found my collection of knives when he entered my bedroom. He then ran through a whole inventory of things he found, including the warranty card for my mother's Waterpik. This was one of the things the prosecution did that had my attorneys and me wondering what they were up to. There was nothing significant about the warranty card. He described the drawings of mine as "very grizzly and gruesome death scenes" and told the jury he found some adult magazines in my room. He claimed it was at this point that they decided to treat me as a suspect and not just as a witness.

They then headed to school and pulled me out of class again. He told the court how he had brought me back to the police station for questioning. He thought it was remarkable that I was "nervous" when he brought me to the station for my second day of questioning. He had taken us into a little room and advised me of my rights. Then he asked my father to leave and interrogated me. Despite my nervousness, he asked me if I would consent to let them search my bedroom—even though they already had—and I told them I had no problem with it. I even signed a form allowing them to do so.

We then talked about my knives and I told him I had six survival knives. He asked about my mother's death and I told him about that. Then we talked about the morning I saw Peggy's body. Again, I had told him I thought it was a Resusci Anne doll and how I had seen it and gone on to school.

He had taken specific notes about the details of what I told him of the body's appearance. This is an example of the prosecution picking and choosing from testimony to make their case seem stronger. From the brief time I had seen Peggy's body, I couldn't remember the kind of detail Dean asked me about that day. I got some of the details right; I got some wrong. I had told him her pants were pulled down to her knees, but I didn't remember seeing her coat. I thought her shirt had numbers on it and that her hand was partially clenched. Dean told the court that I admitted to him that I recognized it as a body when I looked at it. I had never said that.

Dean had kept asking me questions, looking for more and more detail, and I could recall very little. I had only looked at the body for a few moments. He wanted to know: What did her panties look like? How were her arms placed? What pattern was on her shirt? If I didn't know the answer, he wouldn't let me off. He would press: What do you think it might have looked like? He encouraged me to guess.

He asked me if I knew Peggy and I told him no. He asked if I might have ever seen her before. I said no, but if I had it would have been in a crowd or some other place where I didn't notice her or remember her. Dean thought it was significant. It became difficult to follow what facts would surprise Dean. He had asked me what I thought had happened to Peggy, based upon what I had seen. I told him I thought she was raped and killed. After all, her pants had been pulled down. Dean had told me that she had not been raped. Dean recounted to the jury that I "acted very surprised" by this. I was, but why would that be odd?

Dean asked me how I thought Peggy had gotten into the field. I told him I thought she was picked up some-where else and then someone killed her and dumped her body there. Dean asked if it could have been the case that she was attacked in the street and then dragged into the field, and I told him I thought it was unlikely because my dogs would have barked if someone was making a com-motion in the field behind my trailer late at night. Dean wondered if the dogs might not "quiet down" if it was someone they knew. I told him they probably would quiet down if they recognized the person, but I never said they wouldn't bark at all. Still, Dean hinted that this was me telling him that I had done it.

I had asked Dean if they found anyone else's footprints

out in the field. Since I had already been told they had found footprints in the field the day before, I was curious if they had found some closer to the body. I had told them that I had walked over to the body but it seemed to me that whoever killed her would have had to leave footprints as well. Dean found this very suspicious and suggested it made me look guilty to him.

Dean had told me that Peggy must have walked by my house a lot because she walked to work a lot and the guy she dated didn't live far from me either. I had already told him that I didn't remember seeing her walk past the house. When Dean started telling me what times Peggy walked by the house, I mentioned some of the TV shows I watched that were on at those times. I didn't spend my days looking out at the street from my home, watching pedestrians for entertainment. Dean called it an "alibi" that he thought "was unusual."

Before ending his interrogation of me, Dean had come right out and said that I had killed Peggy. He claimed they had much more evidence than he had revealed to me, and he wanted me to admit it. I continued to deny it. Dean found it odd. He told the jury he found my denials too passive and calm.

Dean then told the court about how he had gotten my backpack and that it had contained notebooks of mine and drawings I had made. One of them he found interesting; he called it a "dragging scene."

On cross-examination, my attorney got Dean to admit he was wrong when he told the court I had admitted to him I knew Peggy's body was real. First, he said he would have to look at his report to see what was true. The odd thing was that he didn't feel the need to look at his report when he first made the incorrect statement. Now, he acted as if he had been understandably confused by the passage of time.

"So even at this point, he expressed to you uncertainty as to whether or not it was real or not?"

"During the interview, yes, sir."

His memory started becoming selective, like the other officers' memories, and he started downplaying the evidence that was favorable to me. When asked if it was true that I had told him I had intended to go back after school to see if the body was real, he said, "I believe so, yes."

When asked about his statement that I was too "passive" when being accused of murder, my attorney pointed out to Dean where I had said "I'm worried of being accused of something I didn't do!" And, "If I knew, I would have told somebody!"

Dean said that an exclamation point "generally does not indicate" passivity, when pressed by my attorney. He continued to couch his answers; they became vaguer the longer he testified. When asked if anything of evidentiary value was found in the field he claimed to not know anything. "I don't know about the other investigators. I know I didn't find anything."

"And nothing belonging to Tim Masters was found in the field?"

"Not that I'm aware of, no, sir."

Dean left the stand and the court took a short recess. James Broderick would take the stand next.

BRODERICK RETOOK THE stand next for his big show. From this point forward, his testimony and that of Reid Meloy would really be the foundation of the prosecution's case. But first, he started by telling the court of his twenty years with the Fort Collins Police Department and how he had risen to the rank of lieutenant in order to build their confidence in him as a witness.

Broderick had responded to the scene of Hettrick's murder on the morning of February 11. He had then gone out and questioned Matt Zoellner. He had gotten permission to take the car Zoellner said he had been driving for inspection, and had also gotten blood and hair samples from him. He had then gone and searched Zoellner's apartment. The next day, he had come to my home and searched it as well.

He focused on the "large display" of knives in my room. He described the adult magazines in a suitcase in my room—he called them "pornography"—and also some BB guns I had. He even described a couple of toy guns as if they were dangerous.

The knives became a focal point of his testimony. He testified in great detail about which ones were in sheaths and which were not; which way they were pointed and what order they were in from left to right. It was an amazing amount of detail, considering he did none of those things with the footprints out in the field by Peggy's body.

The prosecution then asked for the adult material to be admitted into evidence and suggested to the court that most of it be sealed, except for one photograph of a "very explicit vaginal shot." Clearly, they wanted the jury to believe that a teenaged boy who found such a photo interesting would also go out and kill a stranger so he could slice off a piece of her vagina.

Then, they moved on to my drawings and stories. For years, I had been sketching and writing little stories, mostly inspired by the movies I liked to watch. I loved *Rambo* and *Friday the 13th* kind of movies. Much of it was oriented toward the military. My father had been a career Navy man, and my sister was in the Army—and, of course, I would go on to join the Navy. I drew a lot of gory stuff, but it wasn't that strange for a fifteen-year-old. I knew other kids who drew stuff like what I drew, and there were friends of mine who complimented my drawings. Some of the drawings grossed people out, but that too was probably an inspiration for me. As a kid who was ignored much of the time, getting a reaction from others was usually a good thing.

Broderick didn't find my drawings or stories amusing. He told the jury he had found more than a thousand pages of drawings and stories of mine. He focused on the goriest of it, telling the jury that "virtually all the drawings I saw was dismemberment, torturous scenes, where people were being tortured, and sometimes captions above it. They were screaming or asking, you know, for it to stop." He also told the jury that he had read some of my short stories—fantasy stuff about teenage soldiers—and had concluded from it that I should be the primary focus of the investigation. In other words, it wasn't evidence of any sort that tied me to the crime; Broderick tied me to the crime based on pictures I'd drawn and stories I'd written over the previous years. Broderick stayed at my home while other officers came to school to interview me. Broderick would spend more than five hours searching my room. Five hours, for a room in a trailer he described as a "relatively small bedroom."

He told the jury that my bedroom window had no storm window, so that someone could climb out of it by removing the screen. Of course, he found no evidence that anyone had done that any time recently, and he found no blood on or near the window and found no footprints under the window—he just made the window sound very suspicious. The prosecutor then walked Broderick through my knife collection, one by one. She would hand one to him, and he would hold it up and tell the jury what it was and where he had found it. When he held up the largest knife in my collection—a big survival knife—a gasp could be heard from the courtroom and the jury. Buried somewhere in this long section of testimony—it takes up eight pages of the transcript—it was briefly mentioned that none of these knives were linked to Peggy's murder in any way.

Broderick then told the court about his interrogation of me. He glossed over how he was the fifth person to interrogate me that day; detectives Dean, Murray, Wagner, and Martinez had already spent the better part of the day yelling at me and accusing me of the murder, trying to get me to confess. Broderick had taken over at 6:30 P.M. Broderick told the jury that I was hard to communicate with.

He found it suspicious that I had been defensive when Martinez had told me my footprints were found out in the field near Peggy's body. I knew exactly where I had walked and I knew my footprints wouldn't incriminate me. I also knew that the plaster cast Martinez had was of a footprint that was a different size than mine. When Broderick asked me what I thought "about all this," I told him the footprints near the body weren't mine. I was merely picking up where Martinez had left off. Even though Broderick was also picking up where Martinez had left off in the tag-team interrogation, he thought my response was suspicious.

He told the jury about how he then focused his questioning of me on the drawings and the stories and how I had told him the stories and the drawings weren't real. No, I had never seen any of the things I drew except in the movies. Broderick didn't believe me. The prosecutor asked Broderick if he had asked me about my "relationships with women." Broderick told the jury he had asked me, and I had told him I was not having any. This is an example of a question I think they asked to try and get the jury to forget that Broderick had been interrogating a fifteen-year-old boy, not the grown man they saw sitting at the defendant's table in the courtroom. What fifteen-year-old boy has had "relationships with women"?

Broderick could find incriminating evidence in anything he looked at. At the time, I didn't think the jury would buy it, but it was remarkable. Broderick had asked me if my survival knives would be "good for stabbing." I thought about it a bit and told him I didn't think so because the jagged edge on the back of the knife—the saw back—would make it hard to pull back out. I had never stabbed anyone, so I was just trying to think about it and give him an honest answer. Broderick told the jury he found that a very strange thing for me to say. "And I thought to myself, I'd never really considered that, pulling the knife back out of somebody that you stabbed." Of course, he added the little flourish about pulling it out of someone I had stabbed—something I had not said.

At the time, Broderick hadn't asked me *why* I might think the knife wouldn't be good for stabbing someone. If he had, I would have told him that we had watched the movie *All Quiet on the Western Front* recently at school. There, a World War I officer lectured a recruit who was carving notches into a knife blade, telling him not to do it because it would make it harder to pull it back out of the enemy.

Broderick also told the jury about some of the facts I got wrong, like when he asked me what I saw when I looked at Peggy's body. I didn't remember seeing her breasts so I told him that I thought they had been covered when I walked up to her body. I mentioned that I thought her shoes were pink and I also thought I remembered seeing a number on her shirt—a number like on a football jersey—but it turns out there was no such number on her clothing. Meloy would later turn those mistaken comments of mine into the basis for arguing that I had really killed her.

Peggy had been wearing red boots and pink socks when she was killed. Broderick wanted the jury to believe that I had mistaken her socks for her footwear and that the only way I could have known she was wearing anything pink was if I had killed her. He based this on his examination of the photos of Peggy's body—Broderick had not examined Peggy's body in the field like the other police officers who had shown up that morning.

Broderick also made a big deal of a sketch I had drawn of someone being dragged. I had made the drawing after talking with Wayne Lawson, and Broderick had asked me about it when he interrogated me. He thought it proved I had some kind of specific knowledge of the crime, something only the killer would know. In the drawing, I had put in arrows flying through the air—I have no idea why— and had shown blood dripping from the subject's arm. To make the drawing scarier than it was, the prosecution blew it up really big, and downplayed how the drawing was just a small part of a full page of doodles. Elsewhere on the same page I had drawn a few dinosaurs, Freddy Krueger from *A Nightmare on Elm Street*, and a man with his tongue nailed to a table. At that point, we broke for the day. The prosecution indicated they were about to start a PowerPoint presentation with Broderick that was going to take up quite a bit of time.

29

The Trial: Day Four

THE NEXT DAY WAS TUESDAY, MARCH 23, AND THE PROS-
ecutor announced she was going to be bringing in
some witnesses out of order. I'm not quite sure how juries
are supposed to follow this; Broderick would not continue
his testimony until after three more witnesses testified.

The first was a woman named Janna Koschene I had
not seen since I was nine years old. Her family had lived
next door to us back then but had long since moved away.
I had written a story where I had used her name for a character. When the police found the story, they contacted her
and showed her the story and told her I had written it.
They wanted her to come in to court and tell the jury
about how my story had scared her! My attorney objected
and the prosecutor backed down a little. He got permis-

sion to let her testify that she had lived in my neighborhood and that she did not know me personally. She knew my sister, who had babysat for her family. The prosecutor wanted the jury to make a connection between Janna and Peggy Hettrick because she had brown hair with red highlights. The prosecutor actually asked her to tell the jury what color her hair was.

THE PROSECUTOR THEN called Wynette Payne, a former teacher who was now retired. She was my English teacher, and she told the jury that I often made drawings during class when I should have been doing my work. She said she found the drawings "frightening." She also told the court about the time she had found me reading an Army manual in class. The manual was Serena's and explained how to survive chemical, biological, and nuclear attacks. She took it from me, and when I got upset—it belonged to my sister—she said I got angry. It had been more than a decade since the incident, and she didn't remember the details all that well. I hadn't gotten mad when she took it from me; I had gotten mad after class when she wouldn't give it back. In her mind, it was a "military manual" and described how to "build bombs." She said it was "really scary." She no longer had the manual, so the jury assumed that this retired schoolteacher must be telling the truth. Even the prosecutor knew, however, that Payne was mistaken on this point. In the affidavit attached to my arrest warrant, Broderick had described it as a "1977 Army publication." Obviously, the U.S. Army does not distribute bomb-making manuals filled with "really scary" images in an attempt to find recruits.

On cross-examination Payne admitted that I had not threatened her, physically or verbally, and the only disciplinary problems I had presented at that time were that I was not paying attention in class.

THEY THEN CALLED a school counselor, Pamela Sachs-Kapp. Payne had sent me to her after the incident with the Army manual, and she recalled that I was angry. She confirmed, however, that the "bomb building manual" was really just an Army publication from 1977. She found my drawings to be unusual but did not feel that I was a threat to anyone after she had counseled me.

JAMES BRODERICK THEN returned to the stand. He would take the stand several times during my trial and testify at great length. One thing I noticed was that he showed very little emotion. He testified very calmly and smoothly, regardless of the topic, and it didn't matter who was asking the questions. His demeanor on the stand was very similar to my demeanor when he was questioning me. Somehow, when I acted like that, he said it incriminated me.

He testified that he and the rest of the police force had exhaustively examined all possible suspects in Peggy's murder. They had tracked down her friends and acquaintances and double-checked their alibis. A teletype was sent out to police agencies around the nation, to see if other crimes like this had occurred elsewhere. Known sex offenders were tracked down, and parolees were scrutinized. It really sounded like they had checked everyone.

Broderick told the jury that a person standing in my bedroom could see Peggy's body from my bedroom. Linda Wheeler-Holloway had written in her report that a person could not see the body from my bedroom, and she had stood in my home while Peggy's body was still in the field. Broderick had decided to try and figure this out after Peggy's body had been removed from the field. To test his theory, he took a two-foot long piece of wood and stuck it into the ground near where Peggy's body had been found. He told the court that he could see his two-foot-tall marker from my bedroom window. I assumed the jury would realize that Peggy's body—lying on the ground— was not two feet tall.

Broderick claimed he had little to do with the investigation of this crime until much later. Everyone knew that one of the prosecution's problems was how long it had taken the police to arrest me. If they had a case, why did it take them ten years to arrest me?

Broderick also told the jury about interviewing me in Philadelphia. He told the jury that my demeanor was an "exact duplicate" of my demeanor when I was fifteen. He said that I had changed my story since then but, "I won't go into every single thing." He claimed there were too many inconsistencies to tell them all to the jury. *Really?* The prosecutor asked for an example or two—when you'd think they'd want to show the jury all of these "inconsistencies." He said that my story had changed regarding how the newspaper had gotten into my home the day after the killing. In 1987, I had said I had gotten it. In 1992, I remembered that my aunt had brought a copy over. My story hadn't changed. Dad and I had gone out to buy the paper. Later, my aunt brought a copy of the paper over, not knowing we already had a copy. She subscribed to the paper, and we didn't.

He told the jury about how they had brought an arrest warrant in 1992 but had decided to not arrest me after questioning me about how I had found out about the mutilation of Peggy's body. The arrest warrant said I was obviously the one who had killed her because I had somehow known that Peggy's nipple had been removed. When they questioned me in Philadelphia, I told them I had heard that information from an Explorer Scout who told people at the school that she had been asked to search the field and look for Peggy's nipple. In retrospect, it was idiotic for the police to ask teenagers to help them with such a serious investigation. While they were supposedly protecting vital information in the investigation, their teenage helpers were gossiping about it over the lunch tables at the local high school. And that's where I—and everyone else at school—heard about it. I didn't know it at the time, but Broderick and Linda Wheeler-Holloway had followed up on this and found out that others had heard this from the Explorer Scout too and confirmed it when they were asked. Missing this incriminating piece of evidence, they felt they couldn't arrest me then.

Broderick told the jury about how he'd attended seminars on sexual homicides and met the former FBI profiler named Roy Hazelwood. After speaking briefly with Hazelwood about my case, he claimed that he was directed to Reid Meloy. He did not tell the jury—nor did the prosecution tell my attorneys—that Hazelwood expressed doubts about me being Peggy's killer. We later found out that this was a pattern of Broderick's: when he encountered someone who disagreed with his conclusions, he would ignore them and find someone else who agreed with him.

He told the jury that he gave Meloy a "huge volume" of my drawings and writings and that Meloy helped categorize them. He told the jury that Meloy had already been paid more than $27,000 for his work.

He then described for the jury some crumpled-up papers he had found in my wastepaper basket in my bedroom in 1987. These are the kinds of things that are irrelevant— they don't prove anything—but they made me look bad to a jury. One was a drawing of Freddy Krueger from *A Nightmare on Elm Street*. The other was a cartoon I'd drawn of a woman's head and a gun, with the caption "God damn old Ladies." He then walked the jury through a series of my drawings, one by one, often spending more time analyzing them than I took drawing them.

"What does that depict?" the prosecutor asked him, holding up one of my sketches.

"It's a—the drawing in the lower right-hand corner, it's on some schoolwork called Design B, which is a class that Mr. Masters was taking in 1987. It shows an individual with a handgun to his head, shooting himself in the head, with all the debris and blood coming out the left side." He claimed it was significant to the investigation because I had told Wagner that if I had committed a crime like the one I was accused of, I would have killed myself. Obviously, I hadn't killed myself, but the judge let the prosecution talk about this to the jury and let Broderick tell the jury that my collection contained six or seven depictions of suicide.

After going through another series of my gory cartoons, he told the jury they were connected to the Hettrick murder because they depicted "scratches and body cutting." He had gone through all of my drawings and writing and had counted various details. For example, he found more than 150 references to knives. There were "30 or 40" references to maps. He counted a hundred times I had written the number "10." It was unclear why some of the categories might even be important. Broderick never explained, leaving that for Reid Meloy to do later.

Broderick had also read everything I had written, which included short stories I had been writing for a few years. Most of them were similar to the movies I liked to watch and included war scenes, horror stuff like *Friday the 13th*, or some combination of the two. He summarized some of the stories for the jury. I guess he wasn't just an art critic; he was also a literary critic.

He described one: "From memory, it's a story about an individual by the name of Harry Dagger. He likes to collect weapons. Kids in the neighborhood feel his house is haunted. They get together and shoot arrows into his house, which catches on fire, one which goes through a window and strikes this Mr. Dagger. It talks about how the fire department comes. Mr. Dagger's brought out of the house all burned up, and there's quite a description as to what he looks like."

Broderick claimed it was important for the jury to hear about this story because characters in the story "stashed" weapons in an irrigation ditch. Since the prosecutor was trying to say that the knife found by the young teenager was the murder weapon—even though there was nothing linking it to Peggy or me—there had to be some way to tie it to me. They had no evidence, so the story would have to do. Of course, Broderick loved to let the jury hear the stories I'd written when I was fifteen; they made me sound creepy and scary. Broderick also purposely misinterpreted some of the stories to make me sound worse. In a couple of my stories, I had used a character named "Mace." When Broderick had asked me about it in 1987, I had told him that I had gotten that name from the book *Tex*, by S. E. Hinton. The book was about a fifteen-year-old boy who had an older brother named Mason—nicknamed Mace— and lived in a trailer in the west. Their mother was dead, and times were tough. Their father was away often. I liked the story a lot and had obviously been inspired by it. Broderick had yelled at me that "Mace" was me. During the trial, he actually referred to me as "Mace" but then corrected himself. "In the narratives, Mace, Mr. Masters—I mean, Mace was . . ."

Broderick admitted that Janna Koschene had pointed to the wrong spot on the map when she had been asked where she lived. In my story, I had used the address of

4500 Stover. She had pointed to 3501 Stover. It was a small point but it showed that my writing wasn't as sinister as the prosecutor claimed.

THE PROSECUTION THEN gave Broderick a break so they could call Sherri Murphy, of the Colorado Bureau of Investigation, to the stand. She was an eminently qualified expert in analyzing fibers and hair. She had examined material Broderick had scraped from under my fingernails in 1987. She identified blue cotton material that she said was consistent with blue jeans. She told the jury that these fibers were microscopically consistent with the jeans Peggy had been wearing when she was killed. The police had given her samples from Peggy's jeans for comparison. Of course, I had also been wearing jeans the day I had been questioned by Broderick—I was wearing them when he scraped my fingernails—but no one had told Murphy that. They also had not sent her samples from my jeans to determine if the fibers were consistent with the material from under my nails. Still, Murphy told the jury her findings had evidentiary value, albeit "limited," even though fibers taken from my blue jeans and from Peggy's blue jeans would have been identical.

BRODERICK THEN RETURNED to the stand and continued going through my drawings and stories in excruciating detail. The prosecutor asked him to summarize each story, and the judge let him. The prosecutor asked Broderick about a 150-page story I had written and to explain to the jury what portions of it "had some correlation to the investigation into the murder of Peggy Hettrick." Broderick noted an event where a Radio Shack employee was killed, another where someone was attacked in a ditch, and then one with a river full of blood and bodies. Although Broderick testified these things correlated to Peggy's murder, he never said how or why. He also didn't tell the jury that this story was a fantasy, set in a world where the adults had all mysteriously disappeared, and the characters were all children, like in *Lord of the Flies*.

After summarizing several more of my stories, he then jumped ahead to how he had prepared another arrest warrant for me, in 1998. He told the jury he did this after a review of all my materials and a "consultation" with Meloy. He described arresting me in Ridgecrest and searching my place. When asked what he found in the search of "evidentiary value" to this murder case he said, "a large amount of pornography." My attorney objected, and before he could even say why, the judge told the prosecutor to move on. Broderick then told the jury he had found guns and knives as well as more drawings and stories of mine. They kept referring to my drawings and writings as "productions." Again, he summarized them for the jury and kept telling the jury that the stories—some of which were science fiction and involved space travel—were really me talking about myself and things I had actually done.

Erik Fischer cross-examined Broderick and got him to admit that many of my gory drawings were set in wartime and the characters were soldiers. He also admitted that I was a pack rat and many of the drawings and writing he had found at the time of my arrest could have been written many years earlier. I rarely threw away anything that I had written or drawn.

Broderick admitted that many of the drawings were interpreted by him and could be taken to represent other things to other people. One picture I had drawn showed a man being sawed in half; Broderick had said it showed "genital mutilation." In another example, I had drawn an optical illusion of a knife slicing through the page it was drawn on; Broderick insisted it was an illustration of a knife slicing a vagina. Fischer got him to admit that the photo depicted no legs, pubic hair, or any body parts. There was nothing to indicate it was a person being cut. It was just Broderick's imagination. To defend his position, Broderick said he showed the picture to "others," and they had agreed with him.

Broderick also admitted he considered the picture I had drawn of someone dragging a body as my "confession." Yet the picture showed arrows flying through the air into the person's body. He defended his opinion, saying it was incriminating of me because I showed the body being dragged. How could I have known the body had been dragged if I hadn't killed Peggy? First, police had asked me if I had seen the bloody "drag trail." Second, the newspaper article quoted a police officer saying that Peggy's body had been dragged into the field. Broderick admitted now that the newspaper article included that information, but he still thought it was incriminating. When my attorney asked him if he was aware that the paper also mentioned that Peggy's body had been mutilated, he feigned surprise. He asked to see the article; it quoted the district attorney in 1987 saying Peggy's body had been mutilated. Broderick conceded the point.

Fischer then focused on one of the biggest flaws with Broderick's theory. "Okay. Now. Lieutenant, we went through a lot of pictures this morning, went through a lot of narratives this morning, but there is not a single picture or a single narrative of a woman being sexually mutilated in the manner in which Miss Hettrick was mutilated; isn't that correct?"

"That's correct." He tried to wiggle out of it though. "There's not an exact duplication."

Fischer wouldn't give up that easily. "In fact, there's not a single picture of any woman having her nipple excised; isn't that correct?"

"That's correct."

"In fact, there's not a single picture of any woman being stabbed in the back; isn't that correct?"

"I don't recall such a picture."

Broderick also admitted that in the eight or nine hours total he had spent questioning me, I had always been cooperative and answered every question he asked me. He admitted his five-hour interrogation of me came after I had already been interrogated for five and one-half hours by other police officers. Broderick tried to stick with his story that I had misled the police when—according to Broderick—I didn't tell the second police officer that I had been interrogated previously. Fischer showed Broderick where he had put in his report that I had indeed told the second officer about my first interrogation. Now, under oath, Broderick claimed that his own police report was incorrect.

Broderick was the seventh person to interrogate me at the police station in 1987, and his questioning of me in 1992 lasted eleven hours over two days. Broderick wrote in his report of the interrogation, "generally, the 1992 interview paralleled exactly what was said in 1987." When Fischer asked him about it on cross, he claimed there were "variations" between what I had said at the interrogations.

Broderick admitted he had absolutely no evidence to indicate that I had done anything in the Quonset hut. There was no evidence I had drawn on the walls, shot holes in the pictures, or even set foot in the hut.

It became clear that Broderick had aimed his investigation at me quite early. When he had gone to Matt Zoellner's apartment in 1987, he had found four very large knives with homemade handles and a razor blade. He looked at them and then just decided to not take them into evidence or send them to the CBI or FBI crime labs for testing. I wondered if the jury would notice such inconsistent behavior from the police as they investigated this crime. We believed that Broderick made up his mind to come after me after he had searched my bedroom. From that point forward, he ignored obvious suspects and evidence pointing away from me as if it never existed.

Fischer pointed out that Broderick had ruled out all of my knives from this crime. The FBI had ruled out the ones that weren't survival knives, and when they found the knife in the ditch, they had exhumed Peggy's body to see if it contained a piece of that knife. That knife couldn't be linked to the crime either. Broderick admitted that I was such a pack rat I'd saved the six boxes that matched the six survival knives I owned. If they wanted to claim the knife found in the ditch was mine, they would also have to say that I had gotten rid of the box, too.

Fischer directed Broderick toward his footprint testimony. He admitted that the single footprint of mine had been found in the blood trail in such a way that it fit my story—it was left after I stepped in the trail and could not have been made by someone dragging Peggy's body into the field.

Here, Broderick started giving the fuzzy and indirect answers the other officers had started giving when cross-examined by my attorneys. Wasn't it true there were no footprints from Peggy's body to my home? Broderick responded, "Not that I'm aware of, no," as if there might be some no one told him about. Wasn't it true there were no footprints outside my bedroom window? He claimed he hadn't thought to look for them; he was looking for blood. Wasn't it true that Wheeler-Holloway had written in her report that Peggy's body could not be seen from my home? "I could look at a report, but it may say that."

He admitted they had found hairs on Peggy's body that did not match Peggy, Zoellner, or me. He also admitted he found no blood in my home and they found no evidence on Peggy linking me to the crime. Fischer walked Broderick through the lack of evidence—all of the things that did not point to me. Fibers, blood, saliva, hair, clothing, knives—everything was tested and nothing came back to point at me.

AFTER BRODERICK WAS done, the prosecution called Gregory Schade. On August 31, 1987, he had found a knife that the prosecution was now trying to say was the murder weapon. At the time, Schade was thirteen years old. In court, his memory was hazy, but he remembered finding the knife in a ditch that feeds into Warren Lake. He said he played in the ditch often and would have seen the knife if it had been there on an earlier visit. He played with the knife for a while—he stuck it in the mud a few times and then wiped the mud off—and took it home to show his father. His father called the police. He had nothing further to add and obviously had no idea how the knife had gotten there or whose it was.

LINDA WHEELER-HOLLOWAY TESTIFIED next; she was one of more than a dozen officers who were at the scene the morning Peggy's body was found. She got there at 8:00 A.M. and was one of the officers who canvassed the neighborhood. When the prosecutor asked her if any evidence was gleaned by any of the officers during the canvass, she replied, "No, not that I'm aware of." She did go to my home and speak with my father right around the same time that Sherry Wagner was talking to the Hammonds over on Skysail. Wheeler-Holloway was aware of the Hammonds when she was testifying; she just did not consider Dr. Hammond relevant to Peggy's murder.

Later, she returned to the area and searched underneath the bridge over the ditch. There, she saw some spray-painted drawings underneath the bridge that she testified were "very sexual in nature." I hadn't made them, but the prosecutor wanted the jury to believe I had. What else was the jury going to believe? Wheeler-Holloway had not photographed the drawings, so the jury was left with their imaginations as to what they were. This point—that Wheeler-Holloway hadn't taken pictures of the drawings—even caught Broderick's attention as he prepared for trial. In his notes, he wrote, "Why no photos of bridge?" Without asking her what the drawings looked like, what evidence she had as to the artist, or why she didn't take pictures of them, the prosecution jumped ahead to 1991.

Wheeler-Holloway noted that, at that time, the Hettrick murder was the only unsolved homicide "on the books" in Fort Collins. She referred to her notes and told the court that when she revisited the evidence in the case, she had interviewed Wayne Lawson twice. Even though she said Lawson was a little unclear in how he related the story to her, she believed Wayne said I had told him about Peggy being mutilated "the next day." Lawson told her I was pretty "flipped out" when I was telling him the story—indicating that I knew the body in the field was real.

Wheeler-Holloway recounted her 1992 interview with me. She told the jury how I had told her the same story I had told before: I saw the body, thought it was a manne-quin, and headed off to my bus. I had told her about the

Explorer Scout in this interview when she asked me how I knew Peggy's body had been mutilated. She asked me to walk her through everything that happened and I told her. One thing she mentioned was how I told her I had taken all of my knives out and laid them side-by-side after my father had left me alone the night after the killing.

She had asked me about my drawings, and I told her it was how I used to work out some of my teenage anger. She had asked me what made me angry back then, and I told her that my dad and I didn't always get along. My drawing and writing were my therapy. We had spoken at length about the "drag" drawing, and I told her I had drawn it at school after I saw Peggy's body. She had asked me what it meant and why there were arrows on the page, and dinosaurs. She had asked me how I knew the body had been dragged, and I told her that it would have been obvious to anyone who had seen the trail of blood in the field.

Wheeler-Holloway's interview with me had covered all the same ground as my previous interrogations with Broderick and the others in 1987 and lasted five hours.

On cross-examination, Wheeler-Holloway was explicit: a person could not see Peggy's body from my home. The berm in the field blocked the view. In fact, she had stepped out my back door and looked from there and still couldn't see the body. She also admitted that Wayne Lawson was "a little confused" on the facts every time she had talked to him—so the timing of when he heard about the breast mutilation was suspect. She also admitted she had to end her interrogation of me because she had become "exhausted." After her exhausting five-hour marathon interrogation, she stepped back and let Broderick continue with me for another four hours. Still, after nine hours, Wheeler-Holloway admitted my story had not changed from 1987. She told the court that at the end of the second day, I finally broke down and cried. She hadn't told the jury that on her direct examination. Now she also told the jury that I had always maintained my innocence and had cooperated fully, answering every question she had asked.

THE NEXT WITNESS for the prosecution would be their last. He would also be the fulcrum on which their entire case rested. Dr. Reid Meloy was the psychologist who claimed to be able to see into my drawings and writings and discern that I had killed Peggy Hettrick. It was an astounding suggestion for a psychologist who had never spoken with me, but the court allowed it. He spent an hour telling the court about his qualifications and the schools where he lectured. He had written numerous articles and books and been given all kinds of awards. He was also paid a pile of money to look at my drawings and stories and to say I had killed Peggy. The court deemed him an expert, which allowed him to tell the jury his opinions of me, gathered from looking at my drawings and writing, and from things told to him by Broderick. At this point, the court took its break for the day.

30

The Trial: Day Five

O N WEDNESDAY, MARCH 24, COURT STARTED AT 8:30 A.M.
with Dr. Reid Meloy on the stand telling the court
how he had been initially contacted by Broderick in 1997.
Broderick had promised to send along "all the evidence on
the case," and Meloy had no reason to believe Broderick
had withheld anything from him. He told Broderick he
was going to charge $300 per hour to work on the case.
Broderick sent along piles of documents and statements
and nine three-ring binders filled with 2,200 pages of my
drawings and writings. Meloy also went to Fort Collins
and visited the crime scene and then met with Broderick and the rest of his staff. Before he had been asked about
any of his store-bought opinions, he started giving them.
"And during that time, I talked extensively with them

about my preliminary opinions concerning this case, one of them being that this was a sexual homicide; and two, talking with them in depth about offense characteristics in a sexual homicide, and also motivational aspects of a sexual homicide; in other words, why people do these kinds of acts."

My attorney objected, and Terry Gilmore even agreed with him when they approached the bench and spoke with the judge quietly. Gilmore told the judge—as if Meloy was a loose cannon—"I've told him a hundred time he cannot say an opinion like that."

The court threatened to declare a mistrial and told Gilmore that if Meloy did it again—offered an opinion without being asked for one—he was going to assess the costs of retrying the case against Meloy personally. "You may tell him that," the judge warned Gilmore.

The court sent the jury out, and we took a break so Gilmore could explain to Meloy how he needed to be more careful with what he said. Six minutes later, the jury returned and Meloy continued with his testimony. Meloy said he directed Broderick to go through the 2,200 pages of my stuff and to categorize the items. He did not indicate what psychology training Broderick might have had to help him do this kind of research for Meloy, but he plowed ahead. He admitted that Broderick had come up with some categories of his own, and Meloy had agreed with them. They agreed on 33 categories into which they would subdivide my work. "Preoccupation with death" contained 291 items; the "Knives" category held 186. Some were mundane, like "The color red," and "The number 10."

To impress the jury, the prosecution asked Meloy questions where he could give long discourses on psychology, lectures on things like "sexual homicide." In answering, he rambled on for ten minutes—his answer to that question took up seven and a half pages of the transcript. He told the jury of studies done in England and of researchers who wrote books on the topic and of papers with titles like "Unprovoked Attacks on Women" and "The Sadistic Murderer." He also managed to work in a plug for his own book, *The Psychopathic Mind*. Nowhere in this monologue did he actually come out and say that any of those articles and books applied to me, but the suggestion was clear to the jury.

He did admit to the jury that the methodology for doing research in this field included three sources of information. The first of the three is an interview with the individual. He glossed over—actually, he didn't mention at all—the fact that he never interviewed me.

He then explained a concept to the jury called "sex-violence pairing." He claimed that sexual homicides are committed by people who have come to associate violence with sexual arousal. He admitted that even the forensic psychologists didn't know what could cause such a thing, but he thought it might be inspired by violent pornography or by adolescents seeing adults have sex.

Meloy told the court that the Hettrick murder had been a sexual homicide, particularly because the body—in his opinion—had been "displayed" and "posed" by the killer. "Displaying" means that the body was left out in the open and not hidden. "Posing" means that the killer left the body in a manner meant to degrade the victim. Peggy's body was left in an open field, her pants had been pulled down and her top had been pulled up, exposing much of her body. Meloy claimed this description fit the crime. But again, none of it pointed to me. It didn't matter to Meloy, though. He didn't need evidence; he could see things in my drawings and writing, what he also called my "productions."

Meloy explained to the jury his opinion that Peggy's body was mutilated by a killer who was angry with women. He also said that a killer in a sexual homicide often has fantasies about his desire to kill. He would point to my drawings and writings and say they were evidence that I fantasized about killing.

Meloy gave examples to the jury from "research," but it was clear to the jury who he was talking about. "And then he, perhaps, would be walking down the street and would see a woman who he found sexually attractive; but because of his anger and hostility toward the woman, in his mind he would believe that because of the way she's walking and the way she's dressed, she's deliberately taunting him and flaunting her sexuality, and that might then stoke his anger toward her." He told the jury that he conducted tests on individuals to prove this point but, again, didn't mention that he had never tested me.

Meloy told the jury that sexual homicides were often committed after a "triggering event," something like a job termination or "an emotional upset concerning the death or the loss of somebody." He said there could be an "anniversary reaction." He was setting the scene so he could later tell the jury I had been inspired to kill someone when the anniversary of my mother's death came around. Meloy mentioned Roy Hazelwood from the FBI here, but only that he was a leader in this field of research.

One of the words Meloy introduced to the jury was "*picquerism*," which he said was a form of paraphilia, or sexual deviance. Picquerism, according to Meloy, is a condition where a person finds sexual gratification from cutting or stabbing someone. At this point, Meloy went through pictures I had drawn—the prosecutor projected them onto a screen so the jury could see them—and pointed out knives, cutting, and stabbing, saying these represented my sexual deviance and my desire to cut up women because I hated them so much. My drawing of Freddy Krueger from *A Nightmare on Elm Street*? "[T]hat represents the picqueristic nature or the interest in cutting, stabbing, slicing instruments in this particular drawing."

Meloy also found great importance in the stories I had written about the character named "Mace." Meloy told the jury that Mace and I were one and the same and that I assumed "the role" of the characters I wrote about. Meloy testified that I did the things my characters did—but he gave no examples. Since I wrote about someone killing someone else, and I was Mace—according to Meloy—I must have actually killed someone. After all, I had written about it, and Meloy said my writing was real. It was all unbelievable, but the court allowed it. We just hoped the jury wouldn't buy it.

At one point, Gilmore put up a slide of a drawing I had

made of a building on fire and asked if it connected sex and violence. Meloy said, "Yes." Even Gilmore realized there was no way to say the drawing had anything to do with sex—despite the fact his expert psychologist had just said it did—so Gilmore corrected him. "I don't believe that slide relates to the sex and violence. Excuse me. Would you relate—I'm sorry." He put up another slide without giving Meloy a chance to explain how a burning building portrayed sex.

Nate Chambers cross-examined Meloy and started by asking him, "Doctor, are you ever wrong?"

"Yes," he replied.

Nate asked the doctor about another case in Colorado where Meloy had testified. In that case, he had testified for the defense, saying that the accused didn't "deliberate" in the manner necessary to be guilty. The jury disagreed and found the man guilty anyway.

On the stand, Meloy said that he had already billed $36,000 for his work on my case.

Nate pulled out a copy of Meloy's book and asked him if *The Psychopathic Mind* was something he relied upon in working on my case. Meloy said yes, it provided "background material for my knowledge base."

Nate read to him one of the reviews of the book, by one of Meloy's peers. "Meloy's idea of psychopathy includes such a widely diverse group of individuals that one must question the concept's usefulness as a psychodynamic formulation since it can apply to just about anyone?"

Meloy wasn't amused. "What's the question?"

"You're familiar with that review of your work?"

"Yes. I didn't remember him specifically saying that."

Nate then pulled out stacks of articles and textbooks, all of which questioned how "scientific" Meloy's theories were. One by one, Meloy said he disagreed with them, even though some of them were textbooks he used when he got his PhD. Meloy also admitted he had no idea how many fifteen-year-old boys drew drawings like mine in 1987. He just assumed I was unique.

Nate got Meloy to admit that much of what I had done did not fit the diagnosis he had tried to give me. According to Meloy, a person who harbored this deep-seated hatred of women and fantasized about killing them would have kept those thoughts private. Yet I showed my pictures to my friends and let them read my stories. Meloy said he did not know whether I had shared them with anyone. Of course, he had never spoken to me; he would have known if he had asked Wayne Lawson, but he didn't bother with that either.

Nate read portions of studies to Meloy where other psychologists pointed out that "normal" men often have fantasies involving violence. Meloy tried arguing with Nate, saying that recent work in the field disproved this. Nate had read Meloy's books and had found some of it fascinating, in light of Meloy's testimony. Apparently, Meloy admitted in one of his books that he sometimes had violent and sexually sadistic fantasies.

"In fact, sir, you engage in violent fantasies?"

"In sexually sadistic fantasies," he admitted.

"Violent fantasies?"

"I have at times had angry fantasies where I have violent images in my mind, and I spoke about that actually in my second book."

There was more. "You've had predatory fantasies?"

"I did mention that at times I've had that, yes."

Meloy even admitted to having "occasional homicidal feelings" and had gone so far as to write it in one of his books. His explanation? "Yes. In plain English, I'm talking about getting angry and wanting to hurt some people at different times."

Nate turned to my drawings. Meloy admitted that in the 2,200 pages of my "productions," there was not a single picture of a woman being stabbed in the back. Nate asked him about specific examples where Meloy had claimed I had hundreds of examples in different categories. Nate pulled out one and read a passage to the doctor, a portion of a story about a knife fight in Vietnam. Meloy had counted it as a graphic portrayal of sexual homicide.

Nate asked Meloy about Rorschach inkblots and then put up the picture that Broderick and Meloy had both said was a knife slicing a vagina. He admitted the picture had no pubic hair, no legs, and nothing to indicate it was even a body. "What does that tell you about yourself that when you're shown a drawing of a knife cutting through a flat surface, you see a knife being inserted into a vagina?" It was Nate's last question for Meloy.

.   .   .

At that point, the prosecution rested. That was their entire case against me. We now had the opportunity to put on my defense. We had decided to simply call one witness: a psychologist to counter the theories of Meloy. After all, the prosecution had no evidence against me except for my drawings and writing. Without them, their case should fall apart.

We called John Yuille, a forensic psychologist who taught at the University of British Columbia. Yuille had a résumé longer and more impressive than Meloy's. He had been a psychologist for fourteen years longer than Meloy, and he ran the world's largest forensic-psychology program there. He had sat through Meloy's testimony and had reviewed Meloy's reports and all of my drawings and writing. The court recognized Yuille as an expert.

Yuille explained to the court that forensic psychology was not quite as advanced and accurate as Meloy had claimed. There was not enough research done in the field to prove the link between fantasy and sexual homicide. He pointed out that studies had been done showing "normal" people with deviant fantasies at a surprisingly high rate. One well-respected journal had published an article that reviewed the state of knowledge in the field and had written, "Most important, there is no evidence that sexual fantasies by themselves are either a sufficient or a necessary condition for committing a sexual offense." After pointing out that psychologists could not say there definitely was a link between fantasies and sex crimes, he was done.

Gilmore cross-examined him for a few minutes, but Yuille stuck to his guns. The science of forensic psychology was still in its infancy and could not be considered as exact as mathematics or chemistry.

With that, there was nothing left but closing arguments. The judge told us we had to make our arguments in no more than an hour and a half each.

31

The Trial: Day Six

On Thursday March 25, 1999, closing arguments began at 9:15 a.m. After the judge read the jury some preliminary instructions, Jolene Blair stood at the lectern and faced the jury. "Who would do such a thing as was done to Peggy Hettrick?" She asked the jury a whole set of rhetorical questions like that: Who would attack her, who would come across her body, who lives right next door to that field . . . and then she jumped right into my drawings. "His drawings and narratives, especially given the huge number of both, tell us exactly what he was fantasizing about. His drawings and narratives provide windows into his mind." At this point, she had not addressed any evidence and had not given the jury a reason to tie me to this murder—other than the drawings and stories I had written as a fifteen-year-old.

She pulled out excerpts of my stories and read the goriest parts to the jury. After reading a few of those and telling the jury that I had not "outgrown any of the aggression and the violence and the deviance that we saw in 1987," she turned to the evidence. She told the jury I didn't have any blood on me because the "majority" of Peggy's blood "was lost internally." She told the jury I had come home and washed my clothes and had disposed of all the evidence—the evidence the police never found—in the time between my two interrogations. She was telling the jury they could convict me based on evidence that didn't exist. And there was no evidence to suggest that anything she said was true. There was no evidence that I had disposed of any evidence; she just made that up.

She described me finding the body and told the jury that since I had written about dead bodies before, I must have known what a real one would look like. I wondered if the jury would understand the difference: I had never seen a mutilated, dead body before. Even though I had mentioned them in my stories, my descriptions of them weren't very good. I had only seen them in movies. She then brought up Linwood Hodgdon, the man who saw Peggy's body while riding his bicycle. She told the jury, "His first reaction was, I should help that person." He had actually said his first reaction was that he thought her body was a mannequin, similar to my first reaction.

She told the jury that the mistakes I had made in my

statements to the police—like that Peggy had been wearing a T-shirt—were not mistakes but were me "blurring" reality and fantasy. She then told the jury that I was an "artist," "capable of performing the mutilations with the symmetry that was noted by Dr. Allen." She told the jury I could see the body from my bedroom window, but Linda Wheeler-Holloway had specifically said she had looked and couldn't see it from my home.

She then told the jury that the Thom McAn brand shoe print—she said there was only one—was "nowhere else on the drag trail around the body." She pointed to my footprint—the one going through the drag trail in the wrong direction—and said it implicated me. The problem is that she went from a single footprint that had been identified as mine and started referring to *prints*—in the plural. "Whose prints do you find in that area?" "You don't need an expert to tell you who laid these prints."

Blair's closing argument was filled with so many mistakes and mischaracterizations it would be hard to recount them all. At one point, she committed an error that the court did not correct her on. She told the jury to reenact the stabbing when they were deliberating. Jurors are explicitly told to not try and re-create or act out crimes when deliberating. "And notice in the photos where this stab wound is on Peggy Hettrick? Stand up and turn around and try to re-create a stab wound, as testified to by Dr. Allen." She told the jury that the evidence showed the killer was left-handed and that I was left-handed. At least on that count, she got half the story right. I was left-handed. No one had testified about whether the killer had been right- or left-handed. Here, she was just playing detective and asking the jury to play along with her.

She also tried to tell the jury that I had known about Peggy's mutilation and talked about it with Wayne Lawson before the Explorer Scout had spoken with me about it. Yet Linda Wheeler-Holloway had explicitly told the jury that she had refused to arrest me in 1992 because she had confirmed the story I had told about the Explorer Scout. Blair didn't seem to care whether testimony supported her case. She just plowed ahead with what she wanted to believe. She said Peggy died on the anniversary of my mother's death, which also wasn't true.

At one point in her closing argument, Blair began confusing reality with fantasy. She told the jury, "Tim Masters rehearsed hundreds of killings, literally hundreds of sneak or surprise attacks, where he sneaks up behind someone, a stranger, and slices their throat or stabs them in the gut, turning the blade so that he can watch the pain and agony in their face, or slicing their genitalia—usually men." Of course, I had never rehearsed any such thing. The evidence was that I had written stories that involved some killing. None of them contained events anything like Peggy's murder. Blair was confusing what I had written with what I had actually done.

She closed her argument with a very important statement, one that would come back to haunt her as much as it would me. "The motive is the fantasy, rehearsal fantasy, living out fantasy, the blurring of fantasy and reality. And the opportunity was the proximity to the scene and the possession of the weapons capable of inflicting this kind of injury. *No one in the world had those things except Timothy Masters."*

NATE DELIVERED MY closing argument. We believed that the case against me was so weak we could simply point to the evidence—and the lack of evidence pointing to me—and explain how it didn't make a case against me. Nate reminded the jury I had given ten different statements and had been interrogated for more than twenty hours total. In all of that, my story was consistent.

Nate pointed out that the real reason I became a suspect was that I had not reported the body immediately after I saw it. He explained how I had felt—as a fifteen-year-old—that I was being pranked and that no one would believe me. Even after I had told my friend Wayne Lawson, his first response was to say I was "full of it."

He then went through some of the evidence. He talked about the footprint evidence and very carefully noted my lone footprint—he always referred to it in the singular since there was only one footprint in the field that was ever identified as mine. And that footprint was where it should have been, as I had walked through the field toward the bus, and not oriented as it would have been if it had been by the same person dragging the body.

Nate tried to argue logic with the jury. If I was guilty, why did I leave all my knives out for the police to see? Why didn't I throw away my drawings and writings? And why didn't I return to the crime scene or the cemetery when they staked them out? They had all said that who-ever killed Peggy would come back to visit the scene.

He then finished with the missing evidence, the complete lack of physical evidence tying me to the crime. No blood from Peggy on any of my knives. No blood, no skin, no tissue, no fiber. None of those things were found on me or my clothing or in my home. And there was nothing of mine on Peggy.

He pointed out how the prosecution's theory of me using a flashlight out in the field would have been impossible. Their theory was that I stabbed Peggy and dragged her into the field, where I then pulled her clothes halfway off. I then—with a flashlight in one hand, a knife in the other—sliced off one of her nipples and a piece of her vagina. The doctor who had testified indicated it would take two hands to do the cuts. One hand to hold the knife, one hand to pull the skin. I'd need a third hand to hold a flashlight. And there was no blood on me, my clothing, my knives, or my flashlight.

He pointed out that much of the state's case involved speculation and contained holes. No one knew how Peggy Hettrick got to Boardwalk and Landings. The prosecutors wanted the jury to assume she walked there, but there was no evidence that she had. The only testimony showed she was looking for a ride at closing time in the bar.

Nate pointed out that the prosecutors had not bothered to ask Dr. Allen if the wound to Peggy was caused by a left-handed assailant. It was an interesting question, one which we would not find the answer to for a few more years.

He summarized the case: "It is real clear, ladies and gentlemen, what you're being asked to do here. You're being asked to find a person guilty of first-degree murder because of what he writes and draws. That's what it comes down to." Still, he noted, there was not a single picture or story about a woman being stabbed in the back. The one thing they accused me of doing is the one thing I had never touched upon in 2,200 pages of material.

THE PROSECUTION ALWAYS gets to give a final response—a rebuttal—to the closing argument of the defense. Gilmore told the jurors he wanted them to dig through the evidence and actually handle Peggy's clothing. He told them they would be provided gloves but he did not tell them what they should be looking for when they did it. How could looking at Peggy's bloody clothes help them determine whether or not I was the one who killed her?

Gilmore then started inventing facts to support the people's case. He told the jury that if they looked really close at some of the pictures, they would see "footprints of the defendant coming down to the drag trail." Like Blair saying that no one else could have killed Peggy, this statement about the footprints would come back to haunt Gilmore. There was only one footprint in the field near Peggy's body that had been identified by law enforcement, and it was exactly where I said I had walked: across the bloody trail. There were no footprints of mine alongside the trail. To bolster his case, Gilmore exaggerated what little evidence they had. He told the jury that Peggy's clothing had been "removed" and that she had been left "naked" in the field. He said that the pool of blood by the curb was only "[m]aybe five or six drops" of blood. Those must have been awfully big drops to leave that big of a pool. Of course, he was trying to downplay how much Peggy had bled, to deflect attention away from the glaring lack of blood evidence tying the crime to me.

He then launched into another dissertation on my drawings and my stories. He told the jury they proved my motive, how I hated women and sought one out so I could mutilate her. To make my stories more sinister, Gilmore mixed them in with facts of the crime, as if the two had something to do with each other: "From the little scrapes on the bottom of her right boot to the cigarette lying in the blood pool, the direction in which the perpetrator came from to attack her, the frequency of the fantasy, the facts of the crime." It sounded like he wanted the jury to believe they had found some of my stories out by Peggy's body in the field.

Gilmore also mixed and matched other facts to make me look bad. He told the jury to remember the incidents I'd had with the teacher and the counselor over the Army publication my sister had given me. He then said that this was the triggering event: "The women felt and saw the anger. The date of February 11th, is it just, again, a coincidence, or is there some significance to that date?" He told the jury that the eleventh was the date I had last seen my mother alive, which was true. The event with the teachers had not taken place on the eleventh—it hadn't even happened in February. It had happened months earlier, which was one of the many reasons my attorneys objected to letting the jury hear about it. It had nothing to do with this story.

As he wound up his presentation, Gilmore told the jury to do something strange. He said they should pay particular attention to a jury instruction on measuring the credibility of witnesses. When he first said it, I was curious. Every witness in the trial except for Dr. Yuille had been a witness for the prosecution. Who was he going to tell them to disbelieve? He told them to apply it to me! I wasn't a witness in the trial. Gilmore was really reaching on this one: the instruction is designed to tell the jurors that it is alright to measure a witness's demeanor and manner when testifying. In this case, all of my statements that had been given to the jury had come in through people like Broderick. How could the jury possibly determine my credibility by measuring something repeated to them by a witness hostile toward me?

Gilmore scrambled as he began to run out of time. The judge warned him to wrap it up, so he skipped around.

"The pink socks. No explanation has been given to you as to why the defendant saw the pink socks. Defense counsel said, 'Well, there's a hair on it.' But somehow the defendant knew she was wearing pink socks, and you cannot see her socks standing next to the body." I had never said I saw her socks.

Gilmore, like Blair, also mixed fantasy and fact in his closing argument. I wondered if he knew he did it. While describing one of my drawings to the jury, he said, "He drags the body being held by the armpits." Again, that was a drawing I made; the drawing wasn't real.

He ended on what he considered to be a strong note. He reminded the jury of the drawing I had done of a knife cutting through a nondescript surface. It was a doodle, but Broderick fantasized it was a vagina. "No mention was made in defendant's argument about the drawing we've labeled the—been talked about as the vaginal drawing. Exhibit 125 has been conveniently forgotten. Defense counsel's argued to you that there's no direct evidence of a stab to the back or a nipple being cut. He didn't mention this one." He told the jury to compare Exhibit 125 to Peggy's body and ask themselves, "Is that just a coincidence?" I assumed that when the jury did that, they'd have to acquit me.

AT 2:00 THE jury began deliberating, and by 5:30, they had not reached a verdict. The next day we returned to court, and at 2:05, we were informed they had reached a verdict. The judge brought the jury back in after warning everyone in the courtroom against overreacting when the verdict was announced. The foreperson stood up and read the verdict. "Jury Verdict Count I—First Degree Murder, People versus Timothy Lee Masters. We, the jury, find the defendant, Timothy Lee Masters, guilty of first degree murder." It was unanimous, of course, and the judge went through the jurors one by one and asked them if this was indeed their verdict.

He dismissed the jury, and then the court asked the parties about the next step. Under Colorado law, there was only one possible sentence for a person convicted of first degree murder: life in prison without the possibility of parole. Although many defendants demand to have a hearing to determine an appropriate sentence, what was the use? No matter how much my lawyers and I clogged up the system now, the end result was going to be the same. Nate offered to let the court sentence me immediately. The prosecution agreed. The judge spoke: "Sentence is a mandatory one. It is a life sentence, and the Court hereby does sentence the defendant to the Department of Corrections for the term of his natural life."

At 2:45 P.M. on March 26, 1999, I was led out of court, headed for a life in prison.

As everyone exited the courtroom, Jolene Blair walked out into the hallway pumping her fist in celebration. She stood talking with Broderick, and my aunt Juanita was nearby and couldn't stand it. She looked at them and said, "You should be ashamed of yourselves for sending an innocent boy to jail."

They laughed at her.

Oftentimes, judges will ask jurors if they want to discuss their verdict with the attorneys. Sometimes jurors will stick around and talk, and sometimes they won't. Some attorneys don't bother talking with jurors afterward, but mine did. They found out that when the jury first went back to deliberate, the panel was evenly split. Half wanted to acquit me, and the other half thought I was guilty. The jurors described how adamant the foreperson was. She had adopted Blair's "Nobody else could have done this!" argument. When the jurors pointed out that there was no evidence to tie me to the crime, she would return with that argument: nobody else could have done this. Therefore, convict Tim Masters.

32

Prison

THE DEPUTIES TOOK ME BACK TO JAIL, WHERE THEY PUT me on suicide watch for a week, something they do for anyone who has just been sentenced to life without a chance of parole. Then, in preparation for being shipped to Denver for processing, they gave me back my civilian clothes. These were the same clothes I had been arrested in eight months earlier, they had just been packed up and stuck on a shelf somewhere. Now they were grungy, with eight months' worth of staleness, to put it mildly. They handcuffed and shackled me and loaded me back into a van and drove me down toward Denver for processing. The van also contained a few others who were headed off to prison. All inmates in the Colorado state penal system pass through the Denver Reception and Diagnostic Center, which is not as nice and welcoming as it might sound.

After they removed our restraints, they stuck us into a stark concrete holding cell. The space contained nothing but three rows of flat steel benches and a toilet. The benches didn't even have backrests, and there were already ten guys in there when we got added to the mix. Every hour or so, a few more guys were thrown in. After a few more hours of waiting, they finally started pulling people out of the cell in small groups. I was in a group of three taken out and led to another room, where we were strip-searched.

"Strip down to your birthday suits," a guard hollered at us.

There was only one guard to check each of us, so he did us one at a time.

"Run your fingers through your hair. Behind the ears. Open your mouth. Lift your tongue. Lift your nuts. Turn around, bend over, and spread them."

I would go through that whole humiliating routine so many more times over the next few years that I would lose track of how many strip searches I endured. I would go through so many I would eventually be able to shut off any feelings of degradation.

We then showered and stood there, waiting and shivering from the cold, until they came by to give us our prison clothing. They handed each of us a pair of boxer shorts, a white T-shirt, and an orange jumpsuit. We then got called to a window, where a guard rifled through our stuff, telling us what we could and couldn't keep. There was no logic to it as far as I could see. He let me keep my Bible and some of my papers. Everything else had to be shipped off to a relative. There were some inmates who had no one on the outside; their stuff was just thrown away.

We were then sent to a medical screening, right after they cut our hair and shaved our beards. They took blood and urine samples, but they weren't looking for drugs here. This was to see if we had any medical conditions or diseases they needed to know about. They then examined us for tattoos and distinguishing characteristics and took our mug shots. We were given a sack lunch. A peanut-butter and jelly sandwich that didn't taste quite right was accompanied by a chocolate-chip cookie and an orange. I later wondered if the Department of Corrections (DOC) had bought stock in the citrus industry; it seemed there were oranges with every meal I ever had there.

The footwear they issued us brought back memories. They gave us what are known as "Boon Dockers." Those are boots that are chopped down to the ankles so that they are no higher on your foot than a dress shoe. They were just like the ones I had worn in Navy boot camp. I had sworn to never wear a pair of them again. Of course, I had also sworn to never let anyone have that much control over my life as they'd had in the Navy. Now, fully dressed in prison garb, I was stuck in another holding cell with nine or ten other guys.

They moved us into housing units in a section of the building that was huge. There were four units, and each was three stories tall with maybe twenty cells on each floor.

I actually got a cell all to myself. After being jammed into overcrowded cells all day long, this seemed like a luxury. I was also surprised that they gave us each a hygiene kit that contained razor blades. After the steel door slammed shut behind me, I stood alone in my cell and looked in the mirror. I looked long and hard at the shaving razor and thought about how easy it would be to bust the razor blade out and slash my arm from my wrist to my elbow. I had never seriously considered suicide before, but now I was in prison for life, without any chance of parole. I wasn't scared to die, and at that moment, I really didn't care one way or the other about living or dying. I thought about my sister and my other relatives. How would they cope if I killed myself? But the biggest motivating factor was that I knew I was innocent. I just couldn't let the bastards win that easily. If I killed myself, I would be re-membered as Peggy Hettrick's convicted murderer. I needed to fight to clear my name. I couldn't let Broderick and Blair and Gilmore send me to my death for something I didn't do. I wouldn't die without a whimper. I would fight to the bitter end for what I knew was right.

I SETTLED INTO a routine, but calling it that is really mak-ing it sound more exciting than it was. First, the nights were rough. The guards did regular rounds of the floors and would only pass a cell after confirming that they could see "living, breathing flesh" in the cell. If you slept with a blanket covering you, like a normal person, the guards would shine a flashlight in your face to see if you were breathing. If they could not see your face or any other skin on your body, they would wake you up. At 2:00 A.M., they would turn on all the lights in the unit, filling the air with the buzzing and clicking noises industrial lights make when they warm up. If the noise didn't wake you up, the bright lights would. I would be spending twenty-three hours a day in that cell by myself for quite some time. I spent my time reading my Bible—which I did, from Genesis to Revelation in the first month—and going over the trial in my head. There seemed to be so much wrong with what happened at the trial that I began making an outline of all the things I thought should be addressed on appeal.

Another overriding sensation during this time was one of hunger. I was starving the entire time I was in that cell. The small amount of food I was given was nowhere near enough, and it still seemed odd to not be able to just eat whenever I was hungry. Every night I went to bed hungry. I would get so hungry that I would drink water to try and fill my stomach with something.

After a few days of sitting in my cell, I was granted the privilege of going to the gym during my hour outside my cell. The first thing I did was weigh myself. I had lost 40 pounds since I was arrested, down to 175 from 215 pounds. A few days later, we were fitted for DOC uniforms. I was measured with a thirty-four-inch waist, a size of pants I hadn't worn since 1993. They also had us take the TABE aptitude test to see what kinds of things we'd be allowed to do in prison. I hoped that if I scored better on the test, I'd be given more opportunities to work behind bars. I took the test very seriously. The test was scored on a scale of 1 to 12.9, to reflect where your education level was. I scored a 12.9, which I thought was pretty good, considering how long I'd been out of school.

We were then sent to case managers for screening. Standing in line in a hallway of government offices reminded me of the military. I then met a young black woman, who asked me a series of questions. Had I been convicted of a felony previously? Did I use drugs? I answered her questions and told her about my case. She seemed astonished that I had been convicted with so little actual evidence against me, but I know she was just humoring me. She heard stories like mine all day long. I also told her how I had become a born-again Christian while in the Larimer County Jail, and she smiled. She'd heard that one from new convicts as well.

She did tell me that she thought the judge was wrong for automatically sentencing me to life with no chance for parole. She said that since Peggy was murdered in 1987, I should have been sentenced under the previous guidelines, which would have made me eligible for parole after forty years. It only took me a moment to do the math and realize I wasn't missing much. I would have been eligible to ask for parole when I was sixty-eight years old. I also doubted they would have paroled a man who had been convicted of brutally stabbing and sexually mutilating a stranger for no good reason.

I HAD MY plan to get out of prison: I was going to appeal. It seemed so clear to me that any rational judges, when shown the lack of evidence in this case, would have to give me a new trial. A new trial without the character evidence and the psychobabble about displaced matricide. One where they wouldn't be allowed to show the jury pictures I had drawn when I was fifteen that had nothing to do with the crime. The problem was that appeals in Colorado routinely take two years. The best-case scenario had an appeals court ruling on my case after I'd spent two years behind bars for a crime I didn't commit.

In the meantime, I just tried to deal with the sensory deprivation of the cell I was in. No television, no radio, no telephone. I hadn't spoken to my sister in ages. She and I had always spoken often, and when we both lived in California, we often made the 360-mile round trips to visit each other.

One by one, the other prisoners were taken away. At night, a jail worker would come by and toss a garbage bag into the cell of the inmate who was about to be moved. You would stuff all your things in the bag, and the next day you'd be transported after breakfast. I had no idea what to expect from prison, so I wasn't looking forward to having the bag thrown into my cell. After a few weeks, it finally happened. They tossed in a bag and said, "Pack it up."

Everything I owned could fit into a single plastic bag. I may have owned things on the outside, but I couldn't see them or touch them. I might never get to again. The DOC inventoried all my stuff and listed it on a property sheet. It seemed like so little. I was more worried about what would happen in prison. All I knew of prison was what I'd seen on TV and in the movies. Would I have to fight people or kill someone to survive? I was scared. I was about to be locked up with rapists, killers, gangbangers—all the worst elements of our society.

THE NEXT DAY I was transported with a group of convicts to another facility, where we would be distributed to our final destinations. We were dressed out in DOC green uniforms. They shackled us, hands and feet, and loaded us onto a huge Greyhound-style bus. I later learned that these groups are usually only handcuffed; the shackling was my fault. Since I was convicted of such a heinous crime, they felt the need to shackle everyone who was traveling with me. If they have to shackle one person, they shackle them all.

On the ride, a short black guy named Domino asked to use the restroom at the back of the bus. The guards didn't move. They kept telling him, "We're almost there," and laughing at him. Domino was diabetic and pleaded with the guards. He said his bladder was messed up from the diabetes. He told the guards he couldn't hold it and if he couldn't use the john, he'd piss on the floor. One of the guards looked at him sternly and said he'd get written up if he did that. Domino panicked, but he didn't want to get written up. He also couldn't leave his seat while he was shackled. He took off his shoe and urinated into it. To this day, it still upsets me how they degraded that man.

We finally got to Territorial Correctional Facility Cell House Five, where we would be held until being shipped for the last time. The cells were tiny, perhaps only six by eight feet, and reminded me of Alcatraz. They had open bars instead of steel doors. The place was ancient. As we walked in line to the chow hall, I saw a guard holding an AR-15 rifle at parade rest. I swear he looked like he wanted a chance to fire his weapon. All those years I served my country and now I'm locked up for something I didn't do. Here's a guy who'd kill me if I tried to leave, and he'd feel good about it.

When they let us out of the cells, I found out that the "yard" was not very large and only contained a basketball hoop and some broken-down free weights. I needed to stretch my legs, but there wasn't much more to do than to just walk circles around the small yard. I'd often be joined by others who were also walking circles. We'd often talk about life outside, the real world, the place we'd been taken from and might never see again.

That day, as I was being brought back to my cell, I looked into another cell I was walking past. "Hey, man, don't look in my cell," a voice barked at me from inside. I was about to respond with a smart-ass comment when I realized he was right. In this world, there was no privacy. The only place that was yours was your cell. When people walked by my cell, I felt like they were intruding when they looked in at me, too. From that point forward—for almost ten years—I did my best to keep my eyes straight ahead when walking down the prison tiers. It also kept me from seeing a lot of things I'd rather not have mental images of now.

That night we got word that about twenty of us were to

be shipped to Buena Vista Correctional Facility, in Buena Vista, Colorado. I heard someone respond to that bit of information by saying, "I heard that place is a fucking gladiator school." This was not the kind of thing I wanted to hear. I'd have to spend the next few years of my life fighting my appeal—and maybe having to fight fellow inmates just to stay alive.

The next day it was back on the bus, feet shackled and chains wrapped around our waists and through our handcuffs. On the plus side, I had a window seat, and the drive was through the mountains. We drove through the Rockies, and the scenery was absolutely stunning. Mountains towered over us, and green forest stretched out below. The peaks of the mountains were still snowcapped. Sitting there in my chains, the images out the window looked like a projection on a movie screen. I told myself it was real, but it didn't seem real. I thought about how I'd like to own a ranch someday. Working from home with no boss, living outdoors. Freedom. I had never worked with cows before, but from where I was sitting, it seemed like a dream job. Looking back on it, there's an irony to this. At trial, I had been accused of fantasizing compulsively. Here, I was in a place where the only escape was to fantasize. And what did I fantasize about? Working outdoors.

After a couple hours, we came to Buena Vista Correctional Facility. What I came to know as "Bueny" consisted of several white-block buildings surrounded by tall fences topped with razor wire. I had been picturing something more like "Shawshank," but this place was no less menacing. There were guard towers with armed guards looking down on the twenty-acre facility.

The bus pulled up to a gate through the outer fence line, and the gate opened. The driver pulled in, and then, as the gate shut behind us, he killed the engine. We were locked in, between the two fences. We had arrived at 11:00 A.M. which is a "count time" at Bueny. They count heads in the facility during that time, and no one comes or goes until the count is completed, and everyone is accounted for. After about forty-five minutes, a guard came out to check the bus. He walked around it and looked under it with a mirror on a stick. What was he looking for? Did they think someone might try to sneak into this place? After a few minutes, he opened the inner gate and waved us through.

Again, we went through the bureaucratic hell of shuffling and processing that prisons and jails have so much of. We started by climbing off the bus, which was no small feat. With shackles and waist chains, it is almost impossible to manage steps without falling. Each step caused the chains to pull tight, and pain shot up my legs from where the shackles pulled my ankles. They eventually removed our restraints and told us to wait in a hallway. Once again, we got sack lunches as the hours passed by.

They then put us into cells. Again, these were small—maybe six by ten—but now there was someone else in the cell with me. My cell mate told me he was a clerk in the housing unit, and as a result, he had some privileges.

He had a television, and he offered me a cigarette. Cigarettes were against the rules, but like I said, he had privileges. He told me that he also got a cell to himself, so my being there must be only temporary. I sat and watched his TV for a few hours, which seemed like an amazing luxury. I hadn't seen television in a month.

A little later, they moved me to another cell, and I saw a familiar face. Ron, my new cell mate, was someone I'd met at the Denver Reception and Diagnostic Center—the place where they decide where the inmates will be sent to serve their sentences—and had eaten with on many occasions. He was missing his front teeth and would not have them replaced for some time. He was waiting for the DOC to make him a pair. As a result, there were a lot of different food items he could not eat, and he had often given them to me. Ron was in his forties but looked much older, and he loved to tell stories. I'm not sure his stories were true, but they were entertaining.

I hadn't been allowed to use a phone now for a month, and when I could, I called Serena. She had some bad news: she had to sell my Trans Am to pay the lawyer's bill. That was rough, but I knew she had no choice. When I got out, I would still have my house and a couple older cars and my dad's old Harley. She did take some of the money and put it in an account that I could use while I was in prison.

When the money came into my account, I ordered a TV set and a bag of tortilla chips. It is difficult to explain how something like that can appeal to you when you've been eating the same bland sack lunches and cafeteria chow day in and day out. When the chips came in, I ate the whole bag that night. At the time, I was convinced they were the best tortilla chips anyone had ever had in the entire world.

We were still waiting to be placed in our regular housing. With two to a cell with open bars at the end, the place got really noisy. What made it worse was that a lot of people passed through A&O—Admission and Orientation—where everyone was first placed before being sent to their permanent housing unit. Some were just placed here until they were sent to "boot camp," an alternative to regular jail where prisoners experienced something meant to look like military training with hard work, marching, and a lot of getting yelled at. This usually meant that they were scheduled to be released soon. They often acted like they were high schoolers in a hotel on spring break. They would yell back and forth through the bars and hold conversations this way at all hours of the night. It was not uncommon to have two or three guys holding conversations like this, yelling to each other even though they were ten cells apart. I gained a newfound respect for quiet. An animosity built up between those of us who were scheduled to be in for a long haul and the boot campers, who could see the light at the end of the tunnel.

One of the other inmates who was fed up with the noisy boot campers would walk up to their cells during free time. He'd lean in and say, "If I hear any yelling or screaming tonight from this cell, I'll shank you both tomorrow." The noise would stop for a while, but eventually the yelling and arguing would begin all over again. Ron and I joked about different ways we'd like to shut the boot campers up. Perhaps a grenade? At one point I made earplugs out of toilet paper. It helped a little.

The second week I was there, my uncle Don came to visit. He had spent some time here as a kid for stealing a car, and he understood how important it was to have visitors. It was good to be able to shake hands with a family member, and visiting the vending machines in the visiting area seemed like a treat. I know the cheeseburgers that came out of the machines were horrible by real-world standards, but to me at that time, they were a delicacy. Don told me about his time there in the 1970s, and we talked about my trial. How could I have been convicted without any evidence?

After a couple of weeks there, a female guard from the kitchen came by and interviewed all the new "fish"—the new inmates—to see if any of us would be suitable to work in the kitchen. Having spent time in the Navy, I had no desire to work in a big kitchen. It didn't matter. Two days later, I got the form telling me I'd been "hired" to work in the kitchen, and the pay rate was a dollar. I looked at Ron. "How on earth can they expect you to earn any money when they only pay you a dollar an hour?"

"That's not a dollar an hour," Ron said. "It's a dollar a day."

"What? That's crazy!" I didn't believe him. Of course, he was right. I'd make a dollar a day in the kitchen. The better jobs in prison paid $3 a day. I'd be working six hours a day, twenty days a month. That $20 I'd make each month was how much I made in an hour in the real world.

After lunch, I reported for work. I stood around for a

few minutes while the guards looked for something I could do. Finally, one of them handed me a bottle filled with vinegar and a sponge, and he pointed at some windows. "Clean those."

As I cleaned the windows—for a dollar a day—I thought about how I had been trained to troubleshoot, repair, and maintain multimillion-dollar military aircraft. Now a guard was watching me wipe windows, to make sure I did it right. How long would it be before they promoted me to wiping down tables?

33

Life at Bueny

LIFE IN PRISON IS UNIMAGINABLE FOR THE AVERAGE PERson. Herded from place to place like cattle, we lived in cramped cells. Prisons remove the last shred of dignity a man might have. You can't have any privacy in prison, for any purpose. The bathrooms all had huge windows on the doors, and the toilets did not have stalls around them. Anyone walking by the door could see you on the toilet. It was the same in the cells. The toilets sit right out in the open, so you have no privacy. Add another cell mate into the mix, and it becomes even more humiliating.

I met some interesting people in prison, as might be expected. Dion was from Oregon and serving a six-year sentence for aggravated assault. He had been heavily into demolition derbies, and one day he lost his temper while driving through a parking lot. Someone took his parking space, so he rammed the other person's car, demolition-derby style. He probably wouldn't have gotten six years if he hadn't then rammed the police car that showed up a few minutes later.

Dion was a little heavyset and very quiet, but he seemed like a nice-enough guy. He was too quiet, though. Some people picked on him because of it: they saw his quietness as weakness. I recall a guy named Tattoo telling Dion that when they got to their units, he was going to "chop" Dion. Chop was prison slang for rape. The guy wasn't actually going to chop Dion, he was just messing around with him, but it was still wrong.

AFTER A LITTLE more than a month, I was moved out of A&O to my permanent cell. This was in the South Unit, a building that had three levels and maybe a couple dozen cells on each side. Again, the cells were six by ten and held two men apiece. Each cell door was a different color: purple, light blue, lime green, pink, yellow. It gave the place a twisted carnival atmosphere. I was assigned 2W13, on the west side. This was good, I would realize, as soon as I looked out the window. We faced the mountains, and not far from the window was a row of tall pine trees. With the windows open, the breeze actually brought in fresh air filled with pine scent. It was the only piece of the real world they allowed us to enjoy.

The cells were Spartan otherwise. Two bunks hung from the wall, two and one-half feet by six feet, and a metal desk and chair were the only pieces of furniture in the cell. There was a toilet and sink combination right by the door; when you ran water in the sink, you could see it drain into the toilet. When you flushed the toilet, it roared as if being sucked out of an airplane.

We had no intercoms, so the only way to get a guard's attention was to bang something on the ground. There were many occasions when I had appointments, but the guards never came to get me until I reached under the door and pounded my shoe on the floor to get them to come over.

I met my new cell mate, Rudart, and had the usual introductory conversation.

"What're you in for?"

"Life, for a murder I didn't commit."

"Really? Okay . . ." No one ever believed me. Why should they? Most of the people there were guilty. Why would they think I wasn't like them? It's a common belief that people in prison will always tell you that they are innocent. Hollywood uses that as a common theme, over and over again. I found that while I was in prison, almost everyone I met told me what they were in for and had no problem saying they were guilty. When I told them I wasn't guilty of the murder for which I'd been convicted, I was the odd man out.

Bueny offered quite a bit in terms of outdoor activities. There were baseball diamonds, a soccer field, horseshoe pits, handball and racquetball courts, a tennis court, basketball, and free weights. I still spent a lot of time just walking around the outside because they wouldn't let us bring books outdoors. One day I was walking around the yard and saw a huge black man pummeling a Mexican who was half his size. By the time the guards broke it up, the little guy was pulverized. It was so bad they cordoned off the area so hazmat guys could clean up all the blood. That was the first fight I saw at Bueny.

Meanwhile, one of my neighbors was being charged "rent" by another prisoner. Rent was a form of extortion common in Bueny, where a prisoner, or a group of prisoners, would simply tell other inmates that if they didn't pay rent, they would get hurt or killed. This guy was paying $10 in canteen money each week to his inmate landlord for the privilege of not being beaten.

I'm not quite sure how I avoided being charged rent or being tested by someone who wanted to prove himself in Bueny. I was kind of scrawny and out of shape when I got there, and I probably looked like a good candidate for someone who wanted to kick someone's ass. I guess I was just lucky and managed to stay below the radar.

In prison, we bought tokens for forty-five cents. Tokens could be used to buy sodas but were also used as currency. Tokens and postage stamps were the basis of the prison economy. I found out that even though haircuts were supposed to be free, it was customary to give the inmate who cut your hair a token as some sort of tip. No one tipped me when I fed them in the kitchen. It seemed like nonsense to me. I also wasn't too crazy about letting another inmate touch my head and cut my hair. For the first time in my adult life, I let my hair grow out.

I managed to move up in the world by getting out of the kitchen and into a computer class run by a man named Jim Osborne. He only accepted people into the class who had scored at least a 10.5 on the TABE test. The class focused on programs an administrative assistant might use, like Windows 95, WordPerfect, Lotus 1-2-3, and then Office 97. There were even advanced classes in Logo, MicroWorlds, and Microsoft Visual C++ 6.0. These basic programming languages interested me quite a bit. I was pleasantly surprised to find the class filled with people who genuinely wanted to learn. It was especially nice because Osborne wanted to teach. He had been a guard for thirty years, though, and approached new inmates with skepticism. He saw so many others come and go that it took him some time to believe that I wanted to learn.

I met a group of inmates in my unit who held a regular Bible study. I attended every night. I was totally caught up in God at the time and was doing my best to live my life the way I thought Jesus wanted me to.

ONE DAY, A friend of mine named Tim and I were walking around the yard talking about what we would do when we got out. Suddenly, a cellophane-wrapped package came flying over the fence and landed on the ground in front of us. Without thinking, Tim picked it up and looked at it. It was filled with pot. Before I could explain to him that he needed to put it down, another inmate came running over and grabbed it. "Hey, that's mine."

As we were walking back to our cells, another inmate walked up to us and asked us to look at his hands. "Do my knuckles look fucked up?" he asked.

"No, why?"

"You didn't see the riot over by the weight pile? Everybody was fighting, and there were weights flying everywhere. That's why they called the yard early."

I didn't wear a watch, so I hadn't realized we had been called in early. That night, they locked us all down in our cells, and the next day they took us all to the gym so they could ransack our cells, looking for contraband.

One day I was standing at the foot of my bunk talking to Rudart, waiting for them to call count, when Griggs came by and banged on the door window; he told me he was issuing me a warning for not being on my bunk during count. They hadn't called count yet. That warning cost me another two months of waiting to get into a single cell.

RUDART HAD LEGAL business to take care of, and he was sent to a county jail. They sent in another inmate to replace him, but the guy was only there one night. I wonder if he somehow got himself transferred out when he heard what I had been convicted of. The next guy was named Ted, and he turned out to be alright. He was a biker who'd gotten into a standoff with the police. It ended when they fired tear gas into his trailer, and he had passed out. The tear gas had caught the trailer on fire, and Ted had been badly burned in the process. He had a lot of stories about his motorcycle days and was always very clear on one thing: he belonged to a motorcycle "club," not a motorcycle "gang." He was the nicest guy in the world, notwithstanding the whole police standoff thing, but his snoring kept me and half the unit awake most nights.

The cells at Bueny were only six by ten, and the first two tiers were all cells that were double-bunked. The place had been built originally as a youth reformatory, and the cells were only designed for one inmate. For whatever reason, the third tier was all single bunk cells. Obviously, those were the most desirable, and after I'd been there a month, I put in a request for one. The wait time to get into one averaged about four months, so I began biding my time.

THE ENTIRE TIME I was in prison, I kept going over the trial in my mind. Whenever I had a thought about something wrong with the state's case against me, I'd write it down. Soon, I had piles of handwritten notes. I bought a typewriter so I could try and organize my notes into something useful. We got two weeks off from the computer classes because the instructor took his Christmas vacation. I spent the time sitting at my metal desk, hammering away at my typewriter. I finished the first draft of my outline right before the end of the break.

I didn't realize it at first but I was also venting as I wrote out my draft. Much of it was laced with sarcasm and anger. "In 1987 I had astigmatism, so unless I developed cat-like vision overnight, I would not have been able to see Peggy Hettrick walk down Landings after 1:00 that morning." I showed the outline to Rudart before he was transferred and also to Tommy, hoping to get some input and constructive criticism. They both told me that no one would sympathize with me the way it was written. I sounded too bitter. I was planning on sending the outline to people who might be able to help me, so I took their advice. I would have to rewrite it and try to make it sound more factual and less emotional.

While I was making a dollar a day working in Bueny, I didn't think my financial situation could get much worse. My sister and aunt would sometimes send me money orders so I could buy things from the canteen, but it turns out that the DOC found a way to make it worse. Within the first year I was at Bueny, the DOC began confiscating 20 percent of everything I earned and everything that people sent me. If I earned $5 for a week's wages, the DOC took a dollar of it to pay back things like the $345 "court costs" I'd been assessed by Larimer County. It seemed so petty on one level, but it was much more than that. They had already stolen everything from me! Now they were stealing more.

34

Wheeler-Holloway Returns

AFTER BEING IN PRISON FOR ABOUT FIVE MONTHS, I WAS pulled out of my cell and brought down to an office in a part of the prison where inmates normally didn't go. I had no idea where I was being taken or why. When I entered the room, I saw a familiar face: Linda Wheeler-Holloway.

"Do you know why I'm here?" she asked me.

"Because you know I'm innocent." I wasn't trying to be argumentative; it was just the first thing that occurred to me. And it was true. I still didn't trust the police, so I was leery of her. She was no longer with the Fort Collins Police Department though; she was now with the Colorado Bureau of Investigation.

She didn't come right out and say she thought I was

innocent, though. She said she had some doubts about the case and wondered if I'd be willing to take another polygraph. She also wanted me to take a sex-offender test. Apparently, that would involve them placing some kind of device over my penis and then showing me a variety of photographs of twisted stuff to see what aroused me. As odd as that all sounded, I was all for it. I told her I would ask my attorneys and go from there. One problem I had was that she still represented the police to me, and the police no longer had my trust. She had even testified against me at my trial. Of course, I was in prison for life with no chance of parole. Things couldn't really get worse.

I didn't know it at the time, but Wheeler-Holloway had been disturbed by my conviction in the Hettrick case. Although she had testified at my trial, she had not sat in court and watched any of the other witnesses or seen the opening statements or closing arguments. Later, she told me she was surprised by my conviction. Even though she was now working for the state at the CBI, she went to her superiors and told them she wanted to see if anything could be done about getting me out of prison. She was convinced I was innocent. She got permission to meet with the district attorney and asked if she could follow up on the matter, even though it was outside of CBI's jurisdiction. They told her they were fine with it and even assigned the case to the CBI so she could work on it officially. They told her they would be open-minded and consider anything she could uncover. They suggested a polygraph and then, if I passed, an evaluation by a well-respected forensic psychiatrist named Dr. McDonald. If I passed the exam and McDonald said he was certain I hadn't done it, they would reevaluate my situation.

My attorney, Erik Fisher, looked at it like I did. It seemed odd for anyone who had testified against me to now come forward, but it could be a good sign. "If she is willing to get involved it may help."

I expressed my doubts to my cell mate, but he disagreed. "She's a CBI agent? She can do a hell of a lot to help you."

A month later, she showed up at the prison with a polygrapher. Part of the deal was that this investigation couldn't cost the state any more money. I had to pay for the polygraph, but I didn't have any money. My cousin Mike volunteered to put the money up when he heard of my predicament. We set up in a private room, and the doctor asked Linda to step outside. I was nervous. I asked the examiner how accurate the test could be considering how nervous I was. He waved off my concerns and asked me to give him all the details of my case. I am not a big believer in lie detectors, and I think he got that impression from some of the questions I asked him. I also asked if maybe he should try doing the examination without getting all of the finer details of my opinions of the case first. Wouldn't that keep his opinions from influencing the results?

He ran the test, but it was different from the test I'd taken before. Among other things, he never ran a baseline and never asked me to lie to him about something obvious. After giving me the test, he walked out and told

Linda, "He's the guy. He's right where he belongs. He committed the crime." They decided to not bother having me take the sex-offender test.

Linda told me the results on the phone. I assumed that this would cause her to lose interest. I didn't hear from her again for a long time. Later, she told me that was one of the hardest and strangest weeks of her professional career. A suspect in a different murder case had offered to take a polygraph and passed his the same week I failed mine. That man is currently serving a life sentence for a murder it turns out he *did* commit.

35

Years in Prison

A MAN NAMED CURT WAS IN A CELL NOT FAR FROM MINE, and we began having discussions about the Bible. I still read it daily and took part in Bible study classes, but Curt challenged me to think about what I believed in. Curt was a Jehovah's Witness and argued that much of the modern church structure didn't come from the Bible itself but had come from the Holy Roman Empire. He said concepts like the trinity and hell were things the Romans had introduced to Christianity; they hadn't come from Jesus. I wasn't about to become a Jehovah's Witness, but I did begin to question what I believed in and why. One of the recurring, nagging doubts I had was how it could be that I was still in prison for something I hadn't done. I prayed my heart out every night and day for God to show the world I was innocent. Why wasn't he doing anything about it?

THE MAIN THING I continued to look forward to were visitors. My relatives visited me often in Bueny, and I could usually count on seeing someone every other week. Aunts, uncles, cousins—they all did their best to visit me and try and keep my spirits up. They were routinely driving one hundred and eighty miles—three hours—each way just to spend some time with me each weekend.

TWICE A YEAR, the Department of Corrections did assessments for each inmate. Each time I saw mine, it recommended some kind of course in anger management. It was lunacy. The entire time I was in prison I never hurt anyone. If anything, I should have been teaching anger management.

In the fall of 2000, I spoke with Fischer, and he told me that television producers from the A&E network had called and said they were doing an investigative report on my case. He asked me to write a statement to make sure I got my side of the story told. I had seen the program and knew that they tended to side with whatever result the jury had come back with. They might mention my side, but they'd spend their time talking to the police and the prosecutors. They did talk to Fischer later, but he told me he had stuck to the legal issues in the case. I was disappointed. The average person doesn't care about the nuance and detail of the legal issues. I wished he could have gone over the evidence with the producers of the show—or, more important, the lack of evidence.

Fischer had to be cautious though. We had filed our appeal, and he had already made his arguments before the court of appeals. We were waiting for the court of appeals to rule on the case. I was sitting in my cell one night when A&E ran their documentary about my case in the series *Cold Case Files*. They crucified me. They spent the whole half hour showing my drawings over and over again and then spoke at length with Broderick, Blair, Gilmore, Meloy, and Reed. They even interviewed Wayne Lawson and blacked out his face so no one would know who he was. Jolene Blair trotted out her closing argument for a national audience this time: "Who else could it possibly be? No one else had the motive, the weapons and the opportunity to commit this crime." The host, Bill Curtis, agreed with her that I was guilty.

Now, everyone in prison knew why I was in Bueny, but since they had learned about it from A&E, most also believed I had done it. I assumed everyone who saw the show believed I had done it. The good news is that a few guys came up to me and expressed sympathy. "Man, that's fucked up how they convicted you with no real evidence." There were others who wouldn't talk to me because they now thought I was guilty and belonged in prison and also because of the sexual nature of the crime.

On February 17, 2001, a friend of mine came by and said he had seen my name in the newspaper under the headline: "Murder Conviction Upheld by Appellate Court." I was a little pissed that my attorney hadn't told me the news; I had to get it thirdhand from someone who had read it in the newspaper. Fischer did call me and then sent me a copy of the opinion written by the court of appeals, explaining why they had ruled against me. Among other things, the court had bought the argument that my mother had red hair! My mother had brown hair. They had gotten several other facts entirely wrong. They wrote that Peggy's body could be seen from my bedroom window. They also bought the nonsense about Peggy's pink socks. According to the court, the knife found by Schade was under the bridge right by the field. In reality, it was found a quarter of a mile away. Somehow, the court of appeals was now twisting and making up facts to support my conviction. Perhaps scariest of all was that the court of appeals found nothing wrong with the prosecution relying so heavily on my drawings and writings to convict me. Since the drawings appeared to show some people being stabbed, they could show them to a jury to prove I stabbed someone.

Amazingly, the court of appeals also upheld the search warrant that Broderick had gotten for my home in Ridgecrest. You may recall that much of what they were searching for were things that Meloy said they might find there. Meloy's beliefs and opinions weren't evidence, however, and we thought the court would have struck the warrant since it wasn't based on evidence. Instead, the court of appeals wrote that Meloy's opinions and beliefs were basis for probable cause because of the prosecutor's theory of the case. It really looked like they were simply writing an opinion to support the conviction, even though they had to ignore common sense to do so.

When I lost my appeal, I lost all faith in God. It was the final nail in the coffin of Christianity for me. I not only stopped believing in him, but I hated him. If he really existed, he was out there, watching me and letting me suffer unjustly. From that point on, I couldn't stand it when people told me to have faith in God.

I also found out that my only hope now was an appeal to the Colorado Supreme Court, and that would take a couple more years as well. Since I had long since spent all my money on legal fees, my sister had been making my mortgage payments on my home in California. I knew now there was no way she could continue to do that, so I talked to her about letting the house go into foreclosure. I made a list of things I'd like to save and sent it to her. Serena made several trips to the house and back and placed my things in storage sheds she put up in her backyard. I knew it was difficult for her. She had helped me get things from our old trailer in Colorado after Dad died; this must have felt the same, cleaning out my place after I had been taken away.

It turns out that you can't just file an appeal with the Supreme Court in Colorado. You first file a petition with the court called a "writ of certiorari," and the Supreme Court then considers whether it will let you file an appeal or not. Some of the things I was learning about the legal system were shocking, and for me, depressing. It turns out that the Colorado Supreme Court only accepts a small percentage of the writs submitted to them. Nate filed the writ on my behalf in April 2001. In the first bright spot of this entire ordeal, the Colorado Supreme Court granted my writ. It was a win for me, but all it really meant was that they would now let me file my appeal with them.

THE A&E PIECE aired in reruns several times a year after that. Each time it ran, I sensed hostility toward me from the inmates who didn't know me. One day I was lifting weights, and a worker from the laundry unit came over to see me. "Hey, Masters, someone fucked with your laundry. I just wanted you to know it wasn't any of us in South Unit. It had to be someone from main laundry who did it."

I went down as soon as I could, and the guy showed me. Someone had taken my shirt and written "Rapist Cho Mo Bastard" on my name tag. I was pissed. The guy kept assuring me that he had no idea who did it, and I believed him. Today, I'm glad I never found out who did it. It was the closest I'd come to losing it in prison. I could have wound up doing something that cost me more in prison. I was also angry that the insults made no sense. I wasn't accused of rape or child molestation, and I knew who my father was.

I was continuing in my computer classes with Mr. Osborne and flourishing. I made it through all the typical stuff and was now into computer programming. Serena even sent me a couple books: *Microsoft Visual C++ 6.0* and *Windows Game Programming for Dummies*.

. . .

IT IS HARD to fathom the level of humiliation and inhumanity in prison. One day I was sitting on the toilet when a guard came by and opened the door. Time for the "monthly shakedown." They'd do these surprise inspections to make sure we didn't have contraband in our cells. I wasn't finished with what I was doing, but the guard told me he wasn't going anywhere. He said he was worried: "You might try to flush some contraband." He stood there and watched me wipe my butt and flush.

On another occasion, several thousand pounds of E coli–contaminated beef was cooked and served to us at Bueny. At the time it was served, something about it just looked wrong, and I didn't eat any. I thought it had been cooked badly, but it was tainted. I knew more than a few guys who got food poisoning from it. A couple guys were laid up for a few days. One inmate told me he was "shitting blood." We later found out that the administrators knew about the bad meat but served it to us anyway. How'd I know? I read about it in the newspaper.

The medical attention we received as prisoners was severely lacking. Around this time I had a physical examination and had some tests run. Hepatitis and tuberculosis were running rampant through the prison population, and I was always worried I could contract something like that. All my tests came back negative, but the nurse noted I had a mole on my left arm that ought to be looked at. I put in a request to have it removed, and a short while later I got sent down to medical. There, a nurse—not a doctor—simply sliced it off with a scalpel. She told me I would have nothing more than a "paper thin" scar. She was wrong. I have a scar that looks like a bullet wound.

My glasses had become so scratched up that I could barely see through them. I put in a request to see the optometrist, but he only came by once a month. He couldn't make it that month, so they shackled and handcuffed us and transported us all over to a minimum-security center to see him. There, the doctor could not get my eyes dialed in at all. He said I needed to actually go to an optometrist's office, where they had a full set of equipment to do it right.

It was a bizarre, otherworldly experience. They dressed me and a few other guys in orange jumpsuits, shackled and handcuffed us, and drove us into town. It was my first trip outside the walls of Bueny in years. Driving through the town was riveting, but it was also a sensory overload. My scenery—inside the walls of the prison—had been bland and hadn't changed in years. It was the strangest thing to be sitting in a comfortable waiting room at an eye doctor's office, chatting with the female secretary, waiting my turn. When I got my prescription, I mailed it to Serena. She spent a small fortune getting me two pairs of glasses. One pair had the tinting that grew darker when exposed to sunlight. At the time, the prison didn't allow shaded lenses, but these got through the mail room because they were inspected indoors. When the guards examined them, it simply looked like I had gotten two pairs of prescription glasses.

.   .   .

IN OCTOBER 2002, I again heard from a fellow inmate that a court had ruled against me. The papers had the story of the Colorado Supreme Court ruling against me. This opinion was much like the one from the court of appeals. The Colorado Supreme Court bought the nonsense of Meloy's and said it was okay for the court to have allowed into evidence all of my drawings and writings. The court said that my attorneys should have asked for a "limiting instruction" to be given to the jury—to tell them that the drawings and writings didn't prove I killed Peggy; they just proved I was the kind of person who could.

I was also surprised to learn that the vote on my case was 4–3. Of the seven Colorado Supreme Court justices, three of them voted to overturn the conviction and grant me a new trial. I lost by one vote! The three justices who disagreed with the verdict wrote a dissenting opinion, including: "Most of these writings and drawings have nothing to do with this grisly murder." "The sheer volume of the inadmissible evidence so overwhelmed the admissible evidence that the defendant could not have a fair trial. . . . There exists a substantial risk that the defendant was convicted not for what he did, but for who he is."

Now, it looked like I was in for the long haul. If we tried to go to the U.S. Supreme Court, that could take many more years. And, like the Colorado Supreme Court, you just don't get to file an appeal and be heard. You have to file the writ and see if they will let you file your appeal.

And the Supreme Court takes very few cases out of all the writs presented to them.

A&E's *Cold Case Files* was still making my life hell by airing their crucifixion of me every few months. After about the sixth time they had aired this show, the unit lieutenant called me down to his office.

He said, "I've been informed that your crime was just shown on TV."

I immediately corrected him by saying, "The crime I was accused of."

He stopped me short by snapping, "The crime you were charged, tried, and convicted of committing."

This man would not entertain the possibility for one second that I was innocent. As far as he was concerned, a jury convicted me, so I was guilty. I suppose that let him sleep easier, with the assumption that everyone in his prison was guilty.

"If you feel you need to be placed in protective custody, you need to let me know."

"No, I'm fine." I told him.

36

The Motion

ALL THE TIME I WAS LEARNING MORE AND MORE ABOUT the legal process. The next step from where I was legally was to file a "35(c)" motion for reconsideration with the state court. Nate told me about it and said that my best bet was to argue that I had been saddled with "ineffective assistance of counsel." He was, in essence, throwing himself under the bus. Not because he had been ineffective at trial; he just thought that this was the argument the court was most likely to grant. The Supreme Court had written in its opinion that my attorneys should have asked for the limiting instruction. Maybe they were hinting at what I needed to do to win an appeal?

Nate sent me a copy of the Supreme Court opinion and the forms to show me what a 35(c) motion looks like. He also sent me the forms to request counsel to be appointed for me. Obviously, Nate couldn't represent me in my motion saying he had been ineffective counsel at trial. I also didn't have any money to pay him anymore, so I would have to rely on counsel appointed for the indigent.

The various time frames of the legal system meant I had a year to file my motion, but I needed it to be heard sooner than that to allow me time to file a habeas corpus petition if I lost that motion. Although I could have hammered it out pretty quickly, I was getting tired of being shot down. I had spent so much time going over the case in my mind that I knew all the details and nuances of my case. I was going to spend every minute of the next six months and file the best damn brief I could, even if I wasn't a lawyer.

Serena sent letters to law schools, looking for any help we could find. I sent Serena a list of schools and addresses, and she mailed out stacks of letters with an outline I had prepared of my case. I had cleaned up my previous efforts in this regard and had gotten the story down to a mere fifteen pages. After sending out about one hundred and fifty letters, we got back eighty or so nice rejection letters. I assume most law schools are overwhelmed with requests like this. I submitted my information to the Colorado Innocence Project as well. There had been some DNA found in my case, but not much was done with it at the time. They sent me an application, and I filled it out with high hopes.

Meanwhile, I hammered away on my motion. I finally wrote it out and raised what I thought were the most important arguments to support my cause. I believe that

Broderick intentionally delayed arresting and charging me with this crime. Although that might not make a big difference in some cases, it was huge in mine. By bringing me to trial later, they presented the jury with a grown man, not a skinny fifteen-year-old kid. The jury would have been more likely to acquit me if they had seen me the way I appeared ten years earlier. And the delay cost me my sole alibi witness: my father, who had passed away shortly before they decided to arrest me. Remember: the Constitution guarantees the right to a fair and speedy trial. What was speedy about mine, coming ten years after the murder?

There were other problems that hadn't occurred to me earlier. The police had interrogated me more than once. In fact, they had questioned me at school, at the police station, and then at the Perkins restaurant. At two of those locations, my father was not present, which was a clear violation of Colorado law. I had been a minor at the time, and the law said they had to get permission from both my father and me before questioning. It wasn't enough to just ask me. What did I know about my rights back then? I was only fifteen!

I also pointed out that one of the jurors had fallen asleep during the trial. Although this was a big deal, my attorneys had not brought it to the court's attention. My uncle had told me about it during the trial, but he told me after the fact.

My strongest arguments, though, hinged on the fact that there was no evidence to support the guilty verdict. And what little the prosecution thought they had—the drawings and the stories—shouldn't have gotten into evidence. They didn't prove anything, and they didn't connect me to the crime.

As I was putting the finishing touches on my motion, I got a letter from the Federal Public Defender's Office. I had corresponded with them about the Colorado Innocence Project, and I hoped the letter would tell me they were taking my case. Instead, the letter said that my case was not a good candidate for them since there appeared to be no DNA to test. The assistant federal public defender who wrote to me said that she was "troubled" by my case, though, and she encouraged me to apply to the courts to have a public defender assigned to help me with my motion. I viewed the letter as another rejection. How could I ever prove my innocence when there was so little evidence to go on?

Now it all depended on my 35(c) motion. I went over it with a fine-tooth comb and typed the cleanest document I could make. Then I had to make copies. The only place an inmate at Bueny could make copies was in the law library, and that was no easy task. I had to skip work for a day and bring a "miscellaneous money" withdrawal form to pay for the copies. I would need three copies of the motion, which was more than thirty pages in length, and three copies of the appendix, which was an additional ninety pages. It would be expensive, but it would be worth it. After standing in line behind all the other inmates in the law library who needed things copied, it was my turn. I handed the huge document to the guard and told him I needed three copies.

He looked at me blankly and said, "I can only copy fifteen pages for you. Which fifteen do you want?"

What?! I tried not to scream at him. "I need all of this copied. This is my 35(c) motion, and it needs to be filed now."

"There is a fifteen-page limit on 35(c) motions. I'm only allowed to copy fifteen pages for you."

This was amazing. There was no page limit on 35(c) motions. The DOC had just set its own page limitations, and it made no sense; we paid for the copies we made. I demanded that he put that in writing, which he gladly did. He handed me a form that indicated he had offered to make copies of fifteen pages for me but I had "refused" his offer. I needed to find some other way. Fifteen pages wasn't nearly enough of the motion.

And if that wasn't enough, I ran into yet another roadblock. The prosecution had argued to the jury that my mother had red hair and this somehow tied me to Peggy, since she had red hair. My mother did not have red hair, and there was nothing in evidence to indicate she had red hair. I hoped that if I could show this to the court, maybe they would see my point. How could I prove the color of my mother's hair? Serena mailed me a color copy of my mother's driver's license. The problem is that the DOC has all kinds of complicated and sometimes ridiculous rules that aren't made clear to you until you break them. One of these rules prohibits inmates from receiving copies of identification cards. I got the envelope from Serena, but the copy of the card was missing. I wound up having to mail my entire motion to Serena so she could copy it and include the copy of the license and then file the motion for me.

Around this time, the state of Colorado began suffering budget problems. One of their cost-saving measures involved them cutting pay to prison inmates. My pay was cut to sixty cents a day. I was now making less money than when I had first gotten to Bueny. Canteen prices were also raised. This double whammy meant that many inmates had so little money that they had to choose between soap and toothpaste or phone time with their family. A lot of inmates started losing weight around this time as well, since they couldn't afford to supplement their meals with food from the canteen.

37

Maria

IN AUGUST, I STARTED GETTING ANXIOUS ABOUT MY CASE. I hadn't heard from the court one way or the other about the motion in the four months since Serena had filed it, so I wrote a letter to them asking for an update. I got a letter back soon after, telling me that a public defender had been appointed to my case back in May. It was news to me. I wondered: Was this a good thing, that they had assigned me a public defender? At least they hadn't just thrown my motion out entirely. Maybe there was hope.

A day or two later, I was called down to my case manager's office. "You need to call your attorney," he told me.

"I don't have an attorney," I started to tell him.

He picked up a phone and started dialing. "Ms. Maria Liu, please," he asked. He handed the phone to me when she got on the line.

"The court told me they appointed me to your case back in May, but I never heard about you until the court sent me a copy of your letter asking for the status of your case," Maria explained. We talked a bit, and I instantly liked her. She seemed very nice and genuinely concerned about my case.

In Colorado, when a 35(c) motion is filed by a prisoner, a judge reviews it, and if it looks like the motion has merit, the judge orders the Office of Alternate Defense Counsel to assign an attorney to the defendant. In murder cases, counsel is almost always assigned. If one hadn't been assigned to me, I never could have afforded an attorney at this point.

A FEW WEEKS later, Maria came by the prison to meet me, and she brought an investigator with her named Elizabeth Hanson. We went over the motion, and Maria told me which claims were strong and which were weak. She did tell me that my motion was the best motion she'd seen filed by an inmate without an attorney. That made me feel good. After she left, I felt better about my case. I didn't harbor any illusions about getting out any time soon, but at least now it seemed like there was hope. Maria also asked the court for permission to bring aboard a couple more attorneys to help me, considering how complicated the case appeared to be. Soon, I had a legal team. A former public defender from Denver named David Wymore was on board, joined by an attorney who specialized in appellate work and legal writing named Mike Heher.

In January 2004, I got word that a box had arrived for me. It was sent "legal mail" so I had to go to the office and open it in front of a guard. It was five thousand pages of documents from my trial, and it included the documents the prosecutors had turned over to my defense team before the trial. I hauled it back to my cell and began going through it. The first thing I noticed is that it was not organized in any meaningful way. A police report from 1987 would be right next to a report from 1998. It looked like the prosecutors had purposely shuffled the documents to make it harder to use them. All of the pages had been "Bates" stamped, meaning that every document had been numbered sequentially and had been in order at one time. The first thing I did was to take out all the pages and put them in order by Bates number. I immediately noticed that some of the numbers were missing. I made a list of the missing documents and sent it to Maria so she could request them.

Then I sat down and began reading the thousands of pages of documents a page at a time. It was overwhelming. I had never seen most of these documents before. There was so much material that I went through it a second and then a third time. I didn't want to miss anything, and each time I went through, I found more information I had missed before.

The first thing I noticed was how much of the information in the files flew in the face of the prosecution's argument. They must have known that many of the things they had presented to the jury were not true. Within the first few pages, I found a copy of my mother's autopsy report.

I had never seen it before. Right at the beginning it described her as a "Caucasian female with brown graying hair." Not red hair. It was right in their own documents that my mother did not have red hair, and still the prosecution and Broderick had said she did. Then the Court of Appeals and the Colorado Supreme Court had bought it as well.

I was always curious about the autopsy; why on earth was that in the paperwork for my case? I later found out from Wheeler-Holloway why it was there. When she was first assigned to the case, she did not know me and had heard all kinds of crazy things about me and how sick I was—from police officers who had focused on my drawings and stories. Someone floated the idea that maybe I had killed my mother, years before I was accused of killing Peggy Hettrick in a "displaced matricide." Wheeler-Holloway had obtained my mother's autopsy report to see if there was any chance that I might have poisoned my mom.

There were all kinds of nuggets like that scattered throughout the five thousand pages, but I had to dig to find them. A delivery-van driver had seen a female matching Peggy's description at 4:15 in the morning the day she died. That would have eliminated Zoellner's alibi, but no one had mentioned it at trial. There were Merit brand cigarettes all over Zoellner's apartment when the police searched it, in the fireplace and in the trash can. The police apparently didn't think that was important. It was unclear if the cigarettes had been smoked by Peggy or Zoellner; they both smoked Merits.

No one outside of Peggy's little circle of friends ever saw her walking around the area where she was killed. People in her own apartment building said they never saw her walking. The prosecution had made such a big deal about how much she walked around there, and how I must have seen her when she was always out walking around.

Ray Martinez's report admitted he had to phone my father to seek permission to interrogate me at the police station. On the stand, Martinez said that my father was at the police station during that interrogation, when he hadn't been there.

Some of the facts I uncovered were more important than others. I now found the report about the footprints in the field. During the trial, Blair had tap-danced around the issue of the Thom McAn footprints in the field. She indicated there was just one, and it probably wasn't relevant to the case. From the reports it became clear: there were at least twelve Thom McAn footprints in the field. Wagner wrote, "It appears as if this person was running down the hill toward the body from initially the point of the blood splatters of the victim." None of this was told to the jury.

Peggy's roommate told the police that Peggy would sometimes go to bars and leave with strangers when she was "mad" at Zoellner. The night she was killed, Peggy had seen Zoellner with another woman.

There were thirteen unidentified fingerprints on the contents of Peggy's purse.

As I read through the documents, a bigger picture emerged. It was clear that Broderick and Reed focused on me almost immediately. When they saw my knife collection, they stopped considering anyone else as a suspect, even when the facts pointed to others. Zoellner was the last person to see Peggy alive, and they'd had a fight that night. Was that suspicious? Not to Reed and Broderick.

Someone had called in a tip to Crime Stoppers saying that another person in the community had confessed to the crime. Marsha Reed brought the man in and confirmed that he was the one who had made the statement, saying he had killed Peggy. He told Reed that he had gone to school with me and had heard that I had done it. Rather than asking him about what he had told others about his role in the murder, she asked him about me!

I found a letter the police had sent to a plastic surgeon in Fort Collins, asking him how difficult it would have been to perform the cutting that had been done to Peggy and how long it would have taken. It was an interesting question, one I had wondered about myself. There was no letter in response to this one, so I assumed that the police had simply dropped the line of inquiry. Either that or the doctor never gave them his opinion. I was very tense reading through the discovery, seeing the messed-up way in which the FCPD looked at me, but it was particularly hard to read through the interrogation. It had been such a traumatic event for me, such a great cause of grief, that I dreaded going through that section. As I read it, all of those feelings I'd felt in 1987 came back to me. All the stress, fear, and anger of what they'd done. Each time I read through the interview was like reliving it.

38

2005

O NE DAY IN 2005, MY FRIEND RUSTY CAME BACK FROM the gym. He was real close to getting released from prison, only a couple months away, so people were hitting him up for his property. A guy they called Looney had asked Rusty for his wristwatch. Rusty told him, "Nah, I already promised my watch to Tim."

"Tim Masters?" he asked. "Oh, dude, I wouldn't give that guy shit. I've heard bad things about him. I heard he has a fucked-up case. I heard he raped and killed a fifteen-year-old girl when he was thirty-six."

I was only thirty-four in 2005.

This wasn't the first time that sort of thing happened. Another guy named Reese once told me guys were talking bad about me, saying something along the lines of, "I heard he raped and killed a fifteen-year-old." It was unbelievable. My case had been on national television, and they still couldn't get the facts right.

It was so bad at times that a guy from work I had been joking with for more than a year told me one day in the hallway of the building, "I can't rap with you anymore." He didn't elaborate, but I knew what it was about. Someone had told him I was a sex offender. If he didn't want to talk to me anymore, it was fine by me. I figured if he wasn't man enough to decide who he could and couldn't talk to on his own, or if he had to rely on rumors to determine who he could socialize with, then I didn't want to "rap" with him either.

Buena Vista decided inmates had too much leeway walking down the passageways. They placed yellow tape along the floors about two feet from the walls on each side. All inmates had to walk on the right side of the passageway, on the two-foot-wide path between the wall and the yellow tape. This forced us to all walk single file. It was just another tool to dehumanize us. I obeyed their rules because I didn't have a choice, and I tried to keep my head up while doing it. But, inside it killed me to be treated like cattle.

To add insult to injury, once again the powers that be got tired of the inmate head count the way it was, and they figured out a way to make count easier for the guards. They implemented a new rule that inmates now had to stand at their door, displaying their ID cards during count. We had to do this for the 1100 hours, 1600 hours, and 2100 hours count times. I guess I should count my blessings that they didn't make us get up in the middle of the night for the 0100 hours and 0400 hours counts. This new count really screwed up some of the kitchen workers who had to get up at 0300 hours to start breakfast.

Oh, the horrible feeling of waking up in a cage. You know that feeling of disorientation we sometimes feel first thing upon waking? That feeling of, "Where am I?" Often I would wake up in Bueny with that feeling, and when the realization of where I was sank in, I would be overwhelmed with depression. I wouldn't even want to get out of bed.

39

2006

MARIA AND DAVE CAME UP FOR AN ATTORNEY VISIT to Bueny on January 27, 2006. Maria, Dave, Josh Hoban (Maria's investigator), and a crime-scene reconstruction expert named Barie Goetz were going over every crime-scene photo in detail to try and find out what really had happened to Peggy Hettrick. My team was looking at the case with a fresh set of eyes, and they discovered several things that no one had realized before. My attorneys had hired Barie to assist in my appeals. Barie had been the lab director of the Colorado Bureau of Investigations until he retired, in 2004. He had spent twenty-three years at the CBI studying crime scenes, and what he saw when he looked at the evidence in my case startled him. He began investigating the case in earnest, reviewing all of the evidence and interviewing witnesses.

He took one look at the crime-scene photos and noticed the drag trail wasn't really a drag trail. It was a drag and carry trail. We could tell from the police crime-scene photos that she had been carried and dragged. At the beginning of the carry/drag trail, there was blood but no furrows in the ground. That was when two people were carrying her. Then, almost immediately after getting her into the field, the person on the legs dropped them, and there was about thirty feet of drag trail, where Peggy's feet furrowed through the soft dirt. Next, you can see where the person on the feet picked them back up, the drag furrows stop, and the blood trail begins again. Since Peggy was stabbed at the top of her lung, it filled with blood. When her feet were on the ground, she was in an upright position and less blood would leak from the wound, but when someone picked up her feet, the wound was then at the bottom, at a low-enough point for the accumulated blood in her lung to escape. Her jacket had become soaked with blood, so when two people carried her, the coat acted like a paintbrush, wiping big trails of blood on the grass as she passed.

I had always assumed that Peggy had been stabbed in a car right near the curb of Landings Drive because of the blood pool and the bloody trail. I reasoned, along with Broderick and everyone else, that she was still alive and bleeding when the blood pool and bloody trail were created. Maria went on to show me crime-scene photos of the cops moving the body. Peggy had already been dead for some time when police moved her body, but each time they rolled her around blood poured out everywhere. They rolled her onto her side, put a white sheet under her, rolled her to her other side, and pulled the sheet the rest of the way under her. By the time they finished, the sheet was a bloody red mess.

"See, Tim," Maria told me, "she could have been dead for hours already when they dumped her body in that field, and it still would have made the blood pool and blood trail when her body was moved around."

I was amazed. How could so many people, myself included, develop such preconceived notions when it was so obvious what had happened? It didn't take a rocket scientist to figure out why police had never seen the truth. The problem was that police didn't want to take me out of the equation. They knew I was a loner in 1987. If two people carried Peggy's body into the field, that eliminated me. They would never look at this case from a perspective that someone other than Tim Masters was the assailant. That's why, even though they had eleven years to look at the crime-scene photos of the carry/drag trail, they didn't notice the obvious.

As THE ATTORNEYS were getting ready to leave, Dave told me, "Tim, I'm sorry. You got fucked, buddy. I want to apologize."

"What for, Dave?" I asked. "You didn't do anything wrong."

"Because someone needs to apologize for what the system did, and those DAs never will. So I'm apologizing for them."

During my many years of prison, Serena would often send me pictures. At first they were mostly just of Little Mario, but then my other niece and nephew came along, and I'd get photos of Summer and Tommy also. It was bittersweet; I wanted the photos, I wanted to see what my new niece and nephew looked like, and I wanted to see how Mario was turning out, but it also killed me. I got to watch my niece and nephews grow up through photographs with the knowledge that I had no part in their lives.

40

Taylor Marris

IN APRIL 2004, I HAD RECEIVED A LETTER FROM A stranger who had seen the A&E show. Taylor "TJ" Marris wrote to me to tell me that he saw the episode and felt that it was unjust, how I'd been convicted on the basis of the drawings and writing. He told me that he had made a "hit list" as a teenager, listing the people he didn't like. He never acted on the hit list, but now he understood that if something bad had happened to someone on the list and the police had found his list, he could be in prison just like me. TJ offered to help me in any way he could. TJ was an accountant in Denver. I wasn't sure how he could help me, but it was nice to know that not everyone bought into A&E's spin.

I was touched by the offer, because until this point I assumed that most everyone who saw the A&E piece sided with the prosecutors. I wrote him back and thanked him but told him I didn't need him to send me anything since my family was taking care of me. From that point forward, TJ and I maintained a correspondence. He would sign his letters to me, "Stay strong." TJ became an activist for my cause. One of the first things he did was start a website devoted to freeing me. He then paid more than $600 to have the trial transcripts copied. After he did that, he made a copy of them and sent them to me. For the first time, I had a complete copy of the trial to work with. Again, I broke out the yellow legal pad and began working.

TJ and I spoke on the phone quite regularly. The phone calls usually revolved around my efforts to get a new trial and the things I found in the transcripts or discovery that he'd recently given to me. I told TJ about the time Linda Wheeler-Holloway had come to visit me and told me she had doubts about my case.

"What?!" he asked. "Why didn't you tell me about that before?"

"It seemed like she lost interest in helping me after the polygraph came back deceptive."

I don't know how he did it, but he tracked down Wheeler-Holloway's phone number and called her. He spoke to her about my case. She told him that she'd be happy to help but had no idea what could be done at this point. He sent a complete transcript of my trial to Linda after she told him that even though she had testified, she hadn't seen any of the rest of the trial. She knew the outcome of the trial, but she didn't have any idea of how far out of line the prosecution had gone to convict me.

He then spoke to Serena and my family and got pictures of me from when I was younger, to put up on the website. I couldn't believe all the effort he put into the website, and the expenses that he was paying out of his own pocket. And even though I had told him to not send me money, I got a $100 money order from him in June 2004.

That month I also got another piece of legal mail, so I went down and opened it in front of a guard and then took it back to my cell. It notified me that there was going to be a hearing on my case and that paperwork was being submitted to have me transferred to the Larimer County Jail so I could attend. My heart stopped. If I left Bueny for even a day, I would lose my cell. I might even lose most of my belongings, because when I left the cell, they would process me out almost like I was leaving for good. I had managed to acquire a lot of stuff in the six years since I'd gotten here, and I didn't want to lose it. Especially since I'd probably be in and out of court in fifteen minutes. I'd also lose the job I now had—in the saddle shop— and when I got back, I'd have to go through the whole process again, having a cell mate and eating in the chow hall, where the inmates scrapped over who sat where.

I spoke with TJ and told him about how it would turn my whole world upside down if I was brought to Larimer County for the hearing, and he told me he would call Maria and talk to her for me. I spoke with him the next day, and he explained to me that I really needed to be there for the hearing. Maria had told TJ that they had been doing a lot of work on my case, and it would mean a lot to them for me to show up. If I didn't show up, it would all seem like they were doing it for nothing. Wheeler-Holloway had also told TJ that if I skipped the hearing, preferring to stay in prison, it would make me look guilty. That was it; I called Maria and told her to put in the paperwork to get me to the hearing.

A full two weeks before the hearing, the night sergeant came by my cell with the trash bag and said, "Go ahead and pack it up." My heart sank. Once again, the dread was upon me. County jail with its nasty food and sack lunches, being locked down with nothing to do, and most likely being packed into cells with other people—all the bad memories came back to me.

I started packing up my stuff, but there was no way a single bag would hold even half of it. I had clothes, appliances, and a huge box of legal stuff, and by the time I was done, I had a whole laundry cart full to take to property. Then I caught a break. The guard said, "You've never caused me any trouble, so I'm not going to sweat the small stuff." He ran down the list and ignored the DOC rule that said that an inmate could not have more property than would fit into a green Navy duffel bag.

In the end, when I left prison in July 2005, they allowed me to take only my legal documents with me. I wasn't even allowed to keep my watch, or the case for my glasses. Everything else went into storage. There was a woman who had just completed boot camp, and she was traveling back to Larimer County to see if she might be released. The two of us were shackled and handcuffed and loaded into a van. I got the seat in the far back, she got the seat nearest the front. This was only my second trip outside of Bueny since I'd gotten here, the first time out being the trip to the eye doctor's.

MARIA CAME TO visit me in the county jail before my hearing and explained to me what her plan was. The legal process that unwound from this point forward was convoluted and bizarre. Even though I had filed a 35(c) motion, my attorneys saw preliminary issues that needed to be resolved before we even got to the heart of the 35(c) matter. First, we had to get a court order to ensure that the evidence from my case was preserved. Colorado law did not require the state to maintain evidence so long after a conviction, and if they wanted to, they could simply dispose of the evidence in my case. The district attorney's office opposed our request.

The judge who would be hearing my case had been a member of the prosecutor's office that had put me in jail. Maria also thought we should be able to get the judge disqualified from hearing my case because of it. I liked her approach. I always felt that the judges in Larimer County and the entire prosecutor's office were suspect. So, before we would ask the judge to hear the 35(c) motion, we would ask to have him recused from the case. In fact, we sought to have the entire bench in Larimer County recused. It took the judge eight months to make a decision on our request, but he granted it. A visiting judge would be brought in to hear my case from this point forward.

41

Discovery

NEXT, WE SOUGHT DISCOVERY. BEFORE A TRIAL LIKE mine, the prosecution had been required by Colorado law to turn over to us all the evidence they had, whether it helped or hurt my case, so that I could prepare for trial. We now knew they had withheld quite a bit of information, and we suspected there was even more they hadn't told us. We asked the new judge to grant us access to the complete prosecution files in my case and also any documents anyone else in the Fort Collins Police Department might have in my case. We had no idea of the extent of the prosecutor's dishonesty at my trial. My defense team had been provided something like 2,100 pages of discovery for the trial. When the court eventually granted

Maria's requests, we received well more than 10,000 pages of documents they should have given us but didn't.

To travel to court, I had to put on a red jail outfit. This was reserved for the most dangerous inmates, which I was classified among because of the nature of the crime for which I had been convicted. I was also shackled and handcuffed, and now they added a shock bracelet to the mix. A neoprene strap went around my forearm, but it was way too small. It had two metal contacts that would allow an officer to shock me by pressing a remote-control device. Even without being shocked by it, the thing hurt like hell.

They shuffled a half dozen of us out to a van, which I had never seen before. The back of it was a stainless steel cage, and there were benches inside it. There was a Plexiglas window in the front, and small air holes had been drilled in the back. It was like a dog kennel! In that, they took us to the new courthouse, which I had never seen before. The entire lower floor of the building was a holding facility: the courthouse, in essence, had its own jail in the basement.

After a few more hours in the basement, I was finally brought up to a courtroom. When I was led in, I was greeted by a gallery packed with my relatives. Some of them applauded. I nodded greetings to them as I was being led to the defense table, where Maria sat.

"Mr. Masters, turn around. Stop greeting your family." The female deputy leading me to my chair wanted me to just sit down. "If you don't turn around, I'll remove everyone from the courtroom."

I sat down.

After exchanging greetings, Maria told me that the prosecutor's office had agreed to disqualify a judge who had worked in the prosecutor's office during my trial. "So now we need to ask to have the entire district recused because two of your witnesses in the 35(c) motion hearing are fellow judges. You'll have to stay in the county jail until the next hearing."

Maria had no idea what a nightmare the county jail was, but it wasn't her fault. She was doing what she could.

The hearing lasted ten minutes.

In August 2005, local and regional newspapers ran articles about me and my case. It really is amazing how newspapers can spin and twist stories. The *Rocky Mountain News* ran a nice article about Wheeler-Holloway helping me, entitled "Former Lead Detective Comes Forward." Another paper ran an article headlined "Murderer Seeks New Trial." Shortly after, Maria called to let me know that the district attorney had agreed with her that the entire district should be recused from my case, and the matter would be heard by a visiting judge, one from another county. This also meant I'd get shipped back to Bueny after all.

A few other guys were going to be shipped back at the same time as me. As we were getting our property back, they told one guy they had lost his wedding band. He was pissed and said he wanted to stay until they found it. It was pretty clear that the ring wasn't really lost or, at least, they didn't act like there was any chance they were going to find it anytime soon. One of the guards told him he was going to Bueny then, like or not. His only choice was whether he went back in shackles and cuffs like the rest of us or if he went back strapped to a gurney. The guard wasn't joking. The inmate surrendered and went back in shackles and handcuffs like the rest of us.

IN A CRIMINAL prosecution, when the prosecution team turns over all the evidence they have—regardless of whether it supports their case or not—a defendant can adequately prepare a defense to the accusations against him or her. In my case, the nature of the evidence they withheld from us indicated that they knew all along I had not killed Peggy Hettrick. Much of what they kept from us pointed to other suspects, and some of it simply showed how sloppy or misguided their investigation was. For example, we were only given some of Meloy's reports before the trial. We should have received them all. Meloy's reports would have been a gold mine for my attorneys when it came their time to cross-examine him.

42

Barie Goetz

As part of his work investigating my case, Barie Goetz studied Dr. Allen's autopsy and all of the reports created by the people who were present during the autopsy. The morning Peggy's body was found, Allen had gone to the field and seen the blood at the curb and the "drag trail" and had initially examined Peggy where she was found. His first conclusion was that she had been killed somewhere else and then brought to the curb and dumped there before being brought out into the field. He hadn't noted that in his written report, however, because the police had come to the conclusion she had been killed at the curb. His job wasn't to determine where she died, just how. When he first saw the cut on Peggy Hettrick's breast, he told the police who were present that it looked like it had been done by a doctor. Later, when he found the injury to Peggy's clitoris he said, "A doctor did do this." He was so convinced the cuts were inflicted by someone with medical training that he jokingly said, "I hope you guys don't think I did this." What struck him about the cuts was how precise they were. The depth of the cut to Peggy's clitoris never went deeper than the upper layer of skin. At least three different doctors who examined the body or the photos of the autopsy said it was certain the cut was made by someone with surgical training. None of this was ever told to my defense team, even though the autopsy was observed by Jack Taylor and Terence Gilmore, one of the men who would prosecute me for the crime.

Later, even Meloy commented on how difficult the cuts looked to make, and he asked the detectives to consult with a surgeon to see if it was something a fifteen-year-old boy could have done in the dark, by himself, out in a field. We know now that the consultation was made with Dr. Christopher Tsoi, a plastic surgeon, but when his opinion conflicted with the prosecution's theory of the case, they simply ignored him and failed to tell my attorneys about him.

To test the theory about how many people were involved in hauling Peggy into the field, Barie and some members of my defense team went out into a field and dragged Maria around in various ways to see which ways worked and how hard it would be for a single person to do it. Even the bigger members of the group had a hard time hauling Maria around by dragging her. And all of them were stronger than I was when I was a one-hundred-and twenty-pound fifteen-year-old.

Whenever I had made a mistake while talking to the police, they had turned it around and tried to make it look like my mistakes were somehow proof that I had killed Peggy. When I thought her shirt had a number on it, they found some sinister motive in it. I had just glanced at her in the field, and I don't have a photographic memory. Goetz pointed out that the trained police officers and detectives who came to the scene also got many of their facts wrong in their reports. Broderick wrote in his report that Peggy's legs were "spread apart." They weren't; they were closed in the field. Her pants were still above her knees, and we have dozens of photos to prove it. Detective Hal Dean made the same mistake. "Her pants and panties were pulled down around her knees and her legs were spread as wide as possible." What crime scene was he investigating? He also wrote that Peggy's blouse was covering the injury to her breast. Again, that was incorrect; later, the coroner moved her around as he examined the crime scene. When the police first arrived, we know from the photographs that her injured breast was exposed.

Another knife expert, Herb Gardner, had already concluded that the "sawtooth" back of my knife would have cut Peggy's clothing quite differently from how it was actually cut. Gardner had been asked about the injuries by the Fort Collins police. He gave them his opinion, and they simply ignored it. Worse, they never told my attorneys that one of their own experts had ruled out my knives.

Barie also reconstructed Peggy's travels the night she died. The police version of what happened was based on a lot of guesswork, and Barie pointed out where their theory fell apart. According to the prosecution, Peggy had walked from the Prime Minister to Zoellner's apartment and then stood outside for two hours waiting for him to show up. Barie found witnesses who said they saw her around a "Comedy Works" show, at a separate room within the Prime Minister. The prosecution claimed I had seen Peggy when she walked back and forth in front of my house going to or coming from Zoellner's apartment. I never saw her, and the facts don't even put her walking by my trailer that night. For Peggy to walk by my home, whether she was walking to Zoellner's or the Prime Minister, the route by my place was always longer than the obvious route. There were better lighted ways for her to walk, and the walk along Landings would have put her in the road, since much of it had no sidewalk at the time.

One of the more puzzling things we may never know is who Peggy called before she finally left the Prime Minister the night she was killed. Sometime between 12:30 and 1:00 A.M., Peggy made a phone call from the bar. She was no longer locked out of her apartment, so she wouldn't have been trying to wake up her roommate like before. She may have simply been trying to call someone for a ride, but the walk home was only a fifteen-minute walk she'd made countless times before. This was a weeknight. Most people don't make phone calls after midnight unless they are calling someone they know is awake or someone who won't mind being woken up. Was Peggy calling another man, since she was mad at Zoellner? She had the next day off from work.

Barie believed Peggy had been stabbed in a car. After examining the crime-scene photos and the autopsy photos, he noticed that the bloodstain on her back spread out from the knife wound; it didn't just run down her back. It spread out evenly, so he knew it was the result of her bleeding while her back was pressed flat against a surface that pressed evenly over that area. The road surface would not have done that. A car seat would have. He believed she had been in a car and was turning to get out of the car when she was stabbed.

Barie was amazed by the evidence he found in the files about the footprints at the scene of the crime. Michael Swihart and Sherry Wagner had spent the morning photographing footprints out in the field, and then many of the footprints were cast in plaster. At my trial, the police and the prosecutors had told the jury that my footprints were found in several places in the field but that there were no other relevant footprints.

The evidence in the file proved that there were more than a dozen footprints made by a Thom McAn shoe and that there was only one footprint of mine, which was right where I said it would be. Broderick knew about the Thom McAns but hid the evidence from us. Wagner and Officer Gonzalez noticed there were twelve Thom McAn shoe prints, which went from the road next to the blood pool to where the body was left. The two of them even measured the distance between the prints to get a gauge for how fast the person was running or walking. There were also Thom McAn prints along the blood trail. The implication is clear: the man in the Thom McAn shoes helped carry and drag Peggy into the field and then he ran from the body back to the curb, probably because that was where his car was parked.

Much of the shoe print evidence was withheld from my defense, and we only found out about it after Maria and David fought with the prosecutors about it in court. We found in Broderick's notes that he had known all along about the Thom McAn shoe prints along the drag and carry trail. When the police sent the castings and photographs to the FBI for examination, they had only sent them my shoes to compare, and they did not mention to the FBI that they knew some of the prints came from a known Thom McAn. The FBI sent back a report to the police indicating that the only print they could positively tie to my shoes was the one we knew about all along. The FBI said that there were "horizontal lines" in a couple of the other prints, which ruled out my shoes. Those were the Thom McAns. When he got the report, Broderick wrote his notes on it and noted that a third print that somehow the FBI missed also had horizontal lines on it. All of this was withheld from my defense team.

At the time of trial, Broderick knew there were several Thom McAn shoe prints in the field. The jury never heard about them. Sherry Wagner and Francis Gonzalez had both noted the footprints with the "lines" running across them. Wagner was never called as a witness, and Gonzalez simply acted confused by the questions, as if the shoe prints were irrelevant. He answered a question asked of him by Fischer and said, "Specifically, it's this one right here, number 1. That's the only identifiable print that matched the Thom McAn shoe." Broderick knew of more Thom McAn prints in the field. He just knew that if he told the jury that, his case would have fallen apart.

The credit card that had been found under the bridge was also intriguing. It had been reported missing from the owner's home several months earlier, and then it got thrown in the ditch on February 15, hours after the ditch had been searched by police. Near the card were footprints with the telltale horizontal lines from the Thom McAn shoes out by the body. The shoe prints were fresh. The owner of the credit card lived two doors down from the Hammonds on Skysail.

IN THE FALL of 2006, Maria Liu sent a letter to Reid Meloy. In Meloy's report, he referred to an FBI profile that had been created in response to a request made by the Fort Collins PD after the murder of Peggy Hettrick. An FBI profile used by the police in their investigation is something that should have been turned over to my trial attorneys before the trial. My attorneys never received any such profile. During the appeals process, my attorneys had asked the prosecutor's office to provide them with the profile, and they were told over and over again that no such profile existed. They claimed that there was confusion because someone at the Fort Collins PD had simply spoken to someone over the phone and had a phone conversation with a profiler at the FBI. It was all very informal, and that explained why there was nothing to give my attorneys.

After Maria got Meloy's report—and paid $1,000 for it—she found a reference to an FBI profile. According to the report, there was a full report created by the FBI Behavioral Science Unit that ran for several pages. It raised ten points about the killer of Peggy Hettrick and contained quite a detailed analysis. It certainly didn't look like a simple list of notes made during a phone conversation.

It was a few months before Meloy responded to Maria's letter, but he did not deny that a full profile existed. He claimed he lost his copy but suggested that she contact the prosecutor's office. After all, Meloy pointed out, that's who had given him his copy. The prosecution still claimed there was no such profile. This was the kind of thing we ran into time and time again. The prosecutor's office threw up roadblock after roadblock in front of us, denying us access to even the most innocuous things.

43

Remembering
Dr. Hammond

Linda Wheeler-Holloway attended a conference and was approached by Dr. McDonald, the one who would have evaluated me if I had passed the polygraph at Buena Vista. When the topic turned to my case he asked her, "What about that Hammond guy?" Wheeler-Holloway had been a patrol officer for Fort Collins when the Hammond situation came to light, but she hadn't been involved in the investigation directly. As she thought about it, she wondered why my attorneys had not tried pointing a finger at Hammond during my trial. After all, he was a pervert whose bedroom window overlooked the spot where Peggy's body was dumped, and he had surgical skills. Did my attorneys even know Hammond existed? I certainly didn't know. Wheeler-Holloway called the district attorney's office and asked them if they had provided the Hammond files to my defense team, as they were required to do with any alternative suspects. She was told they had not. She asked them why. They had no answer for her.

Wheeler-Holloway began to see the level of misconduct that had occurred in my case. She called Maria and told her what she knew of Hammond, and then she called Kevin Vaughan, a reporter with the *Denver Post*. Vaughan managed to come up with some documents on Hammond, including his autopsy, and he provided them to my attorneys.

Wheeler-Holloway also heard about amazing advances in DNA technology being made by a Dutch couple named Richard and Selma Eikelenboom. She traveled to Holland to meet with the couple and convinced them to get involved in my case.

Later, when we found out about Richard Hammond's strange perversions, we heard that he had gone to a psychiatric hospital and then killed himself. Before he committed suicide, he wrote a letter to his friend Terry Gilmore and waived his right of privacy to those records. He wasn't specific about why he was doing it, but it appeared that he was doing it because he felt he had nothing to hide. Be that as it may, when my attorneys asked the prosecutor to turn over those records of the now-dead Dr. Hammond, they claimed they weren't allowed to turn them over because they were confidential. This, even though he had expressly waived his confidentiality. The prosecutor told the court some nonsense about Hammond waiving his confidentiality in his case but not in other cases. It made no sense; he knew he was about to die. Later, when the prosecutor's office contacted Becky Hammond about the issue, she readily agreed to release the medical records. Without an objection from her, the prosecution had no further arguments to make and finally relinquished the records to us.

Hammond's medical records were enlightening. He admitted that the reason he was at the hospital was not medical in nature; his "Chief Complaint" was he needed a "refuge from the pressures in the media and in the legal system following the revelation that he had secretly videotaped household visitors in the house bathroom and toilet facilities." According to his statement to the hospital when he checked himself in, he had gone to a hotel earlier that day with the intent to kill himself. He had called Becky to say good-bye, and she had talked him out of it. Yet the hospital did not feel he was a suicide risk just a couple days later—when he did exactly what he had started out to do earlier. According to the intake notes, Becky Hammond was "in the process" of filing for divorce—something she never mentioned to the police when they interviewed her. Dr. Hammond claimed he had only been videotaping people for two years, but it was clear by the volume of his video collection that he wasn't telling his doctors the complete truth. The prognosis of the doctor who oversaw his discharge was that he was not at risk of harming himself. Hammond promised to call someone if he had any thoughts of suicide.

One of the problems we faced resulted from the length of time between the crime and the hearings we were having on the 35(c) motion. So many years had passed that some of the evidence had disappeared. This may have been helpful for someone who was guilty, but in my case, evidence that would have helped me was lost. For example, the police had found latent fingerprints on items in Peggy's purse. We don't know for a fact that the prints would lead us to the killer, but we do know that when the prints were first lifted, they did not belong to me, Matt Zoellner, or Peggy. Now, in 2006, we were told that the items bearing the prints had been sent to the FBI. They photographed the prints and sent the items back to the Fort Collins PD. When my attorneys tried to get access to the prints and the photographs, they were told various things. The prints had been "lifted" from the items, but those liftings were lost. The prints had not been lifted but had only been enhanced and photographed. They were still in the possession of the FBI. They were in the possession of the Fort Collins PD. The FBI said they may have lost the photographs. We had to go to court and get a court order forcing the Fort Collins PD and the FBI to at least tell us what they knew about the last-known whereabouts of the prints and the photographs.

It seemed that every time Maria went to court and asked for something from the prosecution team, they would fight her tooth and nail—and lose. The court would order them to turn over more evidence, and once Maria looked at it, she would find even more evidence that the prosecution had failed to produce for us.

44

The DNA Fight

IN OCTOBER 2006, MY DEFENSE SOUGHT TO TEST VARIOUS items for DNA. The prosecution opposed testing any of the items. The only item that had been tested in any way was the cigarette butt found near the curb the day they found Peggy's body, and even that was tested simply for blood type. Since the time of the murder, forensics had come a long way, and the Dutch couple, the Eikelenbooms, believed they could extract DNA from the evidence that had been used at trial. That evidence still existed, but now the prosecutors didn't want to make the materials available to us. My attorneys requested a hearing with the court and even brought in one of the men in charge of the state's legal defender's office. David Kaplan testified about how the state legislature had passed new laws recently, addressing situations like mine. Those who had been convicted and run out of time on all of their appeals could still ask to have DNA tested if it might prove they were innocent.

New methods had been developed in the years since the trial, and the experts from Holland said they could extract identifiable DNA from clothing, and they could extract "touch DNA" even if the clothing was simply handled by someone. Whoever killed Peggy Hettrick had dragged her body into the field from the curb. The experts said that—even though so much time had elapsed since then—they were optimistic they could recover usable DNA from wherever the killer had grabbed Peggy's body to drag it.

To perform this sort of testing, the evidence had to be taken to a laboratory in Holland so the Eikelenbooms could examine it. To ensure the prosecution that nothing inappropriate was done with the evidence, we offered to have Barie Goetz hand carry the evidence to Holland, babysit the examination, and return the materials to the court upon his return.

The prosecution objected to letting us test the evidence this way. They raised all kinds of arguments. My family and TJ went to all of the hearings, and by now I was calling TJ once a week to see what was going on and to chat. When I had a hearing that TJ was able to attend, I would call him that evening to find out how it went. That night after the DNA hearing, when I called TJ, he told me all about what happened.

"You had a pretty good hearing today," TJ told me. He was always so optimistic. "Let me tell you what happened.

It lasted all day long. It was about the DNA testing. The Larimer County District Attorney is fighting us on having the testing done."

That part I already knew.

TJ paraphrased the hearing and told me about the latest person—Cliff Riedel, a prosecutor from the DA's office—to work on my case. "Riedel is claiming some obscure statute that is used for people who have exhausted their state remedies, and he's trying to get the court to apply it in your case. That statute is so tough, it's almost impossible to get DNA testing done if it's applied. But Dave and Maria say the statute has nothing to do with your case since you haven't yet exhausted your state remedies."

Riedel fought our request for DNA testing as if it was the end of the world. He claimed the statute did not allow it. At one point, he even claimed it would be a waste of money. TJ told me how the court granted our motion after hearing the testimony from Goetz and Richard Eikelenboom and listening to the complaints and objections of the prosecutor.

"So it's typical Fort Collins DA trickery?" I asked TJ sarcastically.

"Yep. But the judge is on your side, Tim."

I had to see that to believe it.

"Cliff Riedel started making some argument about how the right to counsel on a 35(c) isn't a constitutional right, so none of your other constitutional rights apply to 35(c) hearings. The judge didn't buy into it for a second."

"Really? Riedel said I have no constitutional rights?"

"Yeah. Riedel also tried to talk the judge out of granting you DNA testing because he said DNA testing is expensive, and he was not going to allow testing to be done on a hope and a dream and waste the taxpayers' money."

An angry thought occurred to me when TJ told me that. "So they want to save the taxpayers' money when it comes to proving my innocence, but when it comes to putting me away for life for something I didn't do, they'll spend a fortune. They'll even hire a psychologist for $300 an hour to interpret my stories and drawing? Unbelievable. What did Dave and Maria say to that?"

"They didn't have to say anything; the judge jumped all over him. He told Riedel that the money comes out of ADC's and public defenders' pockets, not his, so it's none of his business what they do with it."

That was good. Like I said, I didn't buy that the judge was on my side, but maybe we really did have an unbiased judge. The court told us that we would have to sit down with the prosecutor and come up with a written agreement on the precise manner in which the evidence would be tested. Once we had an agreement, we would submit the stipulation to the court, and if the court approved, we would have a court order to follow. Everyone would be on the same page. The prosecutor told the court that he was going to file an appeal to the Colorado Supreme Court, and he asked the court to enter a stay in the proceedings so that nothing could be done with the evidence until the Supreme Court had a chance to rule on the issue. The prosecutor's office insisted that this matter was an emergency and asked the court for a fifteen-day stay so they could file their emergency motion.

They claimed they were worried we would destroy the evidence. They also said they were worried we would find too much DNA—what if someone had sneezed on Peggy Hettrick at the bar earlier in the night, before she was killed? Eikelenboom testified, and explained to the court why none of these objections made any sense. On cross-examination, the prosecutor tried arguing that the jurors had handled the evidence and that any DNA he found could have come from one of them. In this case, he was either lying or mistaken: the jurors had been told they could only handle the evidence if they wore gloves. During one exchange—a hypothetical question about "What if the killer had been a woman?"—the prosecutor boldly told the court, "My evidence shows that Timothy Masters is the one who killed her. That's what my evidence shows."

Eikelenboom was an internationally known wizard in the field of trace DNA. He was often called in on difficult cases, ones where the investigators had come to the conclusion that there was no DNA to be found. He had run tests for the JonBenet Ramsey case in Colorado, and he would later even testify at the Casey Anthony trial in Florida.

At the hearing into whether we were going to be allowed to take the evidence to the Eikelenbooms' laboratory, the scientist had showed the court a PowerPoint presentation about a case he had handled in England. There, a woman was murdered, strangled with her own clothing. When the local police investigated, they could find no DNA to work with and were stymied. Eikelenboom arrived and began using his methods to retrieve trace DNA from places the attacker would have touched the victim. He noted there were twenty places where he thought DNA might be found. Of his twenty targets, he found identifiable DNA in eighteen. Complicating the matter, many of the samples contained DNA from three distinct individuals. Eikelenboom sorted it all out quickly enough: there was DNA from the victim, her partner, and the defendant. Case closed. The key was where Eikelenboom looked for DNA. He would examine a crime scene or a victim and determine where force would have been applied by the perpetrator—someplace that would not likely be subjected to force by the victim or someone else. In the British case, the victim's bra had been pulled by her attacker. The attacker had pulled it in places the victim would not likely have pulled or wrenched the bra herself. Sure enough, Eikelenboom found someone else's DNA there. And, in case there was any question about whose side he would be inclined toward, Eikelenboom pointed out to the court that in Holland, he worked for the government.

At the hearing on the DNA, my attorneys had also asked the court to require the prosecutor to go and get back Peggy's bracelet, which Broderick had simply given away before my trial. The prosecutors argued that the court had no authority to order any such thing. There was a court rule that said that the prosecutor had to turn over to us all the evidence they had in their possession. They now argued that when Broderick gave it away before the trial, it was no longer in their possession. My attorney pointed out to the court that if their argument was correct, the prosecution could simply give away or throw out any evidence they felt like and simply refuse to turn it over because it wasn't in their possession anymore.

My attorneys demanded to find out what had happened with the evidence. During the hearing on the DNA testing, the prosecutor accused Linda Wheeler-Holloway of being the one who released the bracelet to Peggy's grandmother. They were trying to paint Linda in a bad light, knowing she had been supportive of my cause. We called Broderick to the stand to clarify the matter, and he admitted he had been the one who gave it away.

The court ruled in my favor and said he would allow us to test the evidence for DNA. The prosecution immediately announced they would appeal the court's ruling. Arguing that this was a matter of utmost urgency, they filed a request with the Colorado Supreme Court asking for an immediate reversal of the order that had granted the permission to do the testing. The Colorado Supreme Court denied their request.

When word came to the prosecutor's office that their appeal to the Colorado Supreme Court had been denied, Cliff Riedel called Gina Meyer, the court reporter who had transcribed testimony from the hearing. She was also the custodian of the evidence. Riedel told her that the evidence needed to be packaged up so it could be tested. Meyer had no reason to doubt what Riedel told her, since she knew the materials were going to be tested. Meyer packaged up the materials, and a few days later, Riedel came by the court with someone from the police department and retrieved the evidence. Riedel handed Meyer the list of items my attorneys had asked for, and she gave them to him. All along, she assumed it was being done in cooperation with my attorneys. My attorneys did not know that the prosecutor's office was doing this; in fact, my attorneys had not resolved the issues with the prosecutor's office to where we could agree on how the DNA sampling was to be handled.

While Meyer watched, Riedel and the others removed all of the evidence—a piece at a time—from its packaging. Each piece was then photographed and repackaged. Riedel and the others then took the evidence with them and left the building. Later, Meyer testified she believed Riedel and the others were preparing the evidence for my attorneys so it could be sent to Holland for the testing that we had been arguing about at the hearing she had recorded.

Instead, the prosecutor took all of the evidence to a laboratory, and technicians, untrained in extracting touch DNA, collected samples using cotton swabs from all of the places the Eikelenbooms had pointed to as likely locations for usable DNA. They did not bother to run tests on any of the samples they took, which made sense on one level: they weren't qualified to run any such tests. One of the reasons we were taking the clothing all the way to the Netherlands for DNA testing was that the Eikelenbooms had expert techniques for extracting skin cells from clothing, techniques that people in the States didn't have. Many member of the Fort Collins District Attorney's office had just attended a lecture given by Richard Eikelenboom where he told everyone you should not use cotton swabs for extracting this type of DNA because it tends to dislodge the cells, and they are then gone forever. Why did they do this? We thought it looked like they were trying to tamper with the evidence so that by the time it got to Holland, there would be nothing left to test.

We were shocked when we found out what the prosecution had done. Wymore had noted to the court at the previous hearing how fragile the evidence was and that the two sides were going to have to sit down and come to an agreement on how to handle the material so everyone would be able to get testing done. The court had said that both sides could test the evidence for DNA, but the court had not said that the prosecution could do their testing first. My attorneys filed a motion with the court requesting sanctions be levied against the prosecutor's office. At that hearing, the prosecutor had the gall to tell the court that the ruling of the court had been that the prosecution got to test the evidence first! The court had said no such thing. Even so, the court couldn't bring itself to punish the prosecution. The judge stated that the prosecution would have had the right to do their own testing, and if they had asked, the evidence would have been released to them to test. The Eikelenbooms had told the court that cotton-swab testing—like that performed at the CBI laboratory—often damaged evidence and removed what little usable DNA there was on an item being tested.

I was crushed. I could have cried. Even though I didn't get my hopes up too much, they had still been there, and those bastards took this from me. They stole the evidence from the courthouse and ruined it. I was convinced the prosecution had taken the evidence not to test it, but to destroy what little DNA there was on the clothing. I also worried that they had done this to try and plant evidence on the clothing before we sent it overseas. To plant evidence, they would need to make sure no one else's DNA showed up on the clothing, hence the cotton swabs.

I was so angry and depressed that I didn't sleep the next few nights. I was worried they were setting me up. I kept trying to think of an honest, valid reason for them to steal the evidence the way they did, and I couldn't come up with one. I became certain they were trying to plant something on the evidence.

Maria filed a motion with the court requesting that the Larimer County District Attorney's office be recused from the case as well. She argued to the court that the DA's office had deliberately disobeyed the court's instructions on handling the DNA and that their actions were designed to harm my case. The court received the motion but did not rule on it right away.

45

The Evidence Starts to Reveal the Truth

After we found out about Dr. Richard Hammond, we sought all of the information we could find about his case. The more we learned about him, the more we were surprised that we had not heard about him before. When the state prosecutes a criminal defendant in Colorado—and elsewhere for that matter—the defendant is entitled to know of any other viable suspects the police had considered before they had settled on the person they were prosecuting. In my case, the prosecutor had given us a list of other suspects, but Richard Hammond was not on the list. From what we were seeing, he should have been at the top of the list.

We then found out that after Dr. Hammond had committed suicide, the Fort Collins PD had quickly gotten a court order to allow them to destroy all the evidence in his case. Then they continued their stonewalling when we asked for whatever remained of the Hammond files. They sent over files that had all of the names of witnesses redacted. Although it would make sense for them to redact the names of the victims, they took it to the level of absurdity. They redacted the names of everyone involved in the case, including the names of the police officers who had conducted the investigations and written the reports. There was no explanation; they clearly did not want us to be able to follow up on anything in the records. We went to court to get the judge to force them to give us more information. In court, the prosecutor claimed that the redaction of the officers' names hadn't been intentional.

Teresa Ablao, assistant attorney for the city of Fort Collins, claimed the redactions were the result of a change in the computer system where the records were kept. The court asked her directly, "Who did the redacting?"

She answered, "The computer did that on an old version."

The court pointed out that someone had actually gone through the records with a permanent marker. Computers don't use permanent markers. The court ordered them to give us the information we sought.

Barie investigated the Hammond connection to the case as well. He was struck by the fact that Hammond was a surgeon, and the medical examiner, Dr. Allen, had said the cuts on Peggy's body had been made by a doctor. He examined the crime-scene diagrams and looked at where Hammond's house was located in relationship to the body.

One of the things that had puzzled many of us when we looked at the drag and carry trail was how the track went in a fairly straight line until near the very end, where it turned suddenly, as if Peggy's body had been placed in a particular spot for a reason. The police had said it was so I could see it from my trailer, but we know that her body couldn't be seen from my trailer. It could, however, be seen from Dr. Hammond's bedroom window. Barie thought that the person or persons dragging her body may have made the jog at the end of the trail so it could be seen from Hammond's window.

ONE OF THE remarkable aspects about this case, and how the prosecutor's office treated me, was how they treated the evidence—as if they owned it and I had no right to see it or even know about it. During the course of discovery— while I was in prison—Maria saw a reference to the "McLellan Binders." She sent out requests for more information to find out what they were or what they contained. Eventually, she got an e-mail from a Captain McLellan with the Fort Collins police. He told Maria that they had put all of the evidence from the Hettrick murder investigation into binders and had used them as a "prop" in a class he had taught on murder investigation. McLellan told Maria the binders were no longer being used as a prop in the class. They had been given back to Broderick.

Later, at a hearing into other suspects, a list of ninety-four suspects the Fort Collins Police Department had considered was introduced into evidence. Among those listed were Matt Zoellner and Tim Masters. One man made the list because the police caught him driving by and looking at the field where Hettrick's body was found. Several sex offenders were placed on the list even though they were locked up out of state at the time of the murder. It looked like the prosecution had given us an overinflated list to make it harder for us to single out who the viable suspects might have been.

Dr. Hammond was never placed on the list. On the witness stand, Officer Sanchez insisted that Hammond was not a suspect and certainly nowhere near as suspicious as the sex offenders who were known to be locked up out of state at the time of the murder. In fact, there were some outright silly names on the list. When the police wanted to see what kind of shoes made the Thom McAn prints at the crime scene, they went to a local store that sold Thom McAns and found a pair on display that were a perfect match. They asked the salesman if they could take the pair of shoes without paying for them. When the salesman told the officers that he was not authorized to give away the store's inventory, they noted that he was "uncooperative" in their report and added his name—John Gragg—to their list of suspects.

At one point, the judge asked the prosecutor to explain why Hammond wasn't considered a suspect in the Hettrick case. The way he said it let everyone know that the judge thought Hammond was an obvious suspect. We found out now, years after my trial, that the Hammond house had the best view of the field where Peggy's body was found of almost anyplace around. The view was so good that when the police wanted to stake the field out on the second anniversary of Peggy's death to see if anything else might happen there, they asked the Hammonds if they could have an officer sit in the house and watch the field. The officer sat in the Hammonds' bedroom, at 401 Skysail, and watched the field.

John Duval, the assistant city attorney who secured the court order to destroy the property, had expressed concern about how the matter was being handled. Broderick and Sanchez had told him that all of the victims they had contacted had wanted the material destroyed. He had not been told about the ones who had said they wanted to sue. Sanchez and Broderick had also not told Duval that there were underage girls on some of the tapes they had viewed. Simply going off of Hammond's records, twenty-two of the victims had been under the age of sixteen; at least two were thirteen. Broderick and Sanchez had led Duval to believe that the victims were adults and had been given plenty of notice and opportunity to respond to what was happening. Duval also expressed surprise at finding out that the Larimer County district attorney had been conflicted off the case at the time Broderick and Sanchez asked him to file the motion. The representation that Larimer County had no use for the files was deceptive and misleading. If he had known there was a special prosecutor, he would have asked him to sign off on the destruction. It made no sense for the office that was not involved in the case to sign off on it. When pressed on the issue—who at Larimer County made the call to destroy the evidence?—Duval said it was Terry Gilmore.

. . .

AT THIS HEARING, many people heard about Terry Safris for the first time. Safris worked at the Prime Minister, the bar Peggy Hettrick had visited the night before she was murdered. On February 12, 1987, Safris called the police and asked if they could send someone over to her home to take a report. A man had called and threatened to kill her. The police never showed up. Over the next few weeks, the man called a total of six times, often at two and three o'clock in the morning. Although her legal name was Teresa, she went by Terry. The man on the phone addressed her as Teresa. She did not recognize the man's voice, but he threatened to kill her every time he called. He also told Safris that he knew she had a son named Matthew. A few weeks later, she encountered a stranger at the bar who spoke to her; she recognized the voice as being that of the man who had called with the death threat. He had an icicle in his hand and made a stabbing motion at her with it. She did not know him but described him to police as being five feet nine inches tall with an athletic build, green or blue eyes, and sandy brown hair, and he was in his thirties. On that date, Dr. Hammond was thirty-seven and had sandy brown hair and an athletic build. Terry Safris had reddish, strawberry-blonde hair and was in her thirties, which, in many respects, meant she looked like Peggy Hettrick.

When the prosecutors turned over evidence to my defense team before trial, they included a description of the man who threatened Safris but indicated that his name was unknown. They did not divulge the obvious conclusion that Hammond resembled the icicle stabber who threatened Safris.

At this hearing, I got to hear for the first time all about the weirdness with Hammond. The whole story of his perverted videotaping would have been crazy enough, but then to see how he got special treatment from the Fort Collins establishment was astonishing They protected an obvious sex offender and then never told my attorneys about him. Here was a man who lived just as close to where Peggy was found as I did and had surgical skills and a fascination with female genitalia. Now when I remembered Blair asking the jury, "Who else could have done this?" I knew the answer: Dr. Hammond, for one.

ONE DAY, I called Wheeler-Holloway from prison, and she told me she had been doing a little poking around on her own. She spoke with one of the jurors who convicted me, Tom Turner, and she was surprised by some of the facts he had believed to be true. He voted to convict me based upon a few mistaken beliefs. He thought I had written in my stories something about wanting all redheaded women dead. He also thought the "drag" drawing was an accurate description of how Peggy had been brought into the field and that the "boots" in the drawing matched the boots Peggy was wearing. He also told Wheeler-Holloway that someone had testified that I had met Peggy at Albertson's the night she was killed and had seen her walking past my house later. Of course, none of this was true, and nothing like it had ever come out in the trial.

EVERYONE KNEW THAT Reid Meloy was the key to my prosecution. Before Broderick found him, they had decided there was not any evidence to support charging me with the crime. After Broderick met Meloy, he suddenly had enough information to get a new arrest warrant and have me tried for Peggy's murder. Everyone knew that nothing had changed; no new evidence had been found. In fact, Meloy didn't actually bring any new evidence to the table. All he did was claim to be able to look at my drawings and see things in them that weren't there. Since courts allow experts to give their opinions to a jury, Meloy—as an expert—could tell the jury all about his opinions on my drawings. No one else could do that. At the heart of deeming Meloy an expert was the notion that what he was testifying about was science—not just conjecture. Science, as we all know, means things that can be measured and verified by others, and is not biased, slanted, or subjective. Two scientists looking at the same evidence should draw the same conclusion from it, right?

On April 20, 2007, there was another hearing on my case, and TJ called me to let me know it was the best one yet. Earlier, Maria had filed a motion to have the Fort Collins district attorney's office disqualified from handling my case. Among other things, their recent mishandling of the evidence showed they were not following the rules in my case, and their stubborn opposition to getting the DNA tested showed they did not really care about the truth or whether I was innocent.

Barie Goetz continued chasing down leads and speaking with witnesses from the trial. He found Tom Bevel, the blood-spatter expert, and showed him the photographs from the crime scene. Bevel was surprised by how many photos there were; he hadn't been shown all of them. He said that if he had seen all of the photos, he would not have testified as he did at my trial. In his opinion, the photos showed that Peggy was killed somewhere else and her body was brought to Landings and dumped. On top of that, he was upset. Why wasn't he shown all of the photos? In a new report, he said he had "serious concerns and questions" about why the evidence was withheld from him at the time of my trial.

Bevel figured something else out. Peggy had been wearing a jacket and a blouse. The cut in the blouse was an inch and a half over from the stab wound; the cut in the jacket was two and a half inches over. When she was stabbed, Peggy had been turning or twisting away from the person with the knife. Again, this was important because it contradicted the prosecution's theory that I had snuck up on Peggy in a "blitz" attack and stabbed her before she knew I was there. It also matched what Barie had concluded about the manner of the murder.

MARIA ALSO FOLLOWED up on everything she could in the file. She went and spoke with Wynette Payne, the teacher who had taken Serena's Army manual from me. Maria asked her if she had ever known that my father, uncle, and sister were all in the military and that the manual had been published by the Army. Payne expressed surprise and said if she had known those things, she would have testified very differently than she had.

Maria also spoke to my homeroom teacher. She mentioned that the police came by the school every year on the anniversary of Peggy's death and asked her if I was behaving strangely. She told them that I acted normally, and they would leave. This little bit of surveillance was never disclosed to us before, but the teacher was quick to point out to Maria how fond she had been of me. She remembered that on graduation, I had brought her a gift and had been the only student who had done that in her entire career. If she had been called to testify, she would have had nothing bad to say about me. Strangely, Donnie Long— the man who admitted stabbing two other women to death around the time of Peggy's murder—had been in her class years earlier. At one point, he had hidden in her classroom and jumped out from under her desk in an attempt to scare her.

A couple weeks later, the Larimer County DA—Larry Abrahamson—issued a press release about my case. People from his office had been complaining that Maria and my team were trying to use the press to influence public opinion. This was nonsense—hadn't they seen what Blair and Broderick had said on national TV about me on A&E?

Abrahamson's press release was entitled, "TIMOTHY MASTERS—THE PEOPLE'S PROSPECTIVE." I assume he meant "perspective," but even so, it was nonsense. He claimed, "Little has been written or expressed from the viewpoint of the prosecution. . . . because we felt it inappropriate to use the press to influence public opinion." He then claimed, "Every precaution available is taken to ensure that the cases we prosecute are handled justly and fairly and only the guilty are convicted." He knew what they had done to convict me, and it wasn't just and it wasn't fair. And obviously, I wasn't guilty. He also claimed that his office had taken DNA samples simply to help them search for the truth. He didn't mention how they had stolen and tampered with the evidence without the court's permission.

Rather than fight our motion to disqualify, the district attorney's office agreed to be recused. A special prosecutor would be appointed to oversee my case, one who had no connection to it previously. A district attorney from Adams County was appointed. His name was Don Quick.

Barie began assembling all of the information on my case, and he put together a PowerPoint presentation to make it more understandable. At one point, he went through every single photograph from the crime scene and reconstructed the footprint evidence, even though the police had not properly marked or recorded where the various footprints had been found. It was the meticulous kind of police work he had done when he was at the CBI. It was also work the Fort Collins PD hadn't bothered to do. When he was done plotting the footprints on a map of the crime scene, the result was startling. There were footprints—starting at the curb and moving along the drag and carry trail—that were clearly made by one of the people carrying Peggy's body. Then, the same shoes made a straight line back to the starting point by the curb. The shoes were Thom McAns.

At the trial, the prosecutors had argued that there was nothing significant about the presence of the Thom McAn prints in the field and had even told the jury that there were more of my prints out there than they had actually found. Barie pointed out something quite interesting from the footprints that everyone else missed: they indicated the killer or killers likely had a car. Keep in mind that the night Peggy was killed was overcast. It was dark out, almost pitch black. When the killer walked away from her body, how did he manage to walk straight back to his starting point when he had walked away from the starting point in an arching line? When he left her body, he looked up toward the raised road and saw a landmark: his car. Otherwise, there was nothing else for him to navigate by in the darkness.

While studying the shoe print evidence, Barie found some more misconduct by Broderick. In 1996, Broderick had decided to revisit the shoe evidence to see if something else in the field would point to me. There was the one lone footprint I had told them they would find, but Broderick hoped that some of the other shoe prints could be linked to me. He decided to ask the FBI to help. He sent them all of the castings that had been made, and he sent them my shoes. He asked if any of the other castings could be linked to the shoe. Interestingly, he did not bother to ask the obvious follow-up question. If they were not from my shoe, what were they? In 1997, the FBI finally got back to Broderick and told him that the only cast they could link to my shoe was the one they already knew about. Some of the castings were definitely not my shoes. They had parallel lines across their soles. They were from Thom McAns. Even though Broderick had known of the Thom McAns identified in the field previously, he had not told the FBI to see if any of these castings were of Thom McAns.

In his report, Broderick made a handwritten note that the castings with the horizontal lines were all "messed up." Later, at trial, he would pretend he knew nothing of the Thom McAns and he would sit by as other officers and then the prosecutors told the jury about the footprint evidence without mentioning all they knew about the Thom McAns.

46

The Evidence Goes to Holland

IN DECEMBER 2006, WHEN THE JUDGE GRANTED US PERmission to send the DNA evidence to Holland for testing, he had told Barie to escort the materials. Although he was working for my defense team, Barie's reputation was beyond reproach. The district attorney wrote a letter for him to carry with him so he could get the bags of bloody and soiled clothing through security at the airports without it getting contaminated by overzealous TSA screeners. Barie spent eight days in Holland as the Eikelenbooms sampled the items. After he left, it took them six months to come up with definitive answers on what they found. They managed to extract usable DNA samples from all the places they had predicted there would be touch DNA from Peggy's assailants. Maria said they had located more than one

DNA profile, and none of it matched me. I really wanted to solve Peggy's murder. I was convinced that if we couldn't point conclusively at who did it, there would always be a shadow of suspicion hanging over me.

After ruling me out, they kept working. The Eikelenbooms spent the next year doing the painstaking analysis of matching the DNA against known profiles of people who worked on the case or who knew Peggy. The Eikelenbooms found a DNA profile for a male on some of Peggy's clothing in places they suspected her assailant would have touched her. Most notably, they found DNA on the inside of the waistband of her panties and also on the cuffs of her blouse. They started cross-checking it against every DNA sample they had, including those of the police officers and detectives who had worked on the case. If one of them had shown up, an argument could be made that the DNA was simply the result of crime-scene contamination. We all wondered if Dr. Hammond would be a match, but we did not have a sample of his DNA to test. Dr. Hammond had been cremated, but my defense team asked Becky Hammond if she could provide any DNA samples for the Eikelenbooms to test: for example, DNA from their children could be used to possibly rule him out. Becky provided an old envelope that she believed he had sealed by licking the flap. The Eikelenbooms extracted DNA from the sample, but it did not match. We were always curious to know if the envelope really contained the doctor's DNA or not.

Then they got a match. The DNA found on Peggy matched Matt Zoellner, Peggy's ex-boyfriend, who said that he had only talked to her briefly the night she was murdered. Perhaps he could explain the touch DNA on her blouse cuffs; how could he explain the DNA on the waistband of her panties?

I had two more hearings in Larimer County that I didn't attend. Everyone said they went well. Former police officers David Mickelson and Troy Krenning testified at these hearings about how they'd believed I was innocent for years and how they wanted to investigate other people as suspects, but their superiors wouldn't let them.

When I called TJ after those hearings, he was once again in a good mood.

"You had two days of great hearings," he told me. "Troy Krenning and David Mickelson did a great job on the stand. It felt so good for us to hear someone who used to be a Fort Collins police officer talk about how ludicrous your conviction is."

ON JUNE 5, Miles Moffeit from the *Denver Post* came up to Bueny to continue interviewing me for a story he was working on about my case. He had come up one time before, and this time Paula Woodward, from Channel 9 News, also came and brought a film crew. I was so nervous about being on camera that I was convinced I'd done horribly. After the A&E piece though, I was just hoping for a balanced story. At the time, hoping for a "pro-Tim" piece felt like asking too much.

Around this time, Linda Wheeler-Holloway got fired from the coroner's office. She had gone to work at the

Larimer County Coroner's Office after she had retired from the CBI. She had been working with Dr. Allen there. TJ told me about it. We believed it was because of her involvement in my case.

During our fight to get ahold of all the files on my case, we found out that Meloy was far from being unbiased or scientific in his approach to this case. When he was first consulted, he was asked if he was willing to go out on a limb and say that my drawings proved I killed Peggy Hettrick. Meloy said he would be happy to do it. In fact, he wrote a letter to the prosecution in February 1999—again, we did not see this letter until almost a decade after the trial—congratulating them for getting the court to allow him to testify as an expert. He said he hoped his efforts would "result in a successful prosecution."

Meloy did more than simply study my drawings and render an opinion for the prosecution. He visited the crime scene and wrote reports where he gave his opinion on how the crime was committed, and he even suggested courses of investigation for the police. If he had been a crime-scene expert, this would have made sense. Meloy was a psychologist, however, and had no expertise in interpreting crime scenes. One suggestion he made to the police had to do with the two mutilations found on Peggy Hettrick's body. The police had concluded that I had done this in the open field, in the dark. Meloy wondered if an expert would agree with this theory. Why he thought of it and not the police, we don't know.

Following Meloy's suggestion, the investigators had sent the autopsy photos to a plastic surgeon named Dr. Christopher Tsoi and asked him some specific questions. How long would it take someone to make the cuts found on Peggy's body? Tsoi offered his answers and included some detail. For example, the person who did the cutting was right-handed. Tsoi could tell because of the way the nipple had been cut. He said the cuts were made with "high-grade surgical-quality steel" and that the cut to Peggy's clitoris would have been a "hard cut" to make, even for an experienced plastic surgeon like Tsoi. Under proper conditions and using the skills of a surgeon, Tsoi said the two cuts could have been done in six minutes. Because the information Tsoi gave them contradicted their theory, they decided to not give it to my attorneys before my trial.

It is important to remember that in Colorado, the prosecutor's office is under a duty to provide the defendant with all evidence they have—good or bad—before trial. This is not optional; it is required by law. When the prosecutor and the police chose to hide this information from my attorneys, they were doing so in an attempt to convict me unfairly. Their own expert said the killer was right-handed. I am left-handed. Rather than tell the jury what the real experts thought, they hid Tsoi from us and didn't call him as a witness. Instead, they just called the coroner, who was not as experienced in surgery as Tsoi. By the time of closing arguments, the prosecution was telling the jury that the killer was left-handed, even though they knew their plastic surgeon had said he was right-handed.

Tsoi would have been a gold mine for us if we had known about his consultation with the police. During the fight over a new trial, we became aware of Dr. Tsoi. Maria sent an investigator out to talk to Tsoi to see what he had told Marsha Reed about Peggy's injuries and to see what he thought about the murder in general. Later, when we revealed what we had found to the court, some attorneys from the district attorney's office ran over and questioned Tsoi about what he had told the investigator. Did he remember being consulted by Reed? He told them he remembered the photos of Hettrick vividly.

He looked at the autopsy and crime-scene photos and drew another conclusion that contradicted the prosecution's theory. When Peggy was found in the field, her pants were pulled partway down and her legs were together. Tsoi said that her killer could not have excised her clitoris with her pants in that position. He said that her legs had to be splayed—he called it "frog legged"—so that the killer could maneuver the scalpel to perform the cut the way it was made. Tsoi believed that her pants were then pulled partway back up after the cut had been made. All of this pointed to the killing and mutilation taking place somewhere else—these things did not happen in the field, according to Tsoi. If they happened elsewhere, it would have proved I couldn't have done it. The killer used a car to bring Peggy to that curb by the field after he had stabbed her and mutilated her body. I didn't own a car, wasn't old enough to drive, and even the police knew that the use of a car would rule me out as the killer.

47

The Media Becomes Involved

O N JULY 13, 2007, THE *ROCKY MOUNTAIN NEWS* RAN AN article about my case, written by Kevin Vaughan. The article was a bit middle-of-the-road in that it didn't come down on my side or the prosecution's. It left out a lot of stuff, but Vaughan wasn't in the loop either. We had decided early on to give Miles Moffeit exclusive access to me and whatever material we could give him so he could tell the story right. Even though the Vaughan article wasn't pro-Tim, it was enough to get people questioning my conviction. After the article came out, I got a lot of positive feedback from inmates at Bueny, including some who had never spoken to me before.

The *Denver Post* and Channel 9 had been planning on holding their coverage of my story until a later date, probably so they could include all the latest-breaking legal developments, which seemed to be coming fast and furious now. When the Vaughan article came out though, they pulled the trigger. The *Denver Post* article ran on the front page of its Sunday edition, July 14, 2007. It was entitled, "Sketchy Evidence Raises Doubt." Miles Moffeit had reviewed all the legal documents he could get his hands on and spoke with as many people as he could. He talked to Wheeler-Holloway, and he talked to Broderick. He talked to me, and he talked to TJ. He sat through every single court hearing. He then condensed it all into a feature article that spelled out my case. He made it clear that when someone examined the evidence of the Hettrick case, it didn't point to me. Broderick had told Moffeit I was the one who killed Peggy Hettrick. He said he was certain of it. He also said that convicting me of the murder was the high point of his career.

Later, Moffeit followed up this article with some others on how the state of Colorado handled evidence and had trouble dealing with DNA. After his articles came out, he got a visit from "authorities" who were upset with his reporting. The authorities went so far as to demand a sitdown with Moffeit and his boss, to express their displeasure. When other news outlets reported the confrontation, Moffeit and his boss confirmed that the meeting took place but would not give details. They clearly did not back down, however.

Paula Woodward's news piece ran that Sunday night on Channel 9. Now that the information was out in the open, I wrote up a list of our newest discoveries and mailed it to

TJ. I had to handwrite the list because my typewriter had died on me, and it would take me another month to replace it from the catalog.

After the news coverage over that weekend, everyone seemed to think I was getting out of prison. Inmates congratulated me, but I had to tell them I was far from being freed. Linda Wheeler-Holloway—who had told my family at one time that I had a "snowball's chance in hell" of getting out—even told me, "You're outta there, Tim." Don't get me wrong; all of the attention was better than the alternative, but I had learned to not get my hopes up. My lawyers thought like I did: hope for the best but expect the worst.

Maria, Dave, and Barie went to the Adams County District Attorney's office in August 2007 and gave them a presentation, showing all the evidence that pointed to my innocence. Don Quick had just been appointed special prosecutor, though, so it wasn't likely he would just roll over and grant me a new trial so quickly. Still, it was good to let the new guys know what they were actually dealing with.

MEANWHILE, I WAS still sitting in prison, where the food situation steadily declined. During my last year in prison, they began substituting soupy, powdered cheese for the real shredded cheese they had been using. They saved a lot of money by doing this because powdered cheese was much cheaper than real cheddar, and they could cut the powdered cheese with flour to make it go further. I love cheese, so this was especially sad for me. The Thanksgiving meal that year was the worst one yet. However, I took solace in the knowledge that it was probably better than next year's dinner was going to be. The one thing I could count on was that, as time passed, things would always get worse. My first Thanksgiving in Bueny, there had been good food that filled two trays. Even in 2004, we had a tray of food and a Styrofoam tray of desserts. Thanksgiving meals now fit on one tray.

DURING A HEARING on December 20, 2007, a woman approached Josh, Maria's investigator, in the hallway and said she wanted to talk to him about the case. They found a quiet corner to talk, and the woman told Josh she was currently living in Dr. Hammond's old home, on Skysail. She said that Broderick had come by her house recently and asked if he could come into the house to see what the view looked like from their bedroom window. He wanted to look at the field where Peggy's body was found. She was put off by Broderick's demeanor and told him no. He left but called a little while later. He wanted to know if she was willing to go stand where Peggy's body was found and aim a laser pointer at her bedroom window to determine if there was a direct line of sight to the body. She found this request even stranger and said no. She told Josh that Broderick got upset with her and said that he planned on doing his laser test regardless of whether she liked it or not. She actually told Josh she was scared of Broderick, because he was aggressive and overbearing. She found his approach "creepy" and had since boarded up the window that Broderick wanted to look through.

Josh duly noted all of this and passed it along to my attorneys and the prosecutor's office. Obviously, there was a concern about Broderick trying to intimidate potential witnesses.

MY LEGAL TEAM and family members were now so optimistic and so confident that they'd almost shaken my eternal pessimism. But optimism never lasted long when you had to look out of your cage through those cold steel bars. Once my cage door slammed shut, I would again feel depressed, angry, and so damn sick of that place. It was taking every ounce of self-restraint not to snap. I felt like I was walking the razor's edge, trying to keep my sanity, trying not to snap at other inmates or the guards, and trying to put up with all the legal bullshit we kept coming up against.

48

Back to County for a Hearing

THE NIGHT BEFORE A TRIP TO THE LARIMER COUNTY Detention Center, on August 20, 2007, I slept worse than usual. I spent the night wondering what was going to be in store for me the next day. Was I going to get stuck with a messed-up celly? Was I going to end up in a holding cell and intake for three days? How long would I have to hold my pee between the prison and county jail? Were they going to stick me in the hole again? Would I get back into North Unit when I got back? Would I end up in the South or East Unit instead? Would I end up in a fight over a chow-hall table? I was well aware that my current housing unit, filled with all single cells, was mainly a protective-custody unit, and I wasn't there on protective custody. They could bump me at any time to make room for someone with issues. Many questions would run through my mind.

I didn't like going back to county for hearings because of all the worry and hassle. But there had been so much publicity in my case recently that I had no choice but to go back for the next hearing. I never knew the exact day they would come pick me up until the night before, when the unit guards would tell me, "Pack it up."

The night before my trip, I packed up all of my property and left it in a laundry basket in a storage room we had. That part was bad, because I had no clock, no fan, no TV, and no radio to occupy my brain the night before. I was just stuck in an empty cell, with no way to drown out all the prison noise. Once I finally got to sleep, I would dream for about four hours, wake up, and sleep on and off for the next few hours, wondering what time it was and how long I had left to sleep.

That morning, when the cell door opened for breakfast, I went to chow. Just like in 2005, I ate but didn't drink anything because I did not want to be stuck halfway between Fort Collins and Buena Vista with a full bladder and nowhere to pee.

After chow, the unit sergeant, Miss Woods, told me to bring my bedding down and wait on the first tier until work lines were finished. Then a unit guard and I rolled the laundry cart full of my property down the stairs and all the way across the facility to the main property room, where my stuff would be stored until I got back from court.

Next, the unit guard dropped me off in "Receiving" where I was put in a holding cell by myself. I brought my 35(c) motion with me; we were allowed to bring only legal work with us when traveling to the county jail. I lay on the concrete bench in the holding cell reading over my motion again. I noticed a few mistakes that I'd made because I had not had my trial transcripts or discovery when I'd written the motion.

About an hour later, they started bringing other inmates in who were being transported to various jails and facilities. In groups of twos and threes, they were put in my cell. The next thing I knew, the empty holding cell was packed with people. The guys who knew each other were chatting away. I didn't know anyone, so I stayed quiet. I had become pretty quiet anyway by then. All those years of being a societal pariah in prison had made me very withdrawn. I didn't want to make new friends with any of them. I was probably just as quiet as I had been as a kid.

Around 11:00 A.M., various county deputies began arriving and taking people out of my cell. They would come into the facility in pairs, the prison guard would holler "Mesa County" or whatever county had showed up, and take inmates out. I kept waiting to hear "Larimer County," but it didn't come. Jackson County came; Arapahoe County came, but still no Larimer. Jefferson County showed up, and the receiving guard opened our cell door and hollered "Jefferson County, your ride's here."

The cell emptied out as the other six guys who were there with me left, on their way to Jeffco.

"I hate waiting in that damn holding cell at Jeffco," I heard one guy say. "It takes forever to get processed through there."

"Did you hear? The food is so bad they just gave the inmates there food poisoning," a different guy asked.

"No shit!"

"Yeah! I just read in the paper over twenty guys had to get medical attention for food poisoning."

As I listened to the horror stories about Jeffco, I thought to myself, *Man, I'm glad I'm not going to that hellhole. Larimer County is bad, but at least it's not as bad as Jeffco.*

And then the hammer fell.

"Masters!" the receiving deputy said "Come on out, you're going to Jeffco."

My heart sank. They wanted to send me to the hellhole I'd just heard those guys talking about? There must be some mistake!

"What?" I exclaimed. "No, I'm going to Larimer County."

"Nope, you're getting a courtesy ride to Jeffco."

Larimer County would be picking me up when I get to Jeffco. At least I wouldn't be stuck in that hellhole long.

The Jeffco guards strip-searched us all, then shackled and handcuffed us.

Luckily, the guys I was going to Jeffco with were smart enough to get us sack lunches before we left, because Jeffco feeds their inmates even worse than Larimer County, and Larimer starves you. We loaded into a crowded dog kennel of a van in shackles and handcuffs and ate our sack lunches that way. It takes some skill to eat with shackles and hand-cuffs on.

That van was a nightmare. From the outside, except for the Jeffco badge and police lights, it looked pretty much like a normal, full-sized van. From inside, the back of the van had been converted into a cage similar to the Larimer County Sheriffs dog-kennel van they had transported me to court in for my 2005 hearing. This one had three metal benches; two running front to back along each side, and one at the front of the cage going from left to right. The windows had been covered with plate metal. There were two-inch-diameter holes, so to see outside you had to peek through these little holes. I wouldn't get to do much sightseeing riding in that van.

It seemed like I had just settled in for the long ride to Jeffco when we pulled off the road in the tiny town of Fairplay, Colorado. We were stopping at the Park County Jail.

I was hoping we were going to drop off some of the people in the van. It would be a more pleasant trip if the van wasn't so crowded. That wasn't the case. The deputies went inside the jail to pick someone up.

We didn't just pick up one guy; the deputy came out leading five more inmates, and they all crowded into the dog kennel. We were shoulder to shoulder, packed like sardines for the three-hour drive down the mountains. It was a long, hot, cramped ride. One of the guys in the van with us almost immediately became carsick and just barely kept from vomiting.

Before we were halfway down the mountain, my legs

started cramping up from being in the same position too long. Next, my butt started hurting from sitting on the steel bench. I'm not normally a claustrophobic person, but stuffed in the back of that van the way we were, about an hour into the drive I just wanted to scream my head off and yell, "Get me the fuck out of here!" But there was nothing I could do. Freaking out would do me no good. In nine and a half years, that was the worst ride they ever put me through.

We arrived at Jefferson County Jail and spent hours in a first-floor holding cell, where they began the booking process. They gave us all sack lunches there; the food was just as bad as the guys at Bueny had said. One by one, they pulled guys out of there to send upstairs to the second part of that facility's booking process. But every time it cleared out of people, they managed to bring some more in. I was there long after dinner and had to eat another sack lunch of the same nasty stuff. The holding cell was about twenty feet by twenty feet, with a TV in one corner and concrete benches along the walls. In the middle of the holding cell was a block formation with a sink and urinal built in. I was not going to use that open toilet in a room packed full of people. My life had been reduced to a series of concrete blocks and steel doors.

I did eventually get one of the deputies to let me use a single holding cell to go to the bathroom.

After the sack-lunch dinner, they moved me upstairs to the booking area of the jail. They fingerprinted me, took my picture, and dressed me out in a pair of Jeffco orange coveralls. That was my first clue that Larimer was not coming for me that day. The deputy dressing me out asked me, "You're Tim Masters? You were in the paper today. Made the front page."

That was news to me. I hadn't known. I never did get to see that article.

Once in the booking area, I was directed to yet another room, although this one was more open. The same guys who had been downstairs with me were waiting in that room. They had been taken out of the downstairs holding cells hours ago, and they were still up there waiting to get a cell? That was not a good sign.

At around 11:00 P.M. they finally took me up to intake and assigned me to a cell. If I had been in a bad mood before, it was nothing next to the sour turn my mood took when I saw my rack. Jeffco was so overcrowded that they were putting two men in cells designed to be singles. These cells were too small to fit two beds into so I got stuck in a "boat" on the floor of the cell. The "boat" was just a plastic container that was almost big enough to hold a thin mattress.

It's like the whole system is designed to break you. Break you, that is, if you're too poor to make bail. They torture you by taking forever to book you, and then they put you in a hellhole, feed you garbage, and make life such hell that you'll take a plea bargain just to get out of the county jail.

The guy I was celled up with was the guy who had gotten carsick on the ride down. He only got out of his rack to use the toilet and to eat. I never saw anyone sleep as much as he did. That was fine by me, though. I didn't want to make any new friends. They would surely want to talk about my case, and I didn't trust anybody.

I spent the next morning and part of the afternoon lying on the floor "boat" bunk reading books that I could not care less about. Larimer County didn't show up until about two in the afternoon. I never thought I'd be glad to be going to LCDC, but after that one night in Jeffco, I was looking forward to it.

The booking area at LCDC was unlike any other booking I've seen. It had comfortable chairs, rather than concrete benches, and carpeted floors. There was a bathroom off to the side with a door you can close for privacy. Up along one wall were three telephones with free local calls. It was too bad I could not remember my family's phone numbers. I had been using the DOC phones so long that everyone's phone was just a two-digit number to me. Uncle Lloyd was 11, Serena 13, Melvin 17, Aunt Betty 18, Aunt Juanita 16, Uncle Johnny 14, and so on.

There were about ten of us in that room waiting to be booked. They all seemed to know one another. Everyone had their little conversations going on. They mostly talked about the drug scene and partying in Fort Collins. It seemed such a shame that all these resources and lives were wasted on drugs.

The guards didn't like inmates eating out on the carpet because it tended to get very dirty from dropped food, so around 5:30 P.M., they put the men into one large holding cell and the women in another cell and fed us sack lunches.

I opened my sack lunch to find that LCDC lunches had gotten even worse since 2005. It was even worse than

Jeffco's! Now, all we were getting was a thin slice of mystery meat on a homemade blob of bread, an orange, a sugar cookie, and a carton of Robinsons Orange drink that had "Made with no real fruit juice" proudly written on the carton.

It was boring as hell in that holding cell, and they decided to keep us in there for the rest of the evening. One guy in there had already been in booking for more than twenty-four hours. He looked exhausted. I had no idea how long I would be in there. I just hoped I wasn't also in there for twenty-four hours.

At around 11:00 P.M., they finally took me to the back to shower and dress. This time they dressed me in regular LCDC oranges. They didn't "red tag" me. That was good. When you were red tagged, you had to be in handcuffs and shackles wherever you went within the facility.

Upstairs, I signed the normal new-guy paperwork. I was issued a set of bedding—which included sheets; a small, thin blanket; and a mattress cover—and was given a spork for my meals and a foam cup because they had no more regular coffee cups left. I grabbed two cheesy books off the book rack in the conference room and strode off to my new cage. When I looked at the clock, it was after midnight.

I quickly made my bed and crawled under the blanket, still shivering from the shower I'd taken downstairs. I slept for about four hours. Then I catnapped on and off. I'd forgotten how much it sucked being in a cage with the light on all the time. My stomach was grumbling already. I was starving. It felt like déjà vu. I was already dreaming about a big bag of Tostitos and other foods to munch on. I wondered what time it was and how much longer until breakfast. I had no way of knowing since I couldn't see the clock from my cell.

Finally, all the lights came on in the cells, and they began serving us breakfast. One by one, our cell doors opened, and we would go to the main door of the pod and be handed a tray through the food slot. We could put our coffee mug down in the slot and get a cup of coffee if we wanted it. For breakfast that day I had some terrible-tasting sausage, cornflakes, applesauce, coffee cake, and a carton of milk. I normally never ate junk food like coffee cake, but during my stays in county I ate every last scrap of food off the tray. Everything gets eaten, or you go hungry. Even after eating everything, I went hungry. I always came back from county jail thinner than I arrived.

That first day in the hole, I had nothing to do but exercise in my cell and read. I finished my first book and started the second.

Court was on August 23. That morning they escorted me down to transportation right after breakfast for my ride to the courthouse. They brought a bunch of us down there about an hour before we were actually leaving for court. There were numerous holding cells near the sally port where they kept us prior to leaving. Even though I didn't have court until 10:30 that morning, I had to be there first thing in the morning with the rest of the guys who had court. I was no longer red tagged as I'd been in 2005, but because of my life sentence, they still took me to court in the high-security dog-kennel van with a zapper on my wrist. I was the last one down there because my housing unit was the farthest away, so I got stuck with the last available wrist zapper, which was way too small for my wrist. It was so tight that my hand was numb by the time I got to court.

It was very crowded in the dog-kennel van since there were so many of us going to court that morning. Down the streets of my old hometown we went. I could see some scenery through the air holes in the sheet metal. We drove right past my Aunt Juanita's house, and it killed me that we were so close to my family and I could not stop to visit them. At least people couldn't see into the van. They could not stare at us like we were circus animals.

We pulled into the basement of the courthouse and shuffled inside to a twenty by twenty holding cell. I staked out a spot on the concrete bench and sat down for the long wait until my court time.

Over the next few hours, they would pull guys out one by one for their court appearances. Most were gone no more than a half hour; then they were right back in the holding cell waiting. A common theme was: "They're offering me such and such plea bargain; should I take it?" There were a lot of questions about what prison was like. Unlike some people, I would tell them the truth. Very few people were raped in Colorado DOC, unless they were celled up with a predator, and people were not getting shanked every day. The gangs were bad, and people were beat down in prison, some to the point of brain damage and death, but for the most part, prison was better than the county jail.

I met a funny guy in that holding cell. He came across as totally crazy. I don't know if it was an act or not, but he claimed to have broken into a house, laid down on the kitchen floor, and told the people who lived there he was sucking the energy out of the ground. He claimed that he saved their lives. He thought he was a hero. If he hadn't sucked out the energy from that house, it would have built up until it exploded, probably killing them all.

By the time I got up to the courtroom, my wrists and ankles hurt from the cuffs digging into them. Inside the courthouse it was a media circus. When I walked in the room, I could hear cameras clicking everywhere, and flashes lit up the place. I think I got an instant tan from so many flashes. My family stood up and clapped. It took me a second to realize it was my family clapping; for a second I had thought people were clapping to see me brought into the courtroom in prison orange, handcuffs, and shackles. The deputies uncuffed my left hand, and I sat down at the defendant's table next to Maria. She looked a little sad about something. That was when she told me the bad news about TJ.

"TJ tried to commit suicide. He's been charged with sex assault on a child."

49

Bad News

I GOT BACK TO BUENY ON FRIDAY, AUGUST 25. LCDC MUST have wanted to get me the heck out of there because of the media attention. In 2005, they had taken their time getting me back to Bueny. This time, they rushed me off, driving me back all by myself.

Back at Buena Vista, I spoke to TJ on the phone, and he did not sound good. Usually, he was totally upbeat, but this time, he sounded like the weight of the world was on his shoulders. He was so depressed over the charges. In the nearly three years of weekly phone calls with him, I had never heard TJ sound so down.

He told me all about his stay in the Jefferson County Jail. I was now familiar with that jail. It was not a fun place to be. After just one day in there, TJ said he couldn't imagine how I endured the years in jail and prison. He told me he didn't think he could do it.

That kind of talk worried me. Taylor had been suicidal for a while. He had gone so far as to put a noose around his neck. But he never went through with it. Something always kept him from ending his life. I remembered how I didn't care whether I lived or died while I was enduring my trial, and I was worried that this would be the kind of thing that would push him over the edge and make him actually go through with it.

"They showed up at my work and arrested me," Taylor told me. I could imagine how he felt. How degraded he felt, being handcuffed in front of his coworkers. "They led me out of my office in handcuffs, for all of my coworkers to see. Then they put me in a filthy holding cell in the Jefferson County Jail with a bunch of other people. They fed us this nasty lunch with a disgusting sandwich in it. I didn't eat mine; I gave it away. I was so nervous that I couldn't eat anything. I was in that cell with all these thugs; I don't know how you do it, Tim."

He kept telling me that. He kept telling me he didn't have the strength to endure the kinds of things I had. And I kept telling him he was wrong. He did have the strength to endure it. If he didn't do the crime, he had to keep fighting, no matter what they put him through.

"What if they convict me?" he asked. I could tell he was very near tears, and my heart poured out to him. I was understanding a little of what my family had gone through while I went through this. It hurt being so helpless to help my friend.

Taylor was traumatized by his night in jail. Jail is not a fun thing, so I completely understood how he felt. But I was adamant that if he really didn't have anything to do with what they accused him of, he needed to fight it to the bitter end, no matter what happened to him.

"I could lose everything I have," he told me. He couldn't help but cry now. "I can't do it, Tim. I can't spend years in prison. I won't make it."

There was nothing I could say. I wanted to lie to him and tell him there was no way he would be convicted. But I couldn't. If TJ had an accuser coming forward saying he had been sexually assaulted, there was a good chance TJ would be convicted. All I could tell him was that he had to fight these charges. He couldn't just give up.

On October 15, 2007, I was working in the saddle shop. It was near the end of the day when my boss, Duncan, called me into the office and told me, as he made out a hall pass, "Your lawyer wants you to call her. You need to go back to your housing unit."

I rushed back to the unit. As soon as I got up the steps, I went right to the phone and called Maria.

"I've got some bad news for you, Tim," she said in a sad tone. "Taylor committed suicide last Monday."

It was like a slap to the face. I was torn up. My best friend, TJ, committed suicide—plus, I hadn't known until four days after the fact. I felt like bawling my head off. I wished I could still cry like I could as a child, but the tears wouldn't flow like that anymore.

I was in shock. I wanted to be furious at TJ for leaving me like that, for not fighting on. But I couldn't be. I understood, like few others would, why he did it. TJ had been accused of a sex crime and was facing long prison time, followed by lifetime parole and registering as a sex offender. Knowing the system the way I did, I thought there was a strong likelihood TJ would have been convicted. TJ knew this. So he killed himself rather than endure it all.

I couldn't even grieve properly because I was in prison, and I couldn't show weakness in front of other inmates. It's likely I would have spent the rest of my life locked up in prison if TJ had not come along. He saved my life, but I could do nothing to save his.

IT SEEMED LIKE we had an endless series of hearings at the end of 2007. I was out to court again real close to Christmas, from December third to the twenty-fourth. This trip they took me straight to LCDC. Thankfully, there were no side trips to Jeffco. When I arrived at LCDC, they put me in a holding cell with someone who thought his "life was over" because he got a DUI. Why did they always put me in cells with these people? Because I was in DOC greens, it was obvious that I was already serving time, so after he vented to me for a while, he asked me how much time I had.

"I'm serving life."

He didn't feel so bad about his DUI after that.

Maybe that's why they always stuck me in cells with those guys, to make them feel better about their petty DUIs.

We were supposed to have court on Friday, the day after

Christmas, but the Adams district attorney wanted more time to go over the evidence with Blair and Gilmore. I was wondering what kind of concoctions they were coming up with now. If my trial was any indication, they would be spinning some fantastic yarns! How would they blur fantasy with reality this time?

After a week into my stay at LCDC, they wanted to move me to General Population. I refused to go because I did not want to be surrounded by fifty inmates awaiting trial or plea bargains, all asking about my case. There was too much potential for one of them to make up a bogus confession story about me in the hopes of getting a reduced sentence for themselves.

To retaliate against me for refusing to move to GP, they would not grant me library privileges. Other inmates in Segregation were allowed to go to the library, but not me. They told me, "If you want to go to the library, move down to population." Move to GP, where they have a hundred snitches ready to make up stories about how I'd confessed to them. No thanks.

Before I returned to Bueny, Dave apologized to me, telling me, "I'm sorry, buddy, I was hoping to have you out before this Christmas."

That was news to me. I had still expected this fight to go on for several more years in the Colorado District Court, Appellate Court, and State Supreme Court.

My defense team had been very hopeful that the Adams County DA, Don Quick, would concede our motion on discovery rule violations. However, he didn't, and if the recent newspaper quotes by Quick were any indication, it didn't look like he was going to concede anything, even though it was pretty obvious that the FCPD and Larimer DAs did not disclose all the evidence to me.

They drove me back to Bueny on Christmas Eve. I marveled over Dave's words about hoping to have had me out before Christmas. That didn't happen, but it was exciting to think I was that close to getting out. I thought about how wonderful it would be to be a free man and all the things I would do.

Still, I was back in prison as 2008 rolled along. The first few years of the hell that is prison I had dreams all the time about being free. I would dream I was back at my own home in Ridgecrest, or living in the duplex I rented while I was still in the Navy, before I'd bought my own home. By 2007, most of my dreams consisted of prison. So there was no reprise from hell, not even in my dreams. I was stuck in prison all the time. Even if my subconscious tried to sneak in a dream of freedom, I was no longer fooled. I knew immediately that I had not been released from prison and woke up instantly.

50

Released

On Friday, January 18, 2008, I was wondering why I hadn't been transported back to Larimer County for some more court hearings. I found out that they had been adjourned, and I was just starting to wonder if these hearings would ever end when a case manager, Curtis, came to my cell. We were locked down, so he told me through the door, "Your lawyer called and said you need to call her." Of course, I couldn't do anything about it until lockdown was over, so I paced. The last time I had gotten a call like this it was bad news. Twenty minutes later, Curtis came back and said, "Your lawyer just called me, and she wants you to call her right now. She sounded really excited about something. As soon as they clear lockdown, I'll get you out to call your lawyer." At least it didn't sound like bad news.

At 4:00 P.M., the news came on, and a man in a neighboring cell yelled out to me, "Hey, Tim, you're on the news!" I turned to Channel 9. I caught the tail end of a report: "Special prosecutor Quick, appointed to the Tim Masters case, announced that Tim Masters' sentence will be vacated and he will be released on a personal recognizance bond."

Inmates began yelling out congratulatory things to me. I was feeling better, but I was still pessimistic. I yelled back, "You can't believe everything you see on the news. Wait 'til I can talk to my lawyer. Then we can see if it's time to celebrate or not."

Curtis came and took me down to a telephone. I called Maria, and she confirmed it: "Tim, they're vacating your sentence." I was stunned and couldn't believe it. I had experienced so much disappointment in ten years that I would not believe it until I walked out of that prison or the courthouse into daylight wearing civilian clothes. Nothing was certain until it was done.

Curtis walked me down to the warden's office, and as we were walking, he confessed to me, "Tim, I've had many inmates over the years claim to be innocent, but I only believed two of them. One of those two was you."

I had made it nine years at Buena Vista without ever being sent to the hole. Nine years without a write-up. The last weekend I spent at Bueny, they put me in the protective custody of the hole. I didn't mind the isolation, but I was sorry I didn't get a chance to give away my canteen and appliances. Dave had requested they put me in protective custody until I was released. You never know what might happen. Some inmate with little to lose could decide to make a name for himself by going after someone who was about to leave. I did have to spend an extra day in the hole, though. It was Martin Luther King Jr. Day on Monday, so my court date wouldn't be until Tuesday.

With all the activity on my case, there was a flurry of news coverage. At one point, a reporter for the *Rocky Mountain News* tracked down a juror from my case and asked him about it. If I was about to be released, how did that make him feel? Larry Noller was now sixty-two years old and told the reporter that he had been one of the jurors who wanted to vote not guilty for me but that he had changed his mind over the two days of deliberation. Noller admitted he wasn't the last holdout. Another man had hung on for the two days and then broke down crying when he voted to convict me: "[H]e just cried like a baby."

Noller said he convicted me based upon the drawings. "I think we did our best." He said that some jurors were curious about Zoellner, but they accepted the prosecution's position that he had an alibi that checked out. "I guess if they know he's got an alibi, he's got an alibi."

Reporter Kevin Vaughan had tracked down another juror after the DNA evidence had come to light, a man named Tom Turner. He, too, had initially voted not guilty and was surprised that so many fellow jurors would vote guilty before any deliberation had taken place. He watched the A&E piece on me and wondered why so much of what was shown in the piece hadn't been produced at trial.

Turner was concerned enough about it that he attended one of the hearings on my case, and when he walked out afterward, he was "pretty upset." He told Vaughan that the jury was "manipulated" and "cheated."

That Saturday, my lawyers called to talk to me and to get my shirt and pant sizes. It had been so long since I'd worn civilian clothes that I couldn't remember my shirt size. I guessed. Dave also suggested that I shave, so I wouldn't look like an inmate when I was in court for the last time. He told me there would be some press coverage of my hearing, and I would want to look like a real person. He even suggested I think about what I would say if someone asked me to make a statement. "Remember, you're not up there to accept an Academy Award or anything. You probably want to keep it short."

Dave, Maria, Barie, and Josh went out and bought me clothes using their own money. How great is that? How many lawyers go that far out of their way to make sure their client has good clothes to wear on his release date?

I called Serena to tell her the news, and she was thrilled for me. She had bad news though. She couldn't be in Colorado to see me when I got out because she had jury duty! The system was screwing with us once again.

Since I couldn't give away my stuff, my choices were to pay to have it shipped out or to have it destroyed. Although the stuff was priceless in prison, most of it was worthless on the outside. A thirteen-inch TV, a cheap coffeemaker, a single-speaker radio—none of it was worth keeping. I told them to go ahead and throw it all away. The only things I kept were my legal papers and my photographs.

Around 3:00 P.M. on Martin Luther King Jr. Day, deputies showed up to drive me back to the LCDC. I had no idea how out of control the media was going to get. In Fort Collins, there was a camera crew filming me as they took me out of the van and into the sally port. I admit I felt better knowing I was close to being free, but again, I was being filmed while wearing DOC greens, with handcuffs and shackles.

Shortly after I arrived, *48 Hours* asked if they could interview me. I sat down with them for a few minutes. After I got back to my cell, I got to put on some of the new clothes my attorneys had bought me. Everything fit, and it was amazing how good it felt to be dressed like a normal person for once.

For the first time in all of my years of being transported by deputies and guards, the rules were finally relaxed a bit for me. At the Larimer County Jail, I was met by Paula Woodward, from Channel 9 News, and Helen Richardson, from the *Denver Post*, and they were allowed to ride with me to the courthouse. It seemed everyone responded to the presence of so much media attention: the guards were even wearing business suits instead of their uniforms. When they took me down to the transport area, they led me to a holding cell but did not close the door. They didn't want to lock me in another cell. As I stood there in the doorway to the cell, Paula noticed that I stood at the doorway but had not crossed the line.

"Did you notice you're not stepping over the line?"

I hadn't noticed because it was instinctive. For the past ten years, I stood where I was told and stayed where I was put.

We rode to the courthouse, and the cameras were rolling. Paula asked me some questions, but it's all a blur to me now. I have no idea what she asked or what I told her. Once we got to the courthouse, there were more cameras. Inmates in holding cells pressed up against the glass to see what was causing the media circus.

This was the first time I'd gone to court without wearing handcuffs and shackles. I waited downstairs in a holding cell, and soon Josh came down to see me. He had some paperwork for me to sign, and when he entered my cell, he gave me a bear hug. He then handed me a brand-new leather wallet. "This is from Tom Congdon." The wallet had $800 inside. Tom was a stranger who had sent letters of support to me in prison; he'd even told Maria he'd post my bond if need be. Someone else came by with paperwork for me to sign. It confirmed I was about to be released on personal recognizance. I wasn't going to have to post any money before I would be released. The state was going to take me at my word that I would show up for court if I was asked to.

Eventually, they came and got me and led me to the courtroom. I had never seen it so packed. I looked around for familiar faces. I saw Maria and Dave, Josh and Barie. Broderick wasn't at the prosecutor's table for once, and I didn't see my family. Somewhere in the courtroom was

Tom Turner, the juror who felt "cheated" by the prosecution at my trial. As I wondered if my family couldn't get in, the judge asked for the bailiff to go get my family. The room had been so packed that the judge had let my family sit in the jury room until we were ready to proceed. One by one they filed in, and I suspect many people were surprised by how many of them showed up. Then Serena walked in. I almost broke down crying when I saw her.

The hearing was short. The prosecution told the court the People were requesting that my sentence be vacated. My attorneys indicated to the court they agreed, and Judge Joseph Weatherby granted the motion. I was a free man again.

The court took a recess, and we moved into another room for a press conference. Maria, Dave, and Barie gave quick speeches. I got up but felt there was little to add to what my attorneys had already said. I thanked my defense team, the media for finally telling my side of the story, and my family for supporting me all these years.

Most people don't realize that very few people ever get released and walk straight out of the courthouse. Most defendants have to go back to the county jail to be processed out. The sheriff had agreed in my case to have me processed out before I left for court. I actually got to walk out of the court a free man, right out the front door of the courthouse.

Dave and Barie played linebacker for me as we left the courthouse and worked our way through all the spectators and reporters. I saw a couple of my cousins down the street. They waved, and I waved back as we climbed into Josh's SUV, which he had managed to pull to the curb in front of the courthouse.

Technically, though, I was not out of the woods yet. The prosecutor had simply agreed that my conviction should be set aside. Presumably, they could decide to retry me for the murder of Peggy Hettrick. We knew that would be a tough call for the prosecutor to make in light of everything we had learned since the last trial, but we still wondered what would happen next.

For now though, we celebrated. My family threw a party for me at the local Elks Club. Aunts, uncles, cousins, and everyone else who supported me for all these years were there. The reporters even followed us over. My aunt Claudia and uncle Ronald drove from Iowa to be there—a thirteen-hour drive. Serena, who had somehow gotten out of jury duty, was there with Mario, who was now eighteen years old.

LESS THAN A week later, Larimer County District Attorney Abrahamson filed a request with the court to have all charges against me dropped and to have my bond provisions released. The reasons he gave for the motion were interesting. He claimed that I had been cleared by DNA results. Not those of the Eikelenbooms and my defense team, but the tests that had been run by the CBI just that month. He referred to it as "newly discovered DNA evidence." Remember: the prosecution had fought tooth and nail to avoid having to run those tests.

He made no mention of the prosecutorial misconduct at the trial or the overwhelming evidence pointing to other suspects. On January 29, 2008, the governor of Colorado asked the state attorney general, John Suthers, to take over the Peggy Hettrick murder case. It had become clear to everyone that outsiders with no connections to the area had to be brought in to sort out the mess made by the local police and the local courts.

In February, the special prosecutors asked to look at how my trial was handled came to the conclusion that my trial was not "fair." Although this was a nice thing for them to acknowledge, they said that none of the people from the prosecutor's office had broken any laws in how they had run my trial. So I didn't get a fair trial, but they did nothing wrong?

Attorneys are regulated by the Colorado Bar Association, and they have their own rules and regulations. Even if they hadn't broken any laws, I believed they had behaved unethically in my case. After all, they broke the rules by not providing my attorneys with the evidence that would have cleared me.

An investigation into Blair and Gilmore was conducted by the Colorado Bar. When the bar finds misconduct by an attorney, it turns the matter over to the Colorado Supreme Court, which is the final authority on matters having to do with the courts of Colorado. The Colorado Supreme Court censured the two former prosecutors— both had gone on to become judges in Fort Collins. In a process that caused many people outside of the legal profession to scratch their heads, the Colorado Supreme Court entered an order to which Blair and Gilmore consented. The order stated that the conduct of the two "directly impaired the proper operation of the criminal justice system in the trial of Timothy Masters." The two paid a small amount of money and the censure was made public.

51

Outside

ONCE I GOT OUT OF PRISON, I HAD TO ADJUST TO A SOCIETY I had not been a part of for a decade. It was difficult to simply believe I was finally free. I had nightmares about being in prison, or being thrown back in prison. I was pleasantly surprised, though, by the reaction I got from most people I ran into. Many people recognized me from the media coverage of my release and would approach me and say nice things. A woman walked up to me in a Taco Bell and just handed me a hundred dollar bill. Two women walked over to me while I was eating in a restaurant in Fort Collins and handed me checks. Leslie Harms, another random stranger, gave me $2,000 in cash. Peter Coulter gave me a 1988 BMW to drive. More than a hundred people sent me checks and money orders with letters of support. I saved the letters as a reminder that not all of Fort Collins was against me.

An eye doctor gave me free laser eye surgery. A dentist fixed a broken tooth of mine and replaced all my old fillings. He refused to let me pay him. As more and more people encouraged me and gave me support, I felt my bitterness and anger toward society melt away. Not everyone was against me. I've even had people remark on how impressed they are that I'm not more bitter or angry about my time in prison and the years of living under suspicion. I explain to them that I spent almost a decade in prison, as bitter and angry as one man can be. It consumed me. It flowed through my veins and occupied every fiber of my body for almost ten years. Broderick, in particular, motivated me to push a lot of weight on the weight pile at prison, raising and lowering the bar while repeating to myself, "Fucking Broderick, Fucking Broderick," like a mantra.

The people who met me after I was released met a very different person than the one I was a year before I was released. I still have some bitterness and anger about what happened to me, but I don't let it rule my life. Too much of my life has been wasted on that. It was time to move on and find constructive things to think about and to do with my life.

And now that I was out of prison, I was overwhelmed by all the things I could do. My cousin invited me out to her ranch. I remembered the drive to Bueny, when I had thought about how nice it would be to work on a ranch. I went up there and helped her with her cattle. Now, though, all I could think of was how the cattle being moved from place to place was just like how the inmates are moved around inside the prison. The prisoners had gone to chow, then to the yard, then back to the cells. The cows had to get fed, taken to the pasture, and so on.

One thing I noticed was that a decade of my knowledge was missing. My cousin Lexi played me a song on her MP3 player and mentioned, "You've got to know this one; it's so old." I'd never heard it before. The little radio I had in Bueny didn't get many stations, and the ones it did get weren't exactly cutting edge. Another cousin, Seth, played a song that came out when he was in grade school—a lifetime ago for him—and again, I hadn't heard it because Seth's grade school years fell within my Buena Vista years. I had lost almost a decade.

52

The Lawsuit

AFTER I HAD BEEN OUT A FEW MONTHS, I DECIDED I HAD to do something about what had happened. I guess I was naive, but I thought there was a chance that someone official might issue an apology for what had been done to me. Rather than apologize for what they had done, they actually continued telling people that I was still a suspect in the case!

Dave and Maria arranged meetings with a couple of big law firms that could handle a case like mine, and we went and sat down with them. I decided to hire David Lane's law firm. He got along well with my attorneys, and his office seemed to be more of a place where work got done—not just a place filled with expensive furniture and marble floors. He also had a reputation for taking on big defendants on behalf of the little guy. He was exactly what I needed.

He filed a notice of intent to sue in October 2008, another little hurdle they put in the way of people who have been hurt by government agents like Broderick, Reed, Gilmore, and Blair. Once that was filed, the news started up again with coverage of my story. Although most of the reaction was favorable for me, there were some people who didn't get it. A local news station's website had a section where people could comment on recent stories. A few people posted—anonymously, of course—things like, "Masters has never been proven innocent" and "I wouldn't want my kids around him."

One poster raised a point that probably hurts anyone in my position but it illustrates a common misconception about the legal system. "Maybe now we'll see all the evidence that convicted him in the first place." The poster was suggesting that there was more evidence against me than what the public knew about. Although this may be the case in a trial where the court suppresses a confession or throws out evidence because of a bad search warrant, there were no such exclusions in my case. The prosecutors got to introduce every bit of evidence they found—and then some! If my case had gone back to trial, the prosecutor would have had to try the case with less evidence than in the first trial, and I would have gotten to put on a proper defense, with all of the evidence the prosecution had withheld from me in the first place.

During this time, Maria arranged to meet with Reid Meloy. What would the doctor say, now that it was proven he was completely wrong in his theories? When she met with him, the first thing he said to her was, "Why didn't you ever contact me?" It appeared he had been following the developments in my case and was feeling that, like Bevel and the others, he had been misled by Broderick, who had only given him the information that pointed to me. He hadn't been told about Hammond. He told Maria to tell me that he was sorry for what happened. Later, he posted a copy of my lawsuit on his website.

The civil suit I filed in federal court named the prosecutors and the police as defendants, which meant that the City of Fort Collins and Larimer County were also defendants. The feedback I got was mostly positive. Many people told me it was "about time" I did something about what they had done to me.

EARLIER, IN APRIL 2008, a television station in Amsterdam flew me over to interview me on a late-night talk show. They wanted me to appear with Richard and Selma Eikelenboom to discuss how their groundbreaking DNA techniques had gotten me freed from prison. Barie Goetz and reporters Miles Moffeit and Helen Richardson all flew over, and after I did the show, we drove down to Paris. Barie and I continued a tour of Europe after the others left. I got to see Switzerland, Austria, and Germany before heading back to the Netherlands and home. I visited the Alps and stood on the deck of Piz Gloria, the restaurant on top of Schilthorn Mountain. They had filmed scenes there for the James Bond movie *On Her Majesty's Secret*

Service. Just a few months before, I had been looking out at the world through barred windows; now I was standing on the roof of the world gazing in wonder at the snow-covered peaks in the Swiss Alps. I never could have dreamed of being here and seeing this.

I visited the Anne Frank House museum in Amsterdam; earlier, I had visited Dachau, the concentration camp outside of Munich. There are only a couple of the barracks left, but you can walk the grounds and imagine what it was like. Sixty thousand humans locked up in a camp designed to hold six thousand. I saw the ovens where they burned the bodies of the people they'd killed. I stood at the gravestone marking the location of a mass grave where dozens had been murdered. Thinking of how all those men had been ripped away from their families and their lives made me feel a kinship with them. I wasn't crammed into a prison where I had to bunk with three others, I wasn't starved to death, and my family wasn't murdered by Nazis before my eyes. It put into perspective what I had gone through, and in comparison made my ordeal seem a little less horrid.

ONCE I WAS out of prison, I had to find a way to support myself. I couldn't just go out and get a regular job. How could I tell a potential employer that I was arrested for a brutal murder and spent ten years in prison? "Oh, don't worry. I didn't do it." I started buying things at auctions and selling them on eBay. At least I could use my computer skills and I could be my own boss.

In February 2010, the federal judge overseeing my case sent us to mediation. My attorneys and I went to the offices of one of the defense attorneys—he worked out of two floors of a nice skyscraper in Denver—and hashed out a settlement. We sat in one conference room, and all of the defendants and their lawyers sat in their own rooms. A mediator shuttled back and forth between us, trying to get us to come to an agreement that would settle the case. My attorneys and I had concluded that my case was worth $10 million—a million per year for the time I spent in prison. We didn't tell them that. We started high and asked for $25 million.

We also felt that the most culpable defendant here was the City of Fort Collins, as the employer of Broderick. The county was on the hook for Blair and Gilmore, the prosecutors, but we were willing to let them pay a little less. After haggling back and forth, Larimer County agreed to pay $4.1 million dollars to settle my case. Fort Collins was not making us any offers we considered worthwhile at this time, so we agreed to settle with the county. This way, we would also have a war chest if we needed it to litigate the matter against the city.

A few months later, the judge brought us into the courthouse for another shot at trying to get us to settle the case, but now it was just the City of Fort Collins that was left. Their attorneys felt that they shouldn't have to pay as much as the County, while we thought they ought to pay more. We weren't worried about trying the case and left, saying that unless they increased their offer, we'd see them in court. David Wymore and David Lane wanted to take the case to trial. They thought a jury would have loved to see Broderick on the stand, having to answer for what he had done in this case. In June 2010, the City of Fort Collins agreed to pay me $5.9 million dollars to settle the case.

Settling the case with the city and the county granted me some relief. I had been worried I would never be able to make a living and had been barely scraping by financially ever since I got out of prison. Still, the money could not compensate me for the ten years of my life I had lost.

53

Afterward

IN JULY 2010, A GRAND JURY RETURNED AN INDICTMENT
against James Broderick. After hearing testimony and
reviewing the documents—many which had been discovered by my attorneys in the postconviction hearings and
the lawsuit—the grand jury found that Broderick should
be tried for eight counts of felony perjury. The grand jury
finally said what we had been trying to say for years: Broderick lied to get me arrested and convicted. His lies were
part of the affidavit behind my arrest and also in his testimony in court. For example, he had lied in his affidavit,
saying that an FBI profiler had provided an opinion that
pointed to me. There was no such FBI profiler who gave
any such opinion. Broderick had lied in his affidavit and
also at trial about my footprint at the field near Peggy's

body. He kept saying that there was more than just the one and that my prints were found near the curb. Broderick lied about my mother's hair color, falsely swearing in his affidavit that she had red hair. As we know, the color of my mother's hair played a huge role in Meloy's opinions and in the presentation to the jury. Broderick claimed there was only one Thom McAn footprint at the scene—when there were many—and that he had little involvement in the investigation until 1992. Broderick coordinated the surveillance of me on the anniversary of the murder. If convicted of perjury, Broderick could go to jail for six years for each count. He could also be fined $500,000 per count.

The papers wanted to know how I felt now that Broderick was finally facing some consequences for his actions. I released a statement and made it clear that I held myself to a higher standard than the ones Broderick, Blair, and Gilmore held themselves to. I pointed out how Blair had "pumped her fist in the air in victory, at the courthouse in front of my family. I refuse to act like that. I'm not going to celebrate. But I am pleased to see a glimmer of hope that the man most directly responsible for my wrongful incarceration might be held accountable for his actions to some extent."

Blair and Gilmore were still judges, and both were up for reelection in the fall of 2010. A group was formed called the Committee for Judicial Justice with the goal of unseating the two former prosecutors. The organization was registered as a 527 organization, which meant it could raise unlimited money but had to watch how it presented its message. The message they chose was simple: "Remember Tim Masters: No on Judges Blair & Gilmore." I donated $3,000 to the effort. I could have donated more, but I didn't want people to think this was just a personal vendetta of mine against the former prosecutors. I believed there were more people in the community who recognized it wasn't just about me. It was about what the community wanted its courts—the judges and the prosecutors—to stand for. I was right: the voters threw them out of office in the election, even though the Larimer County Judicial Performance Commission had unanimously recommended the two for retention.

In May 2010, the judge overseeing the prosecution of James Broderick for the perjury he was accused of dismissed the charges. The judge ruled that it was unclear from the evidence if too much time had elapsed since the perjury was said to have been committed. The statute of limitations may have expired. If Broderick was to be prosecuted for perjury he committed during my murder trial, the charges would have to be brought within a certain time frame. The prosecution would have to go back and get the evidence to show when the perjury was committed and when it was discovered.

The prosecution went back to the grand jury and presented evidence that Broderick's actions—even if they had occurred more than ten years earlier—had only been discovered in 2007. The newspapers credited Maria and Dave for uncovering the necessary evidence while they were working on my case. The grand jury issued new indictments, charging Broderick with nine counts of perjury. Broderick was placed on administrative leave by the Fort Collins Police Department. His attorney, paid for by the City of Fort Collins, argued that there was not enough evidence to support the charges and asked that they all be dismissed. In December 2011, the court dismissed three of the counts but left six of them in place.

54

Exoneration

O N June 28, 2011, the attorney general for the state of Colorado, John Suthers, did something I thought I would never see. He issued an official statement exonerating me of Peggy Hettrick's murder. In 2008, the governor's office had assigned the Hettrick murder case directly to Attorney General Suthers. It had become clear that because so many people in Larimer County were connected to my prosecution, the only sensible solution was to bring in someone completely disconnected from the earlier activities. The governor agreed, and Attorney General Suthers took over.

Suthers assigned the project to a team within his department. A grand jury was convened. In all, more than one hundred and seventy witnesses were interviewed or gave testimony. Evidence was reexamined, and DNA was tested. Suthers came to the conclusion that I hadn't killed Peggy Hettrick. And, he concluded, it was time to formally announce it. I never thought I'd hear the words.

"Based on the testimony, the forensic analysis and the crime scene analysis, the overwhelming conclusion is that Timothy Masters was not involved in the murder of Peggy Hettrick."

My phone began ringing as word of the exoneration spread through the community. The current district attorney, Larry Abrahamson, also issued a statement. "I believe it is appropriate as the current district attorney and on behalf of the criminal justice system in Larimer County to express our apologies to Timothy Masters, his family and friends for the conviction and sentence he endured 12 years ago."

I got a call from my cousin Larry, who works for the city of Fort Collins, asking if I wanted to come in and speak with the mayor and the interim police chief. I drove over to the city "streets department" building, where I met with Jerry Schlager, the interim police chief of Fort Collins. Mayor Karen Weitkunat was there, along with Abrahamson. We spoke for ten minutes, and they apologized on behalf of their departments. My cousin Larry and I left the meeting with the impression that the apologies were genuinely heartfelt. It was nice to finally hear someone officially tell me they were sorry.

PEGGY HETTRICK'S MURDERER has not been arrested yet. The grand jury operates in secret, so no one can say what, if anything, is developing in that regard.

Penguin Group (USA) Online

What will you be reading tomorrow?

Patricia Cornwell, Nora Roberts, Catherine Coulter,
Ken Follett, John Sandford, Clive Cussler,
Tom Clancy, Laurell K. Hamilton, Charlaine Harris,
J. R. Ward, W.E.B. Griffin, William Gibson,
Robin Cook, Brian Jacques, Stephen King,
Dean Koontz, Eric Jerome Dickey, Terry McMillan,
Sue Monk Kidd, Amy Tan, Jayne Ann Krentz,
Daniel Silva, Kate Jacobs...

You'll find them all at
penguin.com

*Read excerpts and newsletters,
find tour schedules and reading group guides,
and enter contests.*

Subscribe to Penguin Group (USA) newsletters
and get an exclusive inside look
at exciting new titles and the authors you love
long before everyone else does.

PENGUIN GROUP (USA)
penguin.com